KENNETH MUIR
Emeritus Professor of English Literature
University of Liverpool

Shakespeare's Tragic Sequence

LIVERPOOL UNIVERSITY PRESS

Published by
LIVERPOOL UNIVERSITY PRESS
123 Grove Street, Liverpool L7 7AF

First published 1972
in Hutchinson University Library

This edition issued 1979
by Liverpool University Press

CLOTH. ISBN 0 85323 184 2
PAPER. ISBN 0 85323 034 X
Library of Congress Catalog Number 79–52453

Printed in Great Britain at the
University Press, Cambridge

To Philip Gibbons

PREFACE

In the first edition of this book, published in 1972, I expressed my indebtedness to former colleagues G. Wilson Knight, G. K. Hunter, Inga-Stina Ewbank and the late Ernest Schanzer, and I expressed my gratitude to those amateur actors with whom I have been associated in York, Leeds and Liverpool. I mentioned, too, that I had deliberately excluded certain aspects of the subject on which I had written elsewhere. Since then I have collected my essays on the narrative poems and on the imagery of the plays in *Shakespeare the Professional* (1973) and on questions of style, characterisation and staging in *The Singularity of Shakespeare* (1977). With the publication of the companion volume *Shakespeare's Comic Sequence*, which is now in the press, I shall have completed my interpretation of Shakespeare's plays.

Reviewers were kind to the first edition of the present work, and where they disagreed with me on points of detail I have considered each one carefully. In the end I decided not to introduce alterations into the text, not because of my conviction that I was always right, but because they were all matters on which there will always be differences of opinion. One critic pointed out the lack of a theoretical framework to the book. This was indeed true, since I believed, and still believe, that many good books on Shakespeare's tragedies have been damaged by attempting to apply a particular definition to all the plays.

Another reviewer qualified his praise by suggesting that the book was lacking in originality—that I considered many different views on each of the plays before choosing the ones which appeared to be correct. Quite so; but any critic of Shakespeare is bound to build on foundations laid by others. I would claim only, as diffidently as possible, that the interpretation of Shakespeare's tragedies in this book does differ, for better or worse, from that of previous critics.

Acknowledgements are due to *Les Lettres Françaises*, Edward Arnold (Publishers) Ltd., the British Academy and Oxford University Press, the Henry E. Huntington Library, Alfred A. Knopf Inc., Macmillan and Co., Methuen and Co. and Secker and Warburg Ltd. I have tried, in the notes, to indicate my indebtedness to particular books and articles.

Liverpool   KENNETH MUIR
March 1978

CONTENTS

I

INTRODUCTION

A. C. Bradley, when he wrote his book on Shakespearean Tragedy, deliberately excluded not merely the early plays, *Titus Andronicus* and *Romeo and Juliet*, and the doubtful case of *Timon of Athens* from his consideration, but also the English and Roman historical tragedies. He thought that Shakespeare himself would probably[1]

have met some criticisms to which these plays are open by appealing to their historical character, and by denying that such works are to be judged by the standard of pure tragedy. In any case, most of the plays, perhaps all, do show, as a matter of fact, considerable deviations from that standard.

Without presuming to know what Shakespeare might have said, we may raise several objections to Bradley's assumptions. In the first place it is very doubtful whether we should segregate the English and Roman histories, and deny them the title of 'pure tragedy', whatever that may be. In the first quartos *Richard III* and *Richard II* were both entitled as tragedies, and the Roman plays are printed among the tragedies in the First Folio. There is no evidence that Shakespeare regarded the Roman plays as different *in kind* from the other tragedies, or that he was really hampered by the necessity of keeping close to the facts of history. Secondly, both *Macbeth* and *King Lear* were historical tragedies, based in part, like *Richard III* and *Richard II*, on Holinshed's *Chronicles*, even though, in *King Lear*, Shakespeare blended Sidney's fiction with historical or legendary material. Thirdly, by Bradley's assumption that the four tragedies with which he dealt were 'pure' tragedies, while the others were not, he was in danger of exaggerating

1. Superior figures refer to notes at the end of the book (p. 197).

both the resemblances between the chosen four and the differences between those four and the rest. It is misleading to regard even Bradley's great four as belonging to a single category. There is no such thing as Shakespearian Tragedy: there are only Shakespearian tragedies.

Nearly all critics now refrain from the attempt to apply external rules to Shakespeare's plays. No one now laments that he did not obey the three unities and no one pretends that Aristotle's observations on Greek tragedy can be applied without modification to the plays of Marlowe, Shakespeare or Middleton;[2] but attempts are still made, because of the rage for order, to find a formula applicable to every one of Shakespeare's tragedies, defining them and distinguishing them from those of other dramatists. Such attempts have met with little success because, as Coleridge realised, each play of a great dramatist will demand its own individual form. It is plain that the form of *Peer Gynt* is utterly different from that of *Rosmersholm* or *The Master Builder*; that of *Phèdre* from that of *Bérénice* or *Athalie*; that of *King Oedipus* from that of *Oedipus at Colonos*; and that of *The Ghost Sonata* from that of *The Father*. In the same way the form of *King Lear* is unlike that of *Macbeth*, not to mention *Antony and Cleopatra* or *Romeo and Juliet*.

The tragic form will be influenced by a number of different factors, some of them, at one extreme, influencing all the writers of a period, and others, at the opposite extreme, being peculiar to a single poet. Elizabethan tragedy depended on the physical structure of the playhouses, whether public or private, on the heterogeneous nature of the audience, on the talents and limitations of the actors. Most writers seem to have been influenced by ideas derived from the Classics as well as by Christian belief. In addition to such general influences there were particular ones which operated on the writing of individual poets and, of course, there were great divergences of temperament. There was, finally and crucially, the choice of subject and the influence of the material to be dramatised on the form of the play: every poet had to consider how to bring out the full significance of a situation or how best to embody a theme in dramatic form. In solving these problems, each dramatist, however original, would be affected by the example of his predecessors.

Much of what Bradley says in his chapter on 'The Substance of Shakespearean Tragedy' is unexceptionable. The tragedies—apart from *Romeo and Juliet* and *Antony and Cleopatra*—are concerned primarily with one person; they end with the death of the hero; the suffering and calamity that befall him are exceptional; and the tragedies include the medieval idea of the reversal of fortune. Shakespeare's main interest was in the way action issued from character, or character issued in action. In most of his tragedies chance or accident has an appreciable influence. So far so good; but Bradley continues:[3]

In the circumstances where we see the hero placed, his tragic trait, which is also his greatness, is fatal to him. To meet these circumstances something is required which a smaller man might have given, but which the hero cannot give. He errs, by action or omission; and his error, joining with other causes, brings on him ruin.

These words are true of Hamlet and perhaps of Coriolanus, but can they be properly applied to Lear or Macbeth?

The main source of tragedy, Bradley continues, is evil, which is always negative. At the end[4]

We remain confronted with the inexplicable fact, or the no less inexplicable appearance, of a world travailing for perfection, but bringing to birth, together with glorious good, an evil which it is able to overcome only by self-torture and self-waste. And this fact or appearance is tragedy.

Is it really a fact? Is it even an appearance? The unshaken integrity of Edgar and Cordelia, or Coriolanus' overcoming of hatred, may indeed represent glorious good; but when the 'delicate and tender prince', Fortinbras, succeeds Hamlet, or when we see the 'tragic loading' of Desdemona's bed or the sombre exhaustion at the end of *King Lear*, we are much more conscious of the waste. The world does not seem to be travailing for perfection, as though Shakespeare were confident

> that somehow good
> Will be the final goal of ill;

but rather bent on substituting the ordinary for the exceptional.

Shakespearean Tragedy is nevertheless a critical monument which has survived a good deal of battering from more recent critics. Professor Lily B. Campbell, for example, includes in recent editions of her *Shakespeare's Tragic Heroes* two chapters in which she formulates her objections to Bradley's methods—in particular, that he was unhistorical and did not know enough about Elizabethan ways of thought and the difference between them and ours. The criticism has a good deal of

validity. Professor Campbell herself expertly deploys her wide knowledge of Elizabethan theories of psychology so as to demonstrate that
Shakespeare's tragic heroes are slaves of passion, *King Lear* being 'a
tragedy of wrath in old age', *Othello*, predictably, 'a tragedy of
jealousy', and *Macbeth*, less predictably, 'a study in fear'. But even if
Miss Campbell convinced us that Shakespeare's understanding of
human behaviour was circumscribed by the theories of his age, the
light thrown on his plays would be disappointingly narrow.

Even more schematic is Harold S. Wilson's *On the Design of
Shakespearian Tragedy* (1957). He classifies ten of Shakespeare's
tragedies into three groups. Four plays are taken to exemplify the
order of faith—*Romeo and Juliet* and *Hamlet* representing the thesis
and *Othello* and *Macbeth* the antithesis. Of the four plays which
exemplify the order of nature, *Julius Caesar* and *Coriolanus* represent
the thesis, *Timon of Athens* and *Troilus and Cressida* the antithesis. The
remaining plays, *Antony and Cleopatra* and *King Lear*, surprisingly
represent a synthesis of the order of faith and the order of nature. To
produce this neo-Hegelian fantasy Wilson had to ignore the chrono-
logical order of the plays: there is something odd about a synthesis
which actually precedes what it is supposed to synthesise. In this case
it can easily be seen that a respected critic has been seduced by a desire
to find a significant relationship between all the tragedies.

Other attempts, more overtly theological, have been made to
discover a unifying principle in Shakespeare's tragedies. In his *Shakespearean Tragedy* (1969), Roy Battenhouse argued 'that the intellectual
basis of Shakespeare's art was provided by Aristotelian principles
modified and deepened by the Christian concepts of Augustine and
Aquinas', and that 'in tragic art the author must contrive a sympathetic
surface level while hiding the real truth underneath'. So we are asked
to believe that Lucrece wanted to be raped, that the Ghost in *Hamlet*
comes from hell, that Edgar has 'a touch of his father's pleasant vices',
and that Cordelia is self-righteous. Professor Battenhouse turns
Shakespeare into a rather puritanical moralist, which to believe of him,
as the King of France says of Cordelia

> Must be a faith that reason without miracle
> Should never plant in me.

Professor G. R. Elliott has not written a book on Shakespearian tragedy
as a whole, but in his detailed studies of *Hamlet*, *Othello* and *Macbeth*

he declares that they, like the rest of the tragedies, deal with one central theme:[5]

Renaissance tragedy including Shakespearean tragedy is the tragedy of pride. Indeed there is no such thing as *Shakespearean tragedy*, in any deep and inclusive sense, apart from the motif of pride.

Hamlet and *Coriolanus*, however dissimilar,

have a central theme in common: right self-esteem turning into wrong pride. And that is the main theme, more or less, of Shakespeare's tragic and semi-tragic plays from the beginning to the end of his career . . . Pride is no less powerful in Brutus, Hamlet and Othello because it is subtly so.

Professor Elliott is well aware of the substantial difference between one play and another, but he regards such characteristics as the credulity or jealousy of Othello, Macbeth's overweening ambition or Antony's sexual passion as of less significance than their pride.

Another example of a good critic being led astray by a seductive generalisation is Mr John Holloway who attempts, in *The Story of the Night*, to show that the Shakespearian tragic hero, driven into isolation, is hunted down as a kind of scapegoat. The effect of the tragedies, therefore, is to[6]

call forth in depth not only our sense of belonging to a community and drawing our strength from that, but also, and again in depth, all that is most naturally observed when that awareness is kindled: all that reminds us of the price exacted for belonging, in the shape of constant partial self-abnegation.

So in *Macbeth* we see 'the expulsion, hunting down and destruction of a man who has turned into a monster' and in the death of Coriolanus is a '*sparagmos* of the ritual victim by the whole social group'. There are, of course, fundamental differences between the scapegoat and the tragic hero. The audience, suffering with the hero, does not feel it is chastising its own sins in his person. The theory, moreover, seems irrelevant to our experience of several of the tragedies and it does not differentiate Shakespeare's from others, from *King Oedipus*, for example, a real scapegoat, or from *Phèdre*.

Mr T. R. Henn's more complex description of Shakespearian tragedy is less open to this kind of objection.[7] He stresses, quite properly, the traditional values embodied in it derived from the medieval tradition, the disruption of order through evil which is the consequence of sin, and the contrast between the evil generated in the hero and his innate nobility. 'The emergence of evil through persona-

lity into act is the theme of tragedy.' This description is applicable to
tragedy other than Shakespeare's. It does not mention that there is
nearly always the presence of evil outside the tragic hero—for example
in Iago, Edmund, Claudius, Tybalt, Lady Macbeth—which is an
essential part of the tragic pattern; and it does not bring out the enormous differences between *Hamlet* and *Macbeth*, or between *Othello*
and *King Lear*.

Professor Virgil K. Whitaker may be taken as a last example of
recent critics of Shakespearian tragedy. He likewise argues that it is
important to interpret the tragedies in traditional Christian terms, so
that[8]

Aristotle's tragic error becomes a moral error—that is, an act of sin. . . . The
tragic hero's error now consists in an act of will, to which the reason consents, and in the overt deed which results from the act of will. Furthermore,
the Aristotelian dictum that character reveals itself in choice gains a new
urgency. . . . In fact, of course, it would be well-nigh impossible to isolate the
crucial moral act among the thousands of venial sins committed by the
ordinary human being. But the tragic poet could so simplify his action as to
trace cause and effect with dreadful clarity and thereby to provide a powerful
moral *exemplum*.

Although Elizabethan drama was secular in essentials, it is perfectly
true that it was written by poets who had at least been brought up as
Christians, however sceptical some of them became, and that their
audience was likewise Christian. It would therefore be surprising if
Shakespeare had not made use of Christian ideas. This does not
differentiate him from other dramatists of the age or, indeed, from
Racine; and one wonders if Shakespeare, like some of his critics,
regarded the love of Romeo and Juliet as sinful.

The failure of such good critics to produce a theory that is applicable
to all Shakespeare's tragedies and yet differentiates them from those of
other poets should warn us of the difficulties of generalisation. Each of
his tragedies is unique.

Shakespeare's contemporaries agreed about the function of tragedy.
It was, as Sidney put it, to 'make kings fear to be tyrants', and 'to
shew the mutabilitie of fortune, and the just punishment of God in
revenge of a vicious and evill life'.[9] It was to 'include the fatall and
abortive ends of such as commit notorious murders . . . to terrifie men
from the like abhorred practises'.[10] Chapman claimed that 'material
instruction, elegant and sententious excitation to virtue, and deflection

from her contrary' were 'the soul, limbs and limits of an authentical tragedy'.[11] This moral purpose of tragedy was doubtless stressed by Elizabethan writers because of attacks on the stage, but there is no reason to think that they were being insincere. Shakespeare was aware of these ideas and he probably shared them. It is possible to see in all his tragedies warnings against sin, against tyranny, against allowing passion to usurp the place of reason, against pride. We can see in some of them the mutability of fortune. Although Shakespeare's final spokesman declared that his purpose 'was to please', this does not necessarily conflict with the aim of mingling teaching with delight.[12]

Didactic literature is now regarded with suspicion. We hate, as Keats said, poetry that has a palpable design on us.[13] Critics who are not averse to rechristening *King Lear* as *End Game* would shrink from admitting that Shakespeare was guilty of a moral purpose. Certainly, even in the English Histories, he was not a propagandist. His mind was 'a thoroughfare for all thoughts, not a select party'.[14] This disinterestedness is the chief necessity for a dramatist, for he can make his characters come alive only if he is able for a time to see through their eyes. Shakespeare was seldom blatantly didactic: he merely tried to give a faithful picture of life, seeing life steadily and seeing it whole. It need hardly be said that poetry which gives a false picture of life, even in the interests of morality, is itself immoral. That is why the concept of poetic justice is more popular with critics than with the poets.[15]

One other matter must be touched on before we discuss each tragedy in turn. Many critics still refer to the years between 1600 and 1607 as Shakespeare's 'tragic period'. It is true that six of his tragedies, including his greatest, were written during these years; but one should remember not merely that as many tragedies were written outside this period, but that *Twelfth Night* was apparently sandwiched between *Julius Caesar* and *Hamlet*, *Measure for Measure* between *Hamlet* and *Othello*, and that *All's Well That Ends Well* was probably written during the same years. It must be admitted that the tone of the Problem Plays has been used to support the view that the poet was passing through a period of gloom and disillusionment, so that the comedies of these years were sour and sordid. Frailty's name was woman and the universe was merely 'a foul and pestilent congregation of vapours'; and Shakespeare's Hamlet-like melancholy was caused by the experience described in the *Sonnets* of lust and betrayal. But we do not know for certain that the *Sonnets* were based on personal experience; and, even if they were, we are too ignorant of Shakespeare's personal life to be sure that there were not other experiences which had a more significant influence on his development. No man endowed with the qualities of a poet can expect to reach the age of forty without the black ox treading on his feet. But a tragic sense of life—a sense of tears in mortal things—does not depend on personal experience; and the so-called tragic period of Shakespeare may correspond not merely to a period of success in his profession, which Sir Sidney Lee apparently equated with happiness, but to one of happiness in his personal life. We do not know.

Realising this, some critics have supposed that the vogue of tragedy was caused by the disenchantment of the Elizabethans in the last years of the Queen's reign, a disenchantment caused by the prevalence of the plague, by the fear of a disputed succession, and by the Essex rebellion. John Dover Wilson stressed[16] the importance of the fall of Essex for Shakespeare, since it led to the imprisonment of his first patron, the Earl of Southampton.

Theodore Spencer thought[17] that the ideology of the age, in which nearly everyone believed, had suffered a series of shocks: Machiavelli had revealed the sordid truth about man as a political animal; Montaigne had shaken people's self-confidence; and the new astronomy had shown that the earth was not the centre of the universe. These critics can point to a good deal of *fin de siècle* gloom, to satire in prose and verse, to the plays of Marston, to portraits of melancholics by Jonson, Shakespeare and others. Yet the greatest tragedies were written after the death of Elizabeth, when the sad augurs mocked their own presage; and there is no evidence to suggest that tragedies are written especially in times of uncertainty, change and disillusionment.

It seems more likely that Shakespeare wrote a series of tragedies in the early years of the seventeenth century because tragedy was regarded as the highest form of drama and because he felt at the height of his powers. During the last decade of the sixteenth century he had completed nine plays on English history. The whole sequence ends with the Tudor settlement; but three of the plays are tragedies and five others are concerned with the tragedy of civil war. The prevailing note—even in the plays in which Falstaff appears—is more genuinely tragic than in the unhistorical tragedies, *Titus Andronicus* and *Romeo and Juliet*. In one of these Shakespeare aroused horror, in the other pity; but in some of the Histories he succeeded in arousing both.

He had learnt a great deal from Marlowe, obviously in his earliest tragedies. He learnt something about construction from *The Spanish Tragedy*; but he learnt most from his own experiments. There was woe and wonder in *Titus Andronicus*, but too much *grand guignol*. *Richard III* was well constructed but the hero was a villain and the element of ritual softened the dramatic impact. *Romeo and Juliet* relied too much on accident. Richard II was too weak to be regarded as a satisfactory tragic hero. Shakespeare did not make these mistakes again. By 1600 he had forged for himself a wonderfully flexible verse capable of differentiating character and of expressing the most delicate nuances; and his company had evolved a style of acting of comparable subtlety, so that audiences seemed to hear men talking rather than actors declaiming. Shakespeare must have realised that he could produce great tragedies which would be worthily performed.

2

APPRENTICESHIP

Titus Andronicus was immensely popular in the sixteenth century and Ben Jonson, followed by later critics, regarded this as a proof of the shocking taste of Elizabethan audiences.[1] William Faulkner dismayed his admirers when he confessed towards the end of his life that one of his novels had been written as a pot-boiler and that he had deliberately made it as lurid as possible. Some of the same embarrassment is to be found in the comments of Shakespeare critics when confronted with *Titus Andronicus*: the play is so horrific that they would gladly transfer the responsibility to some other dramatist. Could Shakespeare, they asked, at any stage of his career have perpetrated this *grand guignol* melodrama of rape, mutilation, murder and cannibalism? Surely it must have been one of the university wits, or a syndicate of the wits? If Shakespeare had a hand in it at all—and we ignore the evidence of Heminge and Condell at our peril[2]—then we must hope that he merely revised a play by an inferior dramatist. The favourite candidate for the crime is George Peele, whose other works are singularly unlike *Titus Andronicus*: yet there are phrases and tricks of style, especially in the first two acts, which are reminiscent of his style. But Hereward T. Price, who spent many years preparing the Variorum edition, was convinced that the play was wholly Shakespeare's because no dramatist of the time exhibited the same powers of construction.

The success of the production at the Stratford Memorial Theatre in 1955, directed by Peter Brook, and with the title role played by Sir Laurence Olivier, led to a revival of interest in the play. Jan Kott hailed the play as a masterpiece[3] and there were more sober estimates by Eugene Waith, A. C. Hamilton, Nicholas Brooke, and Alan

Somers, some of them written about the same time as the production.[4]

The play is not a masterpiece, though it is partially effective on the stage. It differs in many respects from the later Roman plays in which Shakespeare made a real attempt at historical accuracy. As Professor Terence Spencer wittily observes, the play 'includes *all* the political institutions that Rome ever had. The author seems anxious, not to get it all right, but to get it all in'.[5]

All schoolmasters and critics recommended the Latin dramatists as the best models for tragedy and comedy: so that Shakespeare naturally based one of his first comedies on Plautus and, when he came to write a tragedy, he turned to Seneca. He had read some Seneca in the original and he probably knew the Elizabethan translation to which many modern readers have been led by T. S. Eliot's persuasive essay,[6] and from which they have come away disappointed: for the translations as a whole are terribly pedestrian and often ridiculous. *Titus Andronicus* contains two actual quotations from Seneca in the original Latin; it ends with a banquet, copied from *Thyestes*, in which Tamora's sons are served to her in a pie; and the chain of revenges—from the sacrifice of Tamora's eldest son to the killing of Tamora herself—is similar to that in the Thyestes–Agamemnon story. If we wish to deplore Shakespeare's lack of taste in indulging in gratuitous horror, we should not blame him so much as the 'grand old fortifying classical curriculum' which he underwent at school. Coleridge, indeed, said that the play 'was obviously intended to excite vulgar audiences by its scenes of blood and horror—to our ears shocking and disgusting';[7] and he would have been astonished by the enthusiasm of a not-altogether-vulgar Stratford audience. But it is arguable that Shakespeare was trying by his Senecan horrors to please not the groundlings but what Gabriel Harvey called 'the wiser sort'.

Not that Seneca was his sole model. As Eugene M. Waith demonstrated[8] so brilliantly, Shakespeare was also influenced by Ovid. The rape of Philomel was very much in his mind when he wrote of the rape of Lavinia. Aaron tells Tamora:

> This is the day of doom for Bassianus:
> His Philomel must lose her tongue today.   (II.iii.42–3)

When Marcus comes upon the mutilated Lavinia he immediately guesses what has happened:

> But sure some Tereus hath deflowered thee . . .
> Fair Philomel, why she but lost her tongue,
> And in a tedious sampler sew'd her mind . . .
> A craftier Tereus, cousin, hast thou met,
> And he hath cut those pretty fingers off
> That could have better sew'd than Philomel.   (II.iv.26–43)

Lavinia reveals the truth by pointing to the tale in a copy of Ovid; and in the last act Titus tells her ravishers:

> For worse than Philomel you used my daughter,
> And worse than Progne I will be reveng'd.   (V.ii.195–6)

But, as Professor Waith points out, the influence of Ovid extends beyond the subject-matter to the style. Ovid, by his style, transforms violence 'into an object of somewhat detached contemplation'. In the description of the amputation of Philomela's tongue, for example, we forget the pain in the ingenuity of the description:[9]

> But Tereus did not kill her; he seized her tongue
> With pincers, though it cried against the outrage,
> Babbled and made a sound something like Father,
> Till the sword cut it off. The mangled root
> Quivered, the severed tongue along the ground
> Lay quivering, making a little murmur,
> Jerking and twitching, the way a serpent does
> Run over by a wheel, and with its dying movement
> Came to its mistress' feet.

As Professor Waith suggests, Shakespeare's comparisons, like Ovid's, are 'unexpected, fanciful, and yet exact', as in the description of Lavinia:

>   What stern ungentle hands
> Hath lopp'd, and hew'd, and made thy body bare
> Of her two branches . . .
> Alas, a crimson river of warm blood,
> Like to a bubbling fountain stirr'd with wind,
> Doth rise and fall between thy rosed lips,
> Coming and going with thy honey breath . . .
> And notwithstanding all this loss of blood—
> As from a conduit with three issuing spouts—
> Yet do thy cheeks look red as Titan's face
> Blushing to be encount'red with a cloud.   (II.iv.16–32)

Imagery is normally used to illuminate the thing described, but here the various images—the lopped tree, the river, the bubbling fountain, the conduit, the clouds dyed red—seem designed to prettify the horror and distract our attention from the realities of the situation, the raped and mutilated woman.

Everyone has noticed that *Titus Andronicus* was also indebted to Marlowe. When Aaron is asked if he is not sorry for his heinous deeds, he answers:

> Ay, that I had not done a thousand more.
> Even now I curse the day—and yet, I think
> Few come within the compass of my curse—
> Wherein I did not some notorious ill:
> As kill a man, or else devise his death;
> Ravish a maid, or plot the way to do it;
> Accuse some innocent, and forswear myself;
> Set deadly enmity between two friends . . .   (V.i.124ff.)

One is reminded of the speech in which the hero of *The Jew of Malta* boasts of his improbable crimes:[10]

> As for myself, I walk abroad a-nights
> And kill sick people groaning under walls:
> Sometimes I go about and poison wells: . . .
> There I enrich'd the priests with burials,
> And always kept the sexton's arms in ure
> With digging graves and ringing dead men's knells.

Marlowe must have been aware of the absurdity of these lines, as Shakespeare was of his; and just as Barabas is not wholly evil, not merely a melodramatic villain, so Aaron displays human feeling when he defends his bastard by Tamora:

> Stay, murderous villains, will you kill your brother?
> Now, by the burning tapers of the sky
> That shone so brightly when this boy was got,
> He dies upon my scimitar's sharp point
> That touches this, my first-born son and heir . . .
> What, what, ye sanguine, shallow-hearted boys!
> Ye white-lim'd walls! ye alehouse painted signs!
> Coal-black is better than another hue
> In that it scorns to bear another hue;
> For all the water in the ocean
> Can never turn the swan's black legs to white,
> Although she lave them hourly in the flood . . .
> Look how the black slave smiles upon the father,
> As who should say, 'Old lad, I am thine own'.   (IV.ii.88–121)

Professor M. C. Bradbrook has rightly remarked that the character is

a fusion of the 'medieval devil' and the 'conscienceless Machiavel'.[11]
He is likewise an outsider, belonging neither to the Roman world nor
to the world of the Goths.

If, as has been suggested, Shakespeare was dramatising the struggle
between Rome and the European tradition on the one hand and
barbarism on the other,[12] he did not really succeed; for the ritual
sacrifice of Tamora's son and the slaying of Mutius, although they are
the cause of greater horrors, are themselves barbarous. In any case
Shakespeare's dramatic skill was only intermittent. There are fine
passages of eloquence; in the second act Shakespeare effectively
creates a woodland scene which serves as a background for Tamora's
love-making, the murder of Bassianus, and the rape of Lavinia; the
scenes in which Titus, maddened by his wrongs, tries to send messages
to the gods can still be effective on the stage as the Peter Brook production showed. But in the early part of the play—for which Shakespeare
may not be wholly responsible—characters portrayed with little skill
orate at considerable length in undifferentiated verse.

Apart from the figures of Aaron, who is splendidly theatrical,
Tamora and Titus, the characterisation is not very successful. Perhaps
the play is chiefly interesting as a forerunner, with the mad scenes
looking forward to the fourth act of *King Lear* and the Aaron–
Tamora–Saturninus triangle resembling that of Edmund, Goneril and
Albany.

Renaissance critics, as Professor Waith points out, thought that
tragedy should arouse not pity and terror, but admiration and commiseration. Shakespeare did not have to go beyond Sidney's *Defence
of Poesy* to be aware of this. The horrors and excesses of *Titus Andronicus* can still move an audience to 'admiration', in the sense of wonder.
But Shakespeare seems to have realised that he had not satisfied the
other requirement, for one of the few survivors at the end of the play
declares:

> My heart is not compact of flint nor steel;
> Nor can I utter all our bitter grief,
> But floods of tears will drown my oratory
> And break my utt'rance, even in the time
> When it should move ye to attend me most,
> And force you to commiseration.   (V.iii.88–93)

Shakespeare seems to have hoped to arouse commiseration as well as
admiration by means of effective oratory. It is not the floods of tears

which prevent this, but the oratory itself, which instead of forcing our commiseration, acts as a screen between the horrors and our hearts.

The three parts of *Henry VI* are not tragedies, though they have tragic elements—the British defeat in France and the long agony of the wars of the Roses. Some episodes could be detached and expanded into regular tragedies. The love of Margaret and Suffolk could have been treated like the story of Tristram and Iseult. York's bid for the throne and his downfall could likewise have been treated as a separate tragedy. The saintly King, too ineffective to be a tragic hero, is a moving commentator on the kingdom's tragedy. But the three things which best exhibit Shakespeare's development as a dramatist are his ability to present a character deteriorating under the stress of war, his concern with real and important issues, and his creation of Richard, Duke of Gloucester.

This character, as he emerges towards the end of *Henry VI*, is closely modelled on Marlowe's Guise,[13] for both are dedicated to the ruthless pursuit of power and both are followers of Machiavelli, as that political philosopher was misinterpreted by the Elizabethans. But it is arguable that Shakespeare surpasses his rival, for the portrait of Richard is more subtle and complex than that of Guise. The ruthless evil of Richard is related to his deformity. Deprived of the possibility of love, he dreams of the crown which he can achieve only by a series of crimes. This realisation is expressed in his first great soliloquy in Act III. He boasts that he can 'set the murderous Machiavel to school'. His other soliloquy comes after he has murdered Henry VI: in it he proclaims his detachment from his fellows:

I have no brother, I am like no brother;
And this word 'love', which greybeards call divine,
Be resident in men like one another,
And not in me! I am myself alone.

The protagonist of *Richard III*, which is concerned with the events immediately following, is developed from the Richard of *3 Henry VI*. He is more sardonic, wittier, more resourceful and more engaging; but he remains essentially the conscienceless Machiavel.

Gloucester's repudiation of brotherhood and his boast of isolation and self-sufficiency is a deliberate choice of evil. Fifty years ago *Richard III* could be written off as melodrama, and its hero as an incredible monster. As the other Gloucester remarks, 'I have learned

more since';[14] and if we are tempted to regard Richard with incredulity
we should remember that 'I'm all right, Jack' is not morally different
from 'I am myself alone'.

The opening soliloquy is a kind of prologue to remind the audience
of the situation at the end of *Henry VI* and of Richard's determination
'to prove a villain' as a substitute for love. His evil wit is displayed in
the first scene when he tells Clarence, who is to be his victim:

> Well, your imprisonment shall not be long;
> I will deliver you, or else lie for you.

His rhetorical effrontery is displayed in the wooing of Anne, a scene
which is preposterous to read but always theatrically effective. He
begins his wooing beside the coffin of his victim, Henry VI; Anne has
just called down curses on his head and on anyone who marries him;
and Richard has just admitted that his deformity makes it impossible
for him to be a successful lover. Yet he succeeds by a mixture of
flattery, hypocrisy and demonic power.

He is Shakespeare's first full-scale portrait of a hypocrite and it has
been said that in it he was 'pursuing the psychological secrets of his
craft' as an actor. Buckingham, for example, boasts that he

> can counterfeit the deep tragedian,
> Speak and look back, and pry on every side,
> Tremble and start at wagging of a straw,
> Intending deep suspicion: ghastly looks
> Are at my service, like enforced smiles;
> And both are ready in their offices,
> At any time to grace my stratagems.   (III.v.5–11)

It is implied that Richard has the same ability. The hypocrite is one
who plays a part; and if an actor can pretend to be a king or a saint, a
maiden or a monster, it might well be impossible to tell in real life
whether a man is revealing his real self to the world. Hence the prevalence in the play of imagery drawn from the stage.

The resemblances between *Richard III* and *Macbeth* have often
been pointed out, but the differences, as we shall see, are equally
significant. Macbeth too uses imagery drawn from the stage, but
whereas he laments that he and his wife must make their faces visards
to their hearts, Richard glories in the art of hypocrisy.

Richard III is a carefully constructed play, both in itself and as the
fourth play of a tetralogy. We are continually reminded—especially by

Queen Margaret—of what took place before. Richard is a scourge of God, wicked himself, but punishing the wickedness of others. Clarence, his first victim, for example, has been guilty of treachery, as his dream reminds us. The construction of the play itself is almost too rigidly planned. The prophecies of Queen Margaret, whose husband and son have been killed by Richard and who has herself been guilty of the deaths of Richard's father and brother, are all fulfilled before the end of the play. Edward IV dies of a surfeit; Queen Elizabeth outlives her glory and dies 'neither mother, wife, nor England's Queen'; Rivers, Dorset and Hastings are cut off 'by some unlooked accident'; and Buckingham, who scorns her warning to break with Richard, is told to

> remember this another day
> When he shall split thy very heart with sorrow.

We are reminded of each of Margaret's curses as each is fulfilled.

The same theme is brought home to us in the long scene in Act IV where Elizabeth and the Duchess of York ask Margaret to teach them to curse. The three women hate each other, but they are drawn together by their hatred of Richard. Modern audiences are apt to find this scene tedious, especially when it is played naturalistically; but we may be sure that Shakespeare was deliberately using ritual for choric purposes, as he does in the last act of the play when the eleven ghosts of Richard's victims appear to him and to Richmond on the eve of the Battle of Bosworth.

The theme of retribution is linked with the theme of conscience, which is presented to us in various ways. At first it appears that Richard has completely stifled his conscience and he kills off each of his associates when they exhibit scruples. But Shakespeare shows us the fulfilment of Margaret's prophecy:

> The worm of conscience still begnaw thy soul! . . .
> No sleep close up that deadly eye of thine,
> Unless it be while some tormenting dream
> Affrights thee with a hell of ugly devils. (I.iii.222–7)

We are reminded of this when Anne tells us:

> Never yet one hour in his bed
> Did I enjoy the golden dew of sleep
> But with his timorous dreams was still awak'd. (IV.i.83–5)

But before we are allowed to see Richard in this state, we are shown the operations of conscience in others—in Hastings, somewhat muted in Buckingham, in Tyrell, after the murder of the princes, and above all in the scene of Clarence's murder. Clarence's nightmare is the result of his guilty conscience. Brakenbury, the Lieutenant of the Tower, hopes to evade guilt for the murder of Clarence by an assumed ignorance—he dies on Bosworth Field; and the two murderers debate the question of conscience at some length. This is the only scene of the play in prose, partly because of the social status of the murderers and partly because it is used to provide some black comedy. The two men shrink alternately from committing the murder, although it is the second murderer who repents and refuses his half of the promised reward. The second murderer has earlier been asked what he will do if he is bothered again by conscience, and he replies:

> I'll not meddle with it—it makes a man a coward: a man cannot steal, but it accuseth him; a man cannot swear, but it checks him; a man cannot lie with his neighbour's wife, but it detects him. 'Tis a blushing shamefac'd spirit that mutinies in a man's bosom; it fills a man full of obstacles: it made me once restore a purse of gold that—by chance I found. It beggars any man that keeps it. It is turn'd out of towns and cities for a dangerous thing; and every man that means to live well endeavours to trust to himself and live without it.   (I.iv.133–42)

The last reference to conscience is by Richard himself just before the battle:

> Conscience is but a word that cowards use,
> Devis'd at first to keep the strong in awe.
> Our strong arms be our conscience, swords our law.

Marlowe is reported to have said 'that the first beginning of religion was only to keep men in awe' and he tried to convert others to atheism, 'willing them not to be afeard of bugbears and hobgoblins'.[15] But such ideas were very much in the air in the last decade of the sixteenth century. They are mentioned by Hooker and Sidney, and the author of *Selimus* seems to be echoing Marlowe when he speaks of religious observations as

> Only bug-bears to keep the world in fear.[16]

Richard's final defiance of his conscience is appropriate to the most Marlovian of Shakespeare's characters. But, immediately before this, a new dimension has been given to the character, when he is transformed from what Kierkegaard called 'the most demoniacal figure Shakespeare has created' into a sinner terrified of damnation.

> Have mercy, Jesu! Soft! I did but dream.
> O coward conscience, how dost thou afflict me!
> The lights burn blue, it is now dead midnight.
> Cold fearful drops stand on my trembling flesh.
> What do I fear? Myself? There's none else by.
> Richard loves Richard: that is, I am I.
> Is there a murderer here? No—yes, I am.
> Then fly. What, from myself? Great reason why—
> Lest I revenge. What, myself upon myself?
> Alack, I love myself. Wherefore? For any good
> That I myself have done unto myself?
> O, no! Alas, I rather hate myself
> For hateful deeds committed by myself!
> I am a villain; yet I lie, I am not.
> Fool, of thyself speak well. Fool, do not flatter.
> My conscience hath a thousand several tongues,
> And every tongue brings in a several tale,
> And every tale condemns me for a villain.
> Perjury, perjury, in the highest degree;
> Murder, stern murder, in the direst degree;
> And several sins, all us'd in each degree,
> Throng to the bar, crying all 'Guilty! Guilty!'
> I shall despair. There is no creature loves me;
> And if I die no soul will pity me:
> And wherefore should they, since that I myself
> Find in myself no pity to myself?

It is not accidental that *myself* occurs a dozen times in this speech. There sounds throughout it the dreadful realisation of his complete isolation in the prison of self. In the speech in *Henry VI* in which Richard's character is revealed for the first time, he had repudiated love and boasted 'I am myself alone'. Now he laments that no one loves him and 'I am I' is an admission of damnation. But this soliloquy comes too late to make him into a satisfactory tragic hero. For nine-tenths of the play Richard is a bogey-man—the bogey-man of Tudor propaganda— and he is observed from outside. Although Elizabethan critics and audiences would accept an entirely evil man as the protagonist of a tragedy, provided he paid the penalty for his misdeeds, Shakespeare afterwards relegated such characters to the role of villain. His later tragic heroes may commit deeds as atrocious as those of Richard III, but they are not initially, and never deliberately, evil.

Richard III, though complete in itself, can be regarded as the final play of a tetralogy; *Richard II*, though also complete in itself, can be regarded as the first part of a tetralogy on the causes of the Wars of the Roses. (The date of *King John* is still a matter for debate but all critics would agree that it was written at least before *1 Henry IV*, the sequel to *Richard II*. Although Shakespeare shows us John tempted and falling—not one who deliberately chooses evil—his death is not shown as directly relevant to his actions. The play is less coherent than either *Richard III* or *Richard II*.) In some ways *Richard II* is less effective on the stage than *Richard III*. The action is less exciting, the hero is less dynamic, and there are one or two unexpectedly weak scenes. But in other respects the play represents a considerable advance. Shakespeare made use of a much wider range of sources, including not merely the chronicles of Holinshed and Froissart, but also *The Mirror For Magistrates*, Daniel's narrative poem, *The Civil Wars*, Hall's *Union of the Two Noble and Illustrate Famelies of Lancastre and Yorke* and the anonymous play, *Thomas of Woodstock*.[17] It has even been suggested that Shakespeare followed up marginal references and consulted three French manuscripts. What is certain is that in writing some of the set-pieces—the banishment of Bolingbroke and Gaunt's dying speech—he conflated many passages from his reading of Erasmus, Ovid, Cicero, Valerius Maximus, Lyly, Daniel, John Eliot, Lodge and other writers.[18] *Richard II* was also an advance in the level of its poetry—despite the splendour of Clarence's dream—in the dramatic use of imagery, and in subtlety of characterisation.

Richard II has been responsible for the murder of his uncle, Thomas of Woodstock, but no one would describe him as a villain. Nor is Bolingbroke, the usurper, who is responsible for Richard's murder, a villain. The two protagonists are nicely balanced. Richard is the lawful anointed King, with an exquisite sensibility; but he is irresponsible, indecisive, and misled by flatterers. Bolingbroke is a competent ruler, but he breaks his oath both to his followers and to the King and he has some of the characteristics of a Machiavel. Richard is imaginative and voluble; Bolingbroke is prosaic and taciturn. Our sympathies are therefore divided. While Richard is behaving irresponsibly in the first two acts, banishing Bolingbroke, callous at Gaunt's death-bed and seizing his estates, our sympathies are with the spokesman for England and with his exiled son; but once Bolingbroke returns and Richard's fortunes begin to sink, our sympathies switch to the King. This is partly because the King is given all the best poetry to speak; and his great lyrical arias on the fall of princes, the ritual of his abdication and his separation from his wife are all designed to arouse our sympathy. One cannot, it has been said, take sides against poetry. But it is also plain that Richard learns through suffering. His meditation in prison on two biblical texts, his new humility, and his recognition of his own faults—'I wasted time, and now doth Time waste me'—show that he has become superior to Bolingbroke, though he lost his throne for his previous sins and errors.

Shakespeare's new mastery in the presentation of character can be seen to best advantage in the abdication scene, the more impressive because it follows a tedious exchange of challenges: seven gloves are thrown down, so that in the end Aumerle has to borrow one from a bystander. Of the 155 lines between Richard's arrival and departure, Bolingbroke has only eleven speeches, making a total of less than nine lines. Richard has all the limelight: he plays to perfection the role of abdicator. His ritualistic divesting of his symbols of office, his references to Christ's passion, his rebuke of Northumberland, his smashing of the mirror, and his tears all ensure that he retains the interest and sympathy of the audience. But the 'silent king', Bolingbroke, manifesting his strength by his silences, is also an interesting figure. He restrains Northumberland who is only carrying out his orders and so escapes the odium of Richard's persecutors. He remains quiet, courteous and prosaic; but towards the end surprises Richard and the audience with an unexpected subtlety of mind. When the mirror is shattered, Richard remarks:

> How soon my sorrow hath destroyed my face.

Bolingbroke replies in his longest speech during this scene:

> The shadow of your sorrow hath destroyed
> The shadow of your face.

He implies that Richard is putting on an act; but Richard retorts, as Hamlet was later to do, that the trappings and the suits of woe reflect his inner grief.

Swinburne, who thought the play one of Shakespeare's earliest, complained[19] that the dramatist's interest was concentrated on the character of the hero and that the minor characters in *Edward II* are 'far more solid and definite figures' than such characters as York,

Norfolk and Aumerle. But Norfolk appears in only two scenes and it
is his function which is important rather than his character; and the
other two characters mentioned by Swinburne are drawn with considerable subtlety. York especially is a realistic portrayal of an honest
blunderer distracted by conflicting loyalties. He criticises the King at
Gaunt's death-bed, and protests at the seizure of his property. In spite
of which the King makes him Lord Governor of England during his
absence in Ireland. In Act II Scene ii, York is shown incompetent,
bewildered and perplexed:

> Both are my kinsmen.
> Th'one is my sovereign, whom both my oath
> And duty bids defend; t'other again
> Is my kinsman, whom the King hath wronged,
> Whom conscience and my kindred bids to right.
> Well, somewhat we must do.

Two scenes later he confesses that he lacks the power to arrest the
rebels, so he declares that he is neutral. Immediately afterwards, he
offers them hospitality. Even after he has adhered to Bolingbroke's
cause he sympathises with Richard, and it is he who describes the entry
into London. But the scene in which he reports his son's conspiracy to
Bolingbroke and urges his execution despite the pleading of his wife
is less easy to justify, not because it is psychologically impossible, but
because it is written in rhymed couplets. Some critics have argued that
the scene is a survival from a source-play unfortunately retained by
Shakespeare. Others point to the fact that the poet, whose early plays
have comparatively little rhyme, experimented in rhyme in the plays
written soon after his narrative poems, so that it cannot be assumed
that the scene in question was written earlier, or by some other hand.
Swinburne said the scene was 'the last hysterical struggle of rhyme to
maintain its place in tragedy'. But Shakespeare must have been conscious of the absurdity of the situation with three members of the York
family kneeling to the King and it is obvious that the intention of the
scene was comic. On the arrival of the Duchess, Bolingbroke says:

> Our scene is alter'd from a serious thing,
> And now changed to 'The Beggar and the King'.

We are not expected to take the situation seriously, and the absurdity
is pointed by the rhymes:

> *Duchess* The word is short, but no so short as sweet:
> No word like 'pardon' for kings' mouths so meet.
> *York*   Speak it in French, King. Say 'Pardonne moy.'
> *Duchess* Dost thou teach pardon pardon to destroy?

But audiences, who invariably laugh, are uneasy in their laughter, and Shakespeare seems to have miscalculated.

Another scene which is apt to miscarry is that of the gardeners. It provides a choric commentary on the action, underlining Richard's misgovernment and the passing of his power to Bolingbroke. Moreover it fits in with the recurrent idea of England as a garden, Eden restored, as the Queen addresses one of the men as 'old Adam's likeness'. But, by writing the scene in verse, Shakespeare makes it difficult for us to believe in the gardeners as anything more than a chorus.

The fusion of Richard's tragedy and England's is another way in which this play shows an advance. The last speech of *Richard III* ends with the peace of the Tudor settlement, the marriage of the white rose and the red; but we are not conscious during the course of the play that the future of England depends on its outcome. In *Richard II*, on the other hand, this theme is continually stressed. It appears in the speeches about exile in the first act; in John of Gaunt's prophecy in the second act; in Richard's love for the English earth when he returns from Ireland; in the gardeners' scene; and in the Bishop of Carlisle's prophecy before Bolingbroke ascends the throne. Indeed, the two prophecies are nicely balanced, Gaunt's stressing the damage to England of Richard's government, and the Bishop stressing in phrases echoed from the scriptures and the Homilies the more permanent damage caused by deposing the Lord's anointed.

But it is poetically that *Richard II* is most impressive. This can be illustrated by the greater pregnancy of phrasing, as when in the last scene Exton calls Richard's body Bolingbroke's 'buried fear', which refers back to the earlier phrase, 'living fear'. It can be illustrated by Bolingbroke's speech on his banishment or by a score of Richard's speeches in the second half of the play. But as Professor Altick and others have shown,[20] Shakespeare, in the plays written about this time, began to use imagery in a much more dramatic way. In his earliest plays imagery is decorative rather than organic. We can delight in individual similes and metaphors, without feeling that they are of any greater significance, but, as Coleridge pointed out,[21]

B

images, however beautiful, though faithfully copied from nature, and as accurately represented in words, do not of themselves characterize the poet. They become proofs of original genius only as far as they are modified by a predominant passion; or by associated thoughts or images awakened by that passion; or when they have the effect of reducing multitude to unity, or succession to an instant; or lastly, when a human and intellectual life is transferred to them from the poet's own spirit.

There are traces of iterative imagery in *Richard III*—not merely of imagery drawn from the stage referred to above—but Shakespeare seems to have been struck about this time by the dramatic possibilities of imagery. In *A Midsummer Night's Dream* it is used to create the atmosphere of the wood near Athens. In *Richard II* and *Romeo and Juliet* the various groups of images are used rather to underline or reveal the basic themes of the plays. In *Richard II*, as Richard D. Altick has shown, the symbolism 'is dominated by the related words *earth, land* and *ground*', by the image of the untended garden, by the iteration of *blood* and *tongue*, by the sweet/sour antithesis, by the use of the crown as a symbol. To these we may add the religious images and allusions which are designed to remind us of the divine right of kings. Altick argues that 'thanks to its tightly interwoven imagery *Richard II* has a poetic unity that is unsurpassed in any of the great tragedies; so far as structure is concerned, Shakespeare has levied from iterative language about all the aid that it will give'. Perhaps there is some exaggeration in this statement, but at least it may be said that *Richard II* looks forward to mature Shakespearian tragedy more directly than any previous play had done.

Romeo and Juliet was probably written within a few months of *Richard II*. It differs in many respects from all the tragedies discussed in this chapter. It is Shakespeare's first love tragedy and, as a natural result, the hero and heroine are of equal importance; whatever we may think of Romeo he is much less flawed than the previous tragic heroes— neither a double-dyed murderer like Richard III, nor an irresponsible tyrant such as Richard II; and, although the actions of hero and heroine are partly the cause of their deaths, fate plays a larger part in the catastrophe than in any other of Shakespeare's plays. It is unlucky that Romeo should be confronted on his wedding-day by a quarrelsome bully; it is still more unlucky that the Friar's messenger should be put in quarantine, so that Romeo never receives news of the plan to avert Juliet's marriage to Paris. It is the element of fate which is stressed in one of Shakespeare's rare prologues, which was omitted from the Folio, presumably by inadvertence. Romeo and Juliet are 'A pair of star-cross'd lovers'

> Whose misadventured piteous overthrows
> Doth with their death bury their parents' strife.
> The fearful passage of their death-mark'd love . . .
> Is now the two hours' traffic of our stage.

The influence of the stars is stressed again and again throughout the play. Just before his first sight of Juliet, Romeo fears

> Some consequence, yet hanging in the stars,
> Shall bitterly begin his fearful date
> With this night's revels . . .

When he slays Tybalt, he exclaims 'O, I am fortune's fool!' When he hears the false report of Juliet's death, he cries 'Then I defy you, stars'. In her vault he proposes to

> shake the yoke of inauspicious stars
> From this world-wearied flesh.

Even the Friar, commenting on the tragedy, says

> A greater power than we can contradict
> Hath thwarted our intents.

Many critics believe that *Romeo and Juliet* is an unsatisfactory tragedy because the catastrophe is caused by an unfortunate accident. It may be suggested that the fate of Oedipus depends even less on character than Romeo's does, and not many would question the greatness of *Oedipus Rex*. Other critics, while admitting that accident plays a large part in *Romeo and Juliet*, argue that the lovers themselves are largely responsible for what happens. John Masefield declared[22] that the obsession of love

> brings to an end in two hearts, filial affection and that perhaps stronger thing, attachment to family. It makes a charming young man a frantic madman, careless of everything but his love. It makes the sweet-natured girl a deceitful, scheming liar, less frantic, but not less devoted than her lover. It results almost at once in five violent deaths, and a legacy of broken-heartedness not easily told.

This interpretation of the play is impossible to square with the text. Romeo is turned into 'a frantic madman' not by his love but by the fact that he is banished; Juliet, following the advice of the Friar, can hardly be described as a 'deceitful, scheming liar', especially as her parents behave atrociously to her; two of the violent deaths—those of Mercutio and Tybalt—are not due to Romeo's love, but to the bitter feud between the two families. It is, in fact, Romeo's love that makes him refuse to fight Tybalt until Tybalt has killed Mercutio. Shakespeare, as Peter Alexander has pointed out,[23] 'shows Romeo behaving with exemplary composure and forbearance, though insulted by a quarrelsome bully in the presence of his friends'.

Can we really believe that Shakespeare intended us to blame Juliet for deceiving her parents by her secret marriage? No doubt well-trained girls in Shakespeare's day would marry a man chosen by their parents; and some parents in a sixteenth-century audience might condemn Juliet's behaviour. But it is wrong to generalise. An audience consisted of more than a thousand people, young and old, rich and poor, educated and illiterate, wise and foolish; and we can be sure that there was no unanimity about their responses. The young, at least, would approve of the lovers and blame their families for the murderous feud. No decent parent would force his child to marry against her will; and Elizabethan dramatists almost invariably aroused sympathy for those who made secret marriages, refusing marriages arranged for them.

Shakespeare is careful to direct our sympathies. When Lady Capulet informs Juliet that she must marry Paris on the following Thursday, she asks quite reasonably for a little delay in view of the death of Tybalt and of the fact that her bridegroom is almost a stranger:

> I wonder at this haste, that I must wed
> Ere he that should be husband comes to woo.

Lady Capulet says savagely:

> I would the fool were married to her grave.

Capulet tells Juliet that he will drag her to church on a hurdle, calls her a green-sickness carrion, a baggage, a tallow-face, a disobedient wretch. He tells his wife that it is a curse to have a daughter, calls Juliet more names, and finally tells her that, if she refuses to marry Paris, he will cast her out to 'hang, beg, starve, die in the streets'. It may be said in extenuation that Capulet loves his daughter after a fashion and that he does not mean all he says; but he treats her as one of his chattels and his brutality is shocking. Shakespeare made him like this to intensify our sympathy for Juliet.

To what extent should we regard the Friar as Shakespeare's spokesman? He first appears in the third scene of Act II, carrying a basket which he proposes to fill with weeds and flowers. His soliloquy states clearly that just as a flower may contain both poison and medicine, so in man there are potentialities for good and evil:

> For nought so vile that on the earth doth live
> But to the earth some special good doth give;
> Nor aught so good but, strain'd from that fair use,
> Revolts from true birth, stumbling on abuse.
> Virtue itself turns vice, being misapplied,
> And vice sometime's by action dignified.
> Within the infant rind of this weak flower
> Poison hath residence, and medicine power; . . .
> Two such opposed kings encamp them still
> In man as well as herbs—grace and rude will;
> And where the worser is predominant,
> Full soon the canker death eats up that plant.

We are bound to assume that these couplets are intended to be applicable to the action of the play. Grace and rude will are struggling for mastery of Romeo, as in us all. Perhaps, too, we are meant to think that Romeo's love—in itself a virtue—may turn into vice by being misapplied: or, indeed, that sexual passion, in itself a vice, is dignified by the action, that is, by bringing the feud to an end.

The Friar ends the scene by warning Romeo: 'They stumble that run fast'; and in the next scene in which he again advises Romeo to 'love moderately':

> These violent delights have violent ends
> And in their triumph die, like fire and powder,
> Which, as they kiss, consume.

The Friar also saves Romeo from despair and suicide when he is banished. It is plain that Shakespeare was not following the poem which served as his source, in which Arthur Brooke purported to describe

a couple of unfortunate lovers . . . conferring their principal counsels with drunken gossips and superstitious friars (the naturally fit instruments of unchastity) . . . using auricular confession (the key of whoredom and treason) for furtherance of their purpose, abusing the honourable name of lawful marriage to cloak the shame of stolen contracts.

But, despite the Friar's choric role and the Prince's assurance after the catastrophe that he is a holy man, his involvement in the secret marriage, and his advice to Juliet to take the drug rather than confess the marriage, even though the plot demands these actions, may make it difficult to accept the Friar as a disinterested observer and commentator.

To Professor Caroline Spurgeon the significance of the imagery—light, gunpowder, stars—was that Shakespeare saw 'the beauty and ardour of young love' as 'the irradiating glory of sunlight and starlight in a dark world'.[24] But while this may well be true of the light images, it seems likely that the gunpowder images symbolise the destructive effects of passion and the danger of the Montague–Capulet feud, and that many of the star images are concerned with their astrological influence.

Three other groups of images are also of some importance.[25] Those relating to voyages, suggested perhaps by Brooke's poem, are concerned with the love-quest and with the voyage of life. Those concerned with religion suggest the way in which the lovers substitute the worship of each other for the worship of God. Those concerned with Death as a lover reinforce the idea 'that Juliet is foredoomed to die, that Death, personified, has claimed her for his own'. Capulet tells Paris:

> O son, the night before thy wedding-day
> Hath Death lain with thy wife: see, there she lies,
> Flower as she was, deflowered by him.

And Romeo in his last speech asks:

> shall I believe
> That unsubstantial Death is amorous
> And that the lean abhorred monster keeps
> Thee here in dark to be his paramour?
> For fear of that I still will stay with thee
> And never from this palace of dim night
> Depart again.

The imagery can therefore be used in support of either of the main interpretations of the play—either that the lovers—'two of the most attractive lovers in all literature'—allow passion to usurp the place of reason, earthly love to be substituted for the love of God, so that they ignore their duties to their parents and end up by committing the sin of self-murder; or that their love is a shining contrast to the hatred of their families, and their sacrifice is used by providence to bring an end to the feud. As Hankins remarks:[26] 'The sequence of events is deliberately made so improbable that chance alone cannot explain it. Only fate, or the will of Heaven, affords a sufficient explanation.'

As with so many arguments about Shakespeare's plays, we do not arrive at the truth by taking one side or the other, since the poet himself is on both sides. By the standards of religion, the lovers may be found wanting. But in a world where many are not capable of a firm persuasion of anything, their total commitment to each other deserves our admiration; and in a world devoted to the uncertifiable insanity of hatred, their love is a positive and redemptive good. Even Brooke, despite his puritanical moralising, describes the death of the lovers

> As this our mutual and our piteous sacrifice
> Of life, set light for love.

To Shakespeare, too, the death of the lovers was a sacrifice, a means of reconciling their two families. This is made clear in the lines of the Chorus at the beginning of the play, which speaks of

> The fearful passage of their death-mark'd love,
> And the continuance of their parents' rage,
> Which, but their children's end, nought could remove.

The same point is made at the end of the play when the Prince addresses Montague and Capulet:

> See what a scourge is laid upon your hate,
> That heaven finds means to kill your joys with love!

Capulet calls Montague 'brother' and speaks of Romeo and Juliet as

> Poor sacrifices of our enmity!

In spite of the accidents that destroy the happiness of the lovers, the reconciliation of the warring families prevents us from thinking that the President of the Immortals has been using them for his sport.

In several respects *Romeo and Juliet* is an advance on Shakespeare's previous tragedies. It was the first play in which he outdistanced the greatest of his immediate contemporaries, Marlowe. Nearly all the characters are well drawn and for several of them Shakespeare evolved a characteristic style. The two great triumphs in this respect are Mercutio and the Nurse. Mercutio's vitality and wit are apparent in all the scenes in which he appears—in the speech about Queen Mab, in his conjuring of Romeo, and in the wonderful speech after he receives his death-wound:

No, 'tis not so deep as a well, nor so wide as a church door; but 'tis enough, 'twill serve. Ask for me to-morrow, and you shall find me a grave man. I am peppered, I warrant, for this world. A plague o' both your houses.

Juliet's Nurse is even more remarkable. Much of the part is written in verse, but verse so supple and daring that the first compositors thought it was prose. Shakespeare obtains some subtle effects by the verse rhythm underlying the apparently colloquial speech. Some of the lines, considered in isolation, hardly seem to fit into the pattern of the verse—

Come Lammas Eve at night shall she be fourteen . . .

Sitting in the sun under the dovehouse wall—

but in their contexts the verse form dictates how they should be spoken. In previous plays characters are differentiated largely by what they say: the Nurse is differentiated also by the way she says it.

Some critics have complained of the immaturity of certain scenes. Romeo's scene with the Friar in which he laments his banishment is presumably deliberately hysterical, but it is long-drawn-out and one quibble in it has had no admirers:

Flies may do this but I from this must fly.

But other passages which have been adversely criticised may be defended. The tedious antithesis of Romeo's early speeches—

O brawling love, O loving hate,
O anything, of nothing first create!
O heavy lightness, serious vanity—

were clearly intended to bring out the unreality of his love for Rosaline. The sonnet he shares with Juliet at their first meeting is brilliantly devised to show their love at first sight. Juliet's conceit in her address to Night—

Give me my Romeo; and, when he shall die,
Take him and cut him out in little stars—

reveals a charming whimsicality which is perfectly in character.

The scene which has aroused most complaint is the one in which Juliet's parents and the Nurse lament her supposed death:

Nurse   Alas, alas! Help, help! my lady's dead!
          O welladay that ever I was born!
          Some aqua-vitae, ho! my lord! my lady!
          O lamentable day! Look, look! O heavy day!
Lady C. O me, O me! My child, my only life!
Nurse   She's dead, deceased; she's dead, alack the day!
Lady C. Alack the day, she's dead, she's dead, she's dead!

This goes on for another thirty lines:

    O day, O day, O day! O hateful day!
    Never was seen so black a day as this.

It reminds one inevitably of Pyramus's style in *A Midsummer-Night's Dream* and Shakespeare must have been aware of its absurdity. He showed, moreover, even in this scene, that he could express genuine feeling, as in Capulet's lines:

    Death lies on her like an untimely frost
    Upon the sweetest flower of all the field.

We must assume, therefore, that the ritual wailing for the counterfeit death of Juliet was deliberate, perhaps because Shakespeare was afraid of spoiling the effect of her actual death in the next act.

When Shakespeare returned to tragedy at the turn of the century his art had matured as a result of writing some of his finest comedies and the later Histories. But he had learnt from his own experimental tragedies that it was important to have as a tragic hero a man who was neither a villain nor a saint, and that the catastrophe should depend more on character than on accident. Perhaps the alacrity in suicide displayed by Pyramus and Thisbe may be an oblique comment on the final scene of *Romeo and Juliet*.

3

JULIUS CAESAR

In the most high and palmy state of Rome

By 1599 Shakespeare had completed the sequence of English histories
from John to the first Tudor, the first three Edwards having been
covered by other dramatists. Henry VIII was a dangerous topic, at
least until the death of Elizabeth; so, in looking for other historical
material suitable for dramatising, Shakespeare naturally turned to
Rome, led there by North's translation of Plutarch's *Lives*. He had
read in these at least four years earlier[1] and years before, while still at
school, he would have read some of Caesar's works. He knew, as
every schoolboy did, what Rosalind called 'Caesar's thrasonical brag',
Veni, vidi, vici. There was one tradition in which Caesar was thought
of as a braggart and a tyrant; and although Plutarch admitted[2] 'the
state of Rome . . . being now brought to that pass that it could no more
abide to be governed by many lords but required one only absolute
governor', he sympathised with Brutus. But there was another tradition, equally powerful, which held that the assassination of Caesar was
not merely a blunder, but one of the most heinous crimes ever committed: for Caesar had founded the empire which was the secular
framework of Christendom. That is why Dante, who elsewhere
expressed reservations about Caesar, placed Brutus and Cassius beside
Judas in the lowest circle of hell:

> 'Quell' anima lassù che maggior pena,'
>   disse il maestro, 'è Giuda Scarïotto,
>   che il capo ha dentro, e fuor le gambe mena.
> Degli altri due ch'hanno il capo di sotto,
>   quei ché pende dal nero ceffo è Bruto:
>   vedi come si storce, e nom fa motto;
> e l'altro è Cassio, che par sì membruto.'   (*Inferno*, xxxiv.61–7)

'That soul up there to the worst penance brought
    Is Judas the Iscariot,' spoke my Lord.
'His head within, he plies his legs without.
Of the other two, hanging with head downward,
    Brutus it is whom the black mouth doth maul.
See how he writhes and utters not a word!
Cassius the other who seems so large to sprawl.'   (trans. L. Binyon)

What Shakespeare thought of the assassination is still in dispute. Caesar can be played as a thrasonical tyrant or as a truly great man and both interpretations can be supported by the text. This fact led Professor Schanzer to argue[3] that *Julius Caesar* was one of Shakespeare's Problem Plays and that we are presented by the poet with two conflicting views of Caesar and 'the moral problem of the justifiability of the murder'. Add to this the 'dramatic coquetry' with which Shakespeare 'manipulates our response to the principal characters'. Even if we reject the idea that *Julius Caesar* should be classed as a problem play—in which category Professor Schanzer does not include *All's Well That Ends Well* and *Troilus and Cressida*—he has rightly called attention to certain characteristics of the play.

It has often been pointed out that Shakespeare, while accepting Plutarch's portrait of Caesar as a basis, lays more stress on his physical weaknesses. He adds a deafness in one ear and makes more of the falling sickness. Cassius contrasts Caesar's political power with his physical weakness, revealed by the fever caught in Spain and the swimming-match in the Tiber. But, to an audience, this is more likely to call attention to Cassius's envy than to bring discredit on Caesar. Plutarch, indeed, who has no love for Caesar, comments on the way he overcame his physical disabilities. His soldiers admired him 'that he always continued all labour and hardness'.[4] He

yielded not to the disease of his body, to make it a cloak to cherish him withal, but, contrarily, took the pains of war as a medicine to cure his sick body, fighting always with his disease, travelling continually, living soberly, and commonly lying abroad in the field. For the most nights he slept in his coach or litter, and thereby bestowed his rest, to make him always able to do something.

He refuses the crown offered him by Antony so as to demonstrate that he did not wish to be a king; he postpones the reading of Artemidorus's warning because his personal interests are of less importance than those of the state; and, as Brutus admits, he has never let passion usurp the place of reason.[5] Some of his sayings are splendid:

> Cowards die many times before their deaths;
> The valiant never taste of death but once.
> Of all the wonders that I yet have heard,
> It seems to me most strange that men should fear,
> Seeing that death, a necessary end,
> Will come when it will come.   (II.ii.32–7)

But, splendid as this is, it could be taken as a manifestation of pride, of the 'self-approving self-dramatisation' of which Dr Leavis accused Othello.[6] It is significant that he often speaks of himself in the third person:

> Caesar is turn'd to hear ...
> Yet Caesar shall go forth ...
> Shall Caesar send a lie?

When he warns Antony of Cassius, he adds:

> I rather tell thee what is to be fear'd
> Than what I fear; for always I am Caesar.

It has been argued that an Elizabethan audience would know the way to distinguish a good ruler from a tyrant; and since Caesar surrounds himself with flatterers and yes-men, and rules by caprice rather than by reason, they would certainly have regarded him as a tyrant. Mr Bernard Breyer concludes:[7]

In short he shows himself the very picture of a tyrant—above his fellow men, above the law, above reason itself. No Elizabethan in the theatre could doubt that here was a man ripe for the knife. And none, I believe, could have viewed his ensuing slaughter with anything but complete satisfaction, or could have blamed Brutus for his part in the deed.

One can only envy the assurance that can inform us of the unanimous response of a very heterogeneous audience at the end of the sixteenth century. Doubtless Caesar on the morning of the assassination carries his boasting to absurd lengths:

> Danger knows full well
> That Caesar is more dangerous than he;
> We are two lions litter'd in one day,
> And I the elder and more terrible.   (II.ii.44–7)

In his last long speech he is guilty of dreadful *hubris*. He boasts that he is above the frailties of mankind and almost claims divine attributes:

> I could be well mov'd, if I were as you;
> If I could pray to move, prayers would move me;

> But I am constant as the northern star
> Of whose true-fix'd and resting quality
> There is no fellow in the firmament.
> The skies are painted with unnumber'd sparks,
> They are all fire, and every one doth shine;
> But there's but one in all doth hold his place.
> So in the world: 'tis furnish'd well with men,
> And men are flesh and blood, and apprehensive;
> Yet in the number I do know but one
> That unassailable holds on his rank,
> Unshak'd of motion; and that I am he,
> Let me a little show it, even in this—
> That I was constant Cimber should be banish'd
> And constant do remain to keep him so.
> . . . Wilt thou lift up Olympus?   (III.i.58ff.)

Caesar's boast that he is unmoved by prayers has been shown to be false by his listening to his wife's pleading not to attend the Senate, and his boast of constancy is undercut by his decision to attend after all. But his refusal to pardon Cimber cannot be regarded as proof that he is lacking in clemency for we know that the conspirators are using the appeal as an excuse for getting close to their victim. Some members of the audience would surely have regarded the assassination with horror, especially when they recalled the scene where Caesar invited the conspirators to drink with him:

> Good friends, go in, and taste some wine with me
> And we, like friends, will straightway go together.

In Plutarch's account only Decius Brutus goes to Caesar's house and Shakespeare's addition was designed to arouse pity and horror.

It was argued by Schücking that Shakespeare had no intention of depicting Caesar as a braggart: and he gives that impression to a modern reader only because we do not realise that he is using the 'primitive' technique of self-explanation—that he is informing the audience that Caesar is godlike, not implying that the character is making excessive claims for himself. But Mr J. I. M. Stewart is surely right when he argues[8] that Shakespeare is much more subtle in his method of characterisation here: that he is leading the judicious members of his audience to discern that the 'public Caesar is the creation of an inflexible will', that it 'is a rigid mask'; that the exertion of his will demands an immense effort; and that his

utterances marvellously carry the impression of one physically fretted to decay, and opposing to the first falterings of the mind an increasingly rigid and absolute assertion of the Caesar idea.

Those critics who have regarded the play as a straightforward treatment of tyrannicide may have been misled by supposed parallels with the dictatorships of our own day. But Caesar, as depicted by Shakespeare, has little in common with Hitler or Stalin. Nor do the conspirators themselves accuse him of anything except ambition. Caesar is the victim, not the hero. The hero is, of course, Brutus, 'the noblest Roman of them all', who, as Antony testifies, joined the conspiracy

> in a general honest thought
> And common good to all . . .
> His life was gentle; and the elements
> So mix'd in him that Nature might stand up
> And say to all the world 'This was a man!'

This is a notable tribute from an enemy; but it should not be regarded as more than a choric verdict, spoken by the most important character left alive, to direct the response of the audience. The conspirators themselves realise the necessity of obtaining the support of Brutus, whose obvious integrity and unstained reputation will cover up their own shortcomings. Cassius testifies to his friend's nobility after he has first tempted him and he shows clearly that he hopes to corrupt him:

> Well, Brutus, thou art noble; yet, I see,
> Thy honourable metal may be wrought
> From that it is dispos'd. Therefore it is meet
> That noble minds keep ever with their likes,
> For who so firm that cannot be seduc'd?
> Caesar doth bear me hard; but he loves Brutus.
> If I were Brutus now and he were Cassius,
> He should not humour me.   (I.ii.307–14)

At this stage of the play, an envious man is trying to persuade a man of integrity to murder a man who loves him and who has been generous to him. The tempter wisely makes no direct appeal to baser motives but only to political principle. Brutus can do evil only if it comes to him in the guise of good.

Long after the assassination, he tells Cassius that they murdered Caesar 'but for supporting robbers'. This is the first we hear of it. Immediately after the assassination he cries 'Ambition's debt is paid!' and 'Peace, freedom and liberty!' He tells the citizens that despite his love for Caesar he killed him because he was ambitious. This is the reason he gives in the very curious soliloquy at the beginning of Act II:

> It must be by his death: and for my part,
> I know no personal cause to spurn at him,
> But for the general. He would be crowned:
> How that might change his nature, there's the question.
> It is the bright day that brings forth the adder,
> And that craves wary walking. Crown him?—that!
> And then I grant we put a sting in him
> That at his will he may do danger with.
> Th'abuse of greatness is when it disjoins
> Remorse from power; and to speak truth of Caesar,
> I have not known when his affections swayed
> More than his reason. But 'tis a common proof
> That lowliness is young Ambition's ladder
> Whereto the climber-upward turns his face
> But when he once attains the upmost round,
> He then unto the ladder turns his back
> Looks in the clouds, scorning the base degrees
> By which he did ascend. So Caesar may:
> Then lest he may, prevent. And since the quarrel
> Will bear no colour for the thing he is,
> Fashion it thus; that what he is, augmented,
> Would run to these and these extremities:
> And therefore think him as the serpent's egg,
> Which hatched, would as his kind grow mischievous,
> And kill him the shell.

Brutus has already made up his mind, as the first line indicates. Once he had agreed to holding the meeting at his house he was virtually committed to the conspiracy. The argument of the soliloquy is based on the assumption that Caesar wants to be crowned and that there was a danger that this would change his nature. But we have already been informed that Caesar has thrice refused a crown—however reluctantly—so that Brutus has little justification for his assumption. It is, moreover, preposterous to kill a man for his future crimes when his past has been blameless. Caesar, as Brutus admits, has not disjoined remorse from power, or allowed himself to be governed by his passions. What is even more absurd—as Coleridge pointed out[9]—is that Caesar was already an absolute ruler. He had crossed the Rubicon, entered Rome as a conqueror, and destroyed the power of the Senate. Brutus does not mention these things and is worried only by the fear that Caesar, if he is crowned, will undergo a transformation.

There was a case for the assassination of Caesar, as Shakespeare was aware; but in this crucial soliloquy Brutus is not given a single valid argument. Perhaps a reasoned argument for king-killing would have run foul of the censorship. But it seems likely that the soliloquy was carefully designed to reveal the flaw in the mind of the hero. Brutus is completely blind to the realities of the situation, Caesar's absolute power. He is concerned only with the title of King and the fact that his ancestor and namesake had driven out the Tarquins. It is not that he is unintelligent: he substitutes ideas for realities. As John Palmer remarked:[10]

The reflective idealist, living in imagination, is more impressed by the idea or symbol of power than by the thing itself.

The same characteristics are displayed throughout the play. Against the advice of Cassius, Brutus insists that Antony shall be spared and that he shall be allowed to deliver a funeral oration. He thinks that Antony can be trusted not to blame the conspirators. Brutus always gets his own way, not so much by argument as by moral bludgeoning of his opponents. Gordon Ross Smith lists many occasions in the play when Brutus domineers over his fellows[11]—the refusal to swear (II.i.212), the refusal to invite Cicero to join them (II.i.150), the sparing of Antony (II.i.154ff.), the treatment of Antony (III.i), the quarrel with Cassius (IV.iii), the decision to fight at Philippi.

The dilemmas of an idealist in the realm of *realpolitik* can be observed in every scene in which Brutus appears. Before the murder, for example, he urges the conspirators:

> Let's be sacrificers, but not butchers, Caius.
> We all stand up against the spirit of Caesar,
> And in the spirit of men there is no blood.
> O that we then could come by Caesar's spirit,
> And not dismember Caesar! But, alas,
> Caesar must bleed for it! And, gentle friends,
> Let's kill him boldly, but not wrathfully:
> Let's carve him as a dish fit for the gods,
> Not hew him as a carcase fit for hounds.   (II.i.166–74)

There is irony here, not merely that the murder of Caesar ensures the triumph of Caesarism, but also in the contrast between the pious hope and the deed itself. It is not accidental that Shakespeare should contrast the ritual intended by Brutus with the savage spectacle it turns out to be. The daggers of the conspirators, Antony tells us, hacked one

another in the sides of Caesar. Intoxicated with the deed, Brutus urges
the conspirators to stoop

> And let us bathe our hands in Caesar's blood
> Up to the elbows, and besmear our swords.
> Then walk we forth, even to the market-place,
> And waving our red weapons o'er our heads,
> Let's all cry 'Peace, freedom, and liberty!' (III.i.107–11)

So Calpurnia's dream came true. Caesar's statue,

> Like a fountain with an hundred spouts,
> Did run pure blood; and many lusty Romans
> Came smiling and did bathe their hands in it. (II.ii.77–9)

When Antony takes each of the conspirators by the hand, he refers
again and again to the blood:

> Now whilst your purpled hands do reek and smoke . . .
> Let each man render me his bloody hand . . .
> That I did love thee, Caesar, O, 'tis true!
> If then thy spirit look upon us now,
> Shall it not grieve thee dearer than thy death
> To see thy Antony making his peace,
> Shaking the bloody fingers of thy foes. (III.i.159–99)

Three of Antony's remarks seem especially designed to expose Brutus's
illusions. Brutus had been anxious to be a sacrificer rather than a
butcher, and Antony begs the 'bleeding piece of earth', which is all
that is left of Caesar, to pardon him for being 'meek and gentle with
those butchers'. Brutus had wished to avoid hewing Caesar's body 'as
a carcase fit for hounds' and Antony compares Caesar to a hunted deer:

> here thy hunters stand
> Sign'd in thy spoil and crimson'd in thy lethe.

Brutus had shouted the slogan of Peace and Freedom: Antony prophecies the chaos of civil war:

> Over thy wounds now do I prophecy . . .
> Domestic fury and fierce civil strife
> Shall cumber all the parts of Italy;
> Blood and destruction shall be so in use
> And dreadful objects so familiar
> That mothers shall but smile when they behold
> Their infants quartered with the hands of war;
> All pity chok'd with custom of fell deeds. (III.i.260–70)

The climax of his funeral oration is the exhibition of Caesar's blood-stained mantle, followed by the exposure of his many wounds. This is the reality behind the ritual. At the end of the play both Brutus and Cassius recognise that Caesar is avenged, Cassius by the sword 'that ran through Caesar's bowels'; and there are signs during the last two acts that occasional twinges of remorse disturb Brutus's sense of righteousness.

Brutus's relationship with his wife has been much admired and it has often been contrasted with Caesar's relationship with Calpurnia. Caesar, it is true, breaks his word to his wife and goes to the Senate despite her pleadings; but under the circumstances it is difficult to see how he could have done otherwise and there is nothing in his words to suggest that he treats his wife as an inferior. Brutus is obviously devoted to Portia; but neither her self-inflicted wound, nor her agitated behaviour on the Ides of March, suggest that Brutus was wise to reveal the plot to her.

The most curious episode in their relationship is the scene in which Brutus reacts to the news of her death. After the quarrel scene he tells Cassius that he is 'sick of many griefs' and when Cassius refers to the consolations of philosophy, he tells how Portia,

> Impatient of my absence,
> And grief that young Octavius with Mark Antony
> Have made themselves so strong . . .
> With this she fell distract
> And, her attendants absent, swallow'd fire.

Shortly afterwards Titinius and Messala enter and after some discussion of the execution of a hundred senators, Messala asks Brutus if he has heard from his wife and had any news of her. Brutus says he has heard nothing, and the dialogue continues:

> *Mes.*   That, methinks, is strange.
> *Bru.* Why ask you? Hear you aught of her in yours?
> *Mes.* No, my lord.
> *Bru.* Now, as you are a Roman, tell me true.
> *Mes.* Then like a Roman bear the truth I tell:
>   For certain she is dead, and by strange manner.
> *Bru.* Why, farewell, Portia. We must die, Messala.
>   With meditating that she must die once,
>   I have the patience to endure it now.
> *Mes.* Even so great men great losses should endure.

Granville-Barker and Dover Wilson assumed[12] that Shakespeare did not intend the duplicate revelation of Portia's death; that originally the news was conveyed only by Messala; that he transferred the revelation to make an effective ending to the quarrel scene; and that he meant Messala's account to be cut. The text of *Julius Caesar* is a good one and there is only one other sign that it may have been revised—the discrepancy between Jonson's quotation from it and the line as given in the First Folio.[13] If Messala's account was ever the only one, it is odd that Brutus should not ask Messala to enlarge upon the strange manner of Portia's death; and if, in fact, some lines have been deleted at this point, it is odd that the whole episode was not cut. One is driven to assume that Shakespeare intended the duplicate revelation to stand.

An ingenious explanation and defence of Brutus's behaviour has been propounded by Warren D. Smith.[14] He argues that when Messala reports that a hundred senators have been put to death instead of seventy mentioned to him, Brutus clutches at the hope that the story of Portia's death was false. This hope is increased when Messala asks him if he has heard from his wife, but destroyed by his next question: 'Nor nothing in your letters writ of her?' Brutus is naturally concerned about the morale of his troops and there is no reason why he should reveal his wife's suicide. Mr Smith concludes:

I hold that Brutus most firmly establishes his right to be considered an able general at the moment when the hope that Portia may be alive . . . is snuffed out . . . How reassuring to the ears of the soldier must have been the unshaken courage contained in the quiet observation:
    Why, farewell Portia . . .

There are two main objections to this interpretation: it would be almost impossible for any actor to convey it to an audience and there is no evidence that Shakespeare intended it. It is surely more likely, and perfectly in accordance with Brutus's character as revealed elsewhere, that he should deliberately demonstrate how a great man could endure a bereavement—'a demonstration', as MacCallum puts it,[15] 'in Clinical Ethics'. He 'wants to show Messala that he can remain stoically immovable even when confronted with the deepest shock to his personal feelings'.

In the quarrel scene immediately before the double revelation of Portia's death, Brutus appears in his most self-righteous mood. He has refused to pardon a man for taking bribes, despite Cassius's intervention on his behalf; and he complains that Cassius has refused to send him gold with which to pay his legions:

> There is no terror, Cassius, in your threats,
> For I am arm'd so strong in honesty
> That they pass by me as the idle wind,
> Which I respect not. I did send to you
> For certain sums of gold, which you denied me:
> For I can raise no money by vile means—
> By heaven, I had rather coin my heart,
> And drop my blood for drachmas, than to wring
> From the hard hands of peasants their vile trash
> By any indirection.—I did send
> To you for gold to pay my legions,
> Which you denied me. Was that done like Cassius?   (IV.iii.66–77)

No other of Shakespeare's characters goes as far as this in praising his own virtue and audiences have rightly regarded Brutus unsympathetically at this point in the play. He is revealed as repellently self-righteous and more than usually self-deceived. He cannot stoop to raise money by vile means but he complains that Cassius has refused him money, which he has raised, as Brutus has just indicated, by vile means. He wants to enjoy the spiritual satisfaction of a good conscience, the material benefits derived from the shady dealings of others, and a moral superiority in comparison with those others. He is not, of course, a conscious hypocrite; but this scene shows only too clearly his ability to shut his eyes to unpleasant facts.

One other point about Brutus may be mentioned. It is sometimes said that his oration to the mob is contrasted with Antony's, the one appealing to reason and the other to emotion; and that this is another example of Brutus's misunderstanding of what the situation requires. Plutarch recorded that Brutus was able to make a long discourse in Latin, but that when he wrote in Greek 'he counterfeited that brief compendious manner of speech of the Lacedaemonians'.[16] It has been argued that this remark suggested to Shakespeare the brief compendious style of Brutus's oration.[17] It is not, of course, as effective as Antony's, but it puts the case with considerable skill. Brutus had killed Caesar as a preventive measure; and his defence has to be based on an appeal to emotion rather than on reason, though he pretends he is appealing to the judgement of his audience. He begins by referring to his own honour; he claims that he loved Caesar as much as any man, but that he loved Rome more. Then he asks a rhetorical question: 'Had you rather Caesar were living and die all slaves, than that Caesar was dead, to live all freemen?' But he makes no attempt to prove that they will be less enslaved than they were under Caesar. His appeals are to honour, patriotism and freedom. He confesses that as Caesar loved him, he weeps for him, but that he slew him because he was ambitious. Once again there is no attempt at proof. Then he asks a series of rhetorical questions:

Who is here so base that would be a bondman? If any, speak: for him have I offended. Who is here so rude that would not be a Roman? If any, speak; for him have I offended. Who is here so vile that will not love his country? If any, speak; for him have I offended. I pause for a reply.

It is impossible for anyone to say he is offended, as it would show him to be slavish, barbarous or unpatriotic.

Even in this speech we can see the extraordinary self-satisfaction of the man. He is proud of the fact that he slew his 'best lover for the good of Rome', that he has subordinated personal affection to what he imagines his public duty to be. Shakespeare does not refer to the possibility that Brutus was Caesar's illegitimate son and that the assassination was also a case of parricide. Nor does he mention that Brutus fought on Pompey's side at Pharsalia though Pompey had killed his father—a nice example of the sacrifice of his personal feelings to duty. Nor does he mention Caesar's pardoning of Brutus after the battle. But there are numerous references to Caesar's affection for him and the best known words of the play express the horror of betrayal and ingratitude—*Et tu, Brute!*

Just as our views of Caesar and Brutus are liable to alter in the course of the play, so Cassius, who begins as a Machiavellian tempter of the virtuous Brutus, later enlists our sympathies. In the quarrel scene, the morally superior attitude adopted by Brutus alienates our sympathies; and although there is an element of self-dramatisation in Cassius's appeal for pity—

Come, Antony, and young Octavius, come,
Revenge yourselves alone on Cassius,
For Cassius is aweary of the world;
Hated by one he loves; brav'd by his brother;
Check'd like a bondman; all his faults observ'd,
Set in a note-book, learn'd and conn'd by rote
To cast into my teeth. O, I could weep
My spirit from mine eyes!—   (IV.iii.92–9)

we feel, nevertheless, that his love for Brutus is much stronger than Brutus's love for him. At the beginning of the play he is using Brutus as a tool in his attack on Caesar. At the end everything is subordinated to his love.

In spite of the way our attitude to the main characters changes in the course of the play, it is misleading to regard *Julius Caesar* as a problem play. Whether Caesar was a tyrant or not is not the main point, for it is made clear that his assassination leads to the autocratic rule it was designed to prevent. The conspirators are therefore deluded; and the centre of interest lies in the tragic error of Brutus who is tempted by Cassius to kill a man he loves and to whom he is bound by ties of gratitude. He is vulnerable to this temptation partly, as we have seen, because of his tendency to substitute idealisations for realities, and partly because of pride—pride in his virtue and integrity, pride in his own judgement, pride in his ancestry. How far he falls can be seen from his reciprocal love for his wife, his tender concern for Lucius, the esteem in which he is held by the conspirators, Cassius's growing love for him, and even the respect of his enemies. But even at the end—though the appearance of the ghost is a half-conscious recognition of Brutus's tragic error—there are two last examples of the gulf between the ideal and the reality. He boasts absurdly

> that yet in all my life
> I found no man but he was true to me.

And, before the battle, in successive speeches he declares that he will not, like Cato, commit suicide—'I do find it cowardly and vile'—and that he 'bears too great a mind' to fall alive into the hands of the enemy.

4

HAMLET

*high and excellent Tragedie, that openeth the greatest woundes, and
sheweth forth the Vlcers that are covered with Tissue . . .*[1]

(Sir Philip Sidney)

I

It was, perhaps, Sidney's account of tragedy that led Shakespeare to use
as one of the iterative images of *Hamlet* that of the hidden ulcer. The
sickness imagery has been explained in various ways[2]—as reflecting
the disease of Hamlet himself, as proliferating from the Ghost's
description of the effect of Claudius's poison, as indicating the rottenness of the state of Denmark—but, if the images are considered in
context, it becomes apparent that only the last of these explanations
has any validity. The images, with only one exception, refer either to
the rottenness of the court, to the sin of Claudius and Gertrude, or to
the King's guilty fear of his nephew.[3]

There does not seem to have been any mystery about the play, or
about the character of the hero, until the end of the eighteenth century.
Then Romantic critics and their successors concentrated their attention
on the character of the hero, in which they found the explanation of his
postponement of revenge until it had involved the death of Polonius
and his two children, of Gertrude, Rosencrantz and Guildenstern and
of Hamlet himself. They diagnosed the case in a variety of ways, from
Goethe's parable of the oak-tree planted in a costly vase and Coleridge's
idea that Hamlet thought so much that he 'lost the power of action in
the energy of resolve' to Schopenhauer's 'weakness of will', Bradley's
stress on the traumatic shock of Gertrude's remarriage and Freud's
Oedipus complex.[4] These conflicting views led C. S. Lewis to argue[5]
that critics depicted only themselves when they thought they were
depicting Hamlet and they did this because he was in fact Everyman,
tainted with original sin. Professor Lewis invited the retort that as an
amateur theologian, particularly interested in original sin, he was as

likely to hold this view of Hamlet as Freud was to diagnose Oedipus Complex. 'I have a smack of Hamlet myself, if I may say so', Coleridge admitted.[6] But the tendency of critics to draw self-portraits does not necessarily mean that Hamlet is characterless: it may mean rather that the methods we employ for ascertaining his character are inappropriate.

Side by side with those critics who seek for the reasons for Hamlet's delay in his psychology are those who emphasise the fact that Shakespeare's play was based on an earlier one, possibly by Kyd, and that in the finished product there are traces of the more primitive original.[7] Shakespeare did not quite succeed in effecting a complete transformation of the old play. He retained incidents and motivations proper to a primitive revenge play, but incompatible with the sophisticated hero of his own. The character who meditates on suicide is unlike the one who spares Claudius at his prayers because he wants to be sure of damning his soul, who speaks of Polonius's corpse as 'the guts', or who sends Rosencrantz and Guildenstern to their deaths, 'not shriving time allowed', without pity or remorse. The play, therefore, is deeply flawed by Shakespeare's attempt to pour new wine into old bottles.

Against this view must be set the fact that Shakespeare seems to have taken exceptional pains with the play. The second quarto version is so long that it cannot have been accommodated in the two-hour traffic of the stage, and it may never have been performed without substantial cuts. This would seem to suggest that Shakespeare wrote for his own satisfaction and that, if he retained 'primitive' elements from the old play, he did so deliberately. Nor is it difficult to guess why. By putting a sensitive and sophisticated Renaissance prince—scholar, soldier, courtier—in a situation which requires only a primitive avenger to set the world to rights he provides a tragic contrast fraught with irony. For in such a situation a man's virtues may become liabilities.

In recent years, however, much more stress has been laid on Hamlet's defects. Wilson Knight in *The Wheel of Fire* spoke of him as morbid and neurotic, less healthy than his uncle.[8] Madariaga, who assumed that he had seduced Ophelia, ascribed[9] the cause of his procrastination to his egotism:

Hamlet, in spirit and intention, does not avenge his father; he avenges himself . . . Hamlet could not pour himself into action because he was too egotistic for that. All action—even crime—requires freedom from egotism.

Whatever we may think of this view of Hamlet's character, the last remark is manifestly false: we can all think of criminal egotists. Professor L. C. Knights is another critic who has a low opinion of Hamlet's character.[10] We were told that 'the desire to escape from the complexities of adult living is central' to his character, and that 'his attitudes of hatred, revulsion, self-complacency and self-reproach' are 'forms of escape from the difficult process of complex adjustment which normal living demands'. Professor Knights appears to exaggerate the normality of Hamlet's position. To have an adulterous mother, to have one's father murdered, and to lose one's kingdom to the murderer can happily still be regarded as abnormal. In his later study of *Hamlet* he argues that the Ghost's commands should have been disregarded:[11]

> The Ghost is tempting Hamlet to gaze with fascinated horror at an abyss of evil . . . Hamlet does not merely see the evil about him, does not merely react to it with loathing and rejection, he allows his vision to activate something within himself—say, if you like, his own feeling of corruption—and so to produce that state of near paralysis that so perplexes him.

Hamlet, Professor Knights thinks, is a sterile intellectual whose disgust with himself is used to shock and damage others. He seems not to realise that some of his own actions are sinful. He is fascinated by the lust he condemns in his mother. He indulges in self-dramatisation, dramatising both his melancholy and his grief at Ophelia's death.

This bare summary does not do justice to the persuasiveness of Professor Knights' argument. But even though we may allow that Hamlet is infected by the evil of the world of Elsinore and partially corrupted by the task he has to do—what I have elsewhere called the occupational disease of avengers—the self-dramatisation of which Professor Knights complains can better be explained as Shakespeare's own dramatisation of Hamlet's feelings.

Are we to accept the view that the Ghost is tempting Hamlet to evil? Professor Eleanor Prosser in a well-argued book[12] agrees with Professor Knights. She starts from the condemnation of revenge by Elizabethan moralists and theologians and claims that virtuous characters in Shakespeare's plays 'faced with the wanton murder' of their kin either forgive or leave their cause to heaven. But she plays down the element of personal vengeance in Macduff's determination to kill the murderer of his wife and children. She has some more effective arguments in her discussion of the Ghost's appearances. It departs, apparently offended, when Horatio invokes heaven. On its second appearance, it vanishes on the crowing of the cock, starting 'like a guilty thing upon a fearful summons', though only erring spirits are compelled to depart at cockcrow. When Hamlet confronts the Ghost he is not certain whether it brings 'airs from heaven or blasts from hell'. The Ghost does not appeal 'to Hamlet's love of virtue; it is not arousing his determination to serve the justice of God'. It follows that the Ghost cannot be a penitent soul come from purgatory, acknowledging the justice of his punishment. Here Professor Prosser is surely mistaken for the Ghost laments that he was sent to his account,

> Unhous'led, disappointed, unanel'd,

and confesses that he is

> confin'd to fast in fires,
> Till the foul crimes done in my days of nature
> Are burnt and purg'd away.

She is on stronger ground in her interpretation of the cellarage scene, in which the Ghost speaks from beneath the stage, 'the familiar abode in Elizabethan drama of demons, furies and damned souls'. The Ghost acts like a devil, Professor Prosser thinks, because it is a devil. This leads her to argue that the Ghost intervenes in the closet scene, not to protect Gertrude, but to prevent her from repenting. This interpretation is impossible to accept since the Ghost's words indicate a loving concern for Gertrude; and if the Ghost were a devil in disguise he would not have warned Hamlet not to contrive anything against her but to leave her to the stings of conscience.

Professor Prosser makes one damaging admission. When Hamlet says that if Claudius does not reveal his guilt during the performance of 'The Murder of Gonzago',

> It is a damned ghost that we have seen.

Professor Prosser comments:[13]

There is no hint that a damned ghost might have told the truth . . . Admittedly, the argument of this study would be strengthened immeasurably if Horatio countered with the warning that the instruments of darkness can tell us truths in order to betray us.

It would indeed: and the fact that Horatio does nothing of the kind must make one sceptical of Professor Prosser's main theory. There are other objections too (e.g. Hamlet does not decide in the 'To be or not to be' soliloquy to reject coward conscience). But the fundamental objection both to Professor Prosser and to Professor Knights is that Claudius is an unpunished murderer and usurper; and whether the Ghost is a spirit of health or goblin damned, it is Hamlet's bounden duty, after checking the truth of the story, to execute justice on his uncle. Hamlet is not just a private avenger; and, although we may deplore his hatred and the errors that spring from it, we cannot believe, in the world of the play, that he ought to have accepted the situation and done nothing about it. As the author of *The Hystorie of Hamblet* put it, after warning his readers not to conspire against their lawful sovereign:[14]

If vengeance ever seem to have any shew of justice, it is then, when piety and affection constraineth us to remember our fathers unjustly murdered ... and which seeke the means not to leave treason and murder unpunished.

Even the pious and prolific William Perkins admitted that it was sometimes legitimate to take the law into one's own hands:[15]

when violence is offered, and the Magistrate absent; either for a time, and his stay be dangerous; or altogether, so as no helpe can be had of him, nor any hope of his comming. In this case, God puts the sword into the private mans hands.

In the state of Denmark there was no hope of the Magistrate's coming.

There remains the problem raised by Professor Prosser: why does the Ghost behave like a stage-devil? This is sometimes explained as a survival from the pre-Shakespearian *Hamlet*, or as a device used by Hamlet and the Ghost to put Horatio and Marcellus off the scent. It may be suggested, too, that a devil who wished to convince a man that he was his father's spirit would hardly fall into the mistake of behaving like a stage devil. All the Ghost does is to demand that Hamlet's companions should swear to keep the secret of his appearance—it is Hamlet himself who treats the Ghost as a stage devil. The men swear by grace and heaven, a vow which would not please a devil, but which apparently gives rest to the perturbed spirit.

Apart from this it was necessary for the action of the play that there should be some doubt about the nature and provenance of the Ghost. When Hamlet is first informed of the haunting, he speaks as though it were an evil spirit in the shape of his father:

If it assume my noble father's person,
I'll speak to it, though hell itself should gape
And bid me hold my peace. (I.ii.243-5)

When he first confronts the Ghost he prays for the protection of angels and ministers of grace; but he is convinced by the Ghost's tale that it is 'honest'—not a devil in disguise. Professor Prosser assures us that ghosts from purgatory would be full of joy and tranquillity and would not be vindictive. But it is not certain that Shakespeare was aware of this; or that, even if he was, he would necessarily conform to it in writing a play. Banquo's ghost is not particularly tranquil, nor are the ghosts who appear on the eve of Bosworth Field. In *Hamlet* it seems that Christian teaching about the after-life is contaminated with memories of the Classics, and perhaps of folklore.[16]

Hamlet himself is well aware of the dangers he runs in conversing with spirits. Horatio speaks of the physical dangers, but Hamlet asks:

> And for my soul, what can it do to that
> Being a thing immortal as itself?

Later on, 'lapsed in time and passion', he confesses that there may well be a danger to his soul:

> The spirit that I have seen
> May be a devil; and the devil hath power
> T'assume a pleasing shape; yea, and perhaps
> Out of my weakness and my melancholy,
> As he is very potent with such spirits,
> Abuses me to damn me.   (II.ii.594-9)

It is precisely because he is aware of the danger of damnation that he arranges to catch the conscience of the King by a performance of a play; and the King's reactions to the performance convince both Hamlet and Horatio that the Ghost's story was true. Shakespeare has already let the audience into the secret in the previous scene, when Claudius reveals his guilt in an aside.[17] After that, no member of an audience, however expert in demonology, is likely to believe that the Ghost is a devil in disguise.

We must start, therefore, from the assumption that Hamlet is charged with the duty of killing Claudius.

II

Hamlet is not the sole avenger of the play. Laertes, Fortinbras and Pyrrhus all have injuries to avenge: Laertes, the deaths of Polonius and Ophelia; Fortinbras, the death of his father and loss of some territory;

Pyrrhus, the death of his father. All three are contrasted with Hamlet. The Dido play—which seems to be an oblique compliment to Marlowe's—provides Hamlet with a number of reminders of his own situation. The mobled Queen, weeping for Priam, is contrasted with Gertrude, whose tears for her husband had soon been dried. Pyrrhus, the avenger, is depicted as a figure of evil. His arms are 'Black as his purpose'; his appearance is 'dread and black'; he is 'total gules', covered with the blood 'of fathers, mothers, daughters, sons'; he is, finally, 'hellish'. He is about to kill Priam, when he hears the noise of Ilium's fall.

> For lo! his sword,
> Which was declining on the milky head
> Of reverend Priam, seemed i'th'air to stick.
> So as a painted tyrant Pyrrhus stood,
> And like a neutral to his will and matter
> Did nothing.   (II.ii.471–6)

After this pause,

> Aroused vengeance sets him new awork,

and he slays the old king, while Hecuba sees him

> make malicious sport
> In mincing with his sword her husband's limbs.

This savage and evil avenger, murdering an aged man who was not guilty of his father's death in battle, contrasts with the more civilised Hamlet who finds it difficult to execute the man who has secretly murdered his father, after seducing his mother. The central image of the sword suspended motionless over his enemy is repeated in Act III when Hamlet holds his sword over his kneeling enemy. Hamlet wants to be as ruthless as Pyrrhus, and in the soliloquy after the *Dido* speeches he laments that he is pigeon-livered and lacks 'gall/To make oppression bitter'. He uses the ability of the actor to weep real tears 'But in a fiction, in a dream of passion' as a reproach to himself for being unable to carry out his duty, or as he absurdly puts it, that he 'can say nothing'. He can say a great deal, but not act.

Fortinbras is praised by Hamlet as 'a delicate and tender prince' and he is named by him as his successor. But all the other evidence undercuts these tributes. We hear of him in the first scene as one who has secretly mustered a band of soldiers, who seem little better than brigands, to seize the lands lost by his father. He has

> Shark'd up a list of lawless resolutes,
> For food and diet, to some enterprise
> That hath a stomach in't.   (I.i.98–100)

Voltemand and Cornelius are dispatched on an embassage to the 'impotent and bed-rid' King of Norway, who rebukes Fortinbras but empowers him to use the troops to attack Poland. There is no suggestion that the war is a just one. It is, as one of his captains tells Hamlet, a war of aggression:

> Truly to speak, and with no addition,
> We go to gain a little patch of ground
> That hath in it no profit but the name.
> To pay five ducats, five, I would not farm it;
> Nor will it yield to Norway or the Pole
> A ranker rate should it be sold in fee.
> *Ham.* Why, then the Polack never will defend it.
> *Cap.* Yes, it is already garrison'd.
> *Ham.* Two thousand souls and twenty thousand ducats
> Will not[18] debate the question of this straw.
> This is th'imposthume of much wealth and peace,
> That inward breaks, and shows no cause without
> Why the man dies.   (IV.iv.17–28)

In the soliloquy which follows Hamlet uses the example of Fortinbras' action as a reproach to his own inaction. In the dialogue with the Captain war is thought of as a fatal disease, and the campaign against Poland absurd and irrational; but in the soliloquy Hamlet argues that god-like reason was not given us to fust in us unused, as though the war was the result of a rational decision. Fortinbras is

> a delicate and tender prince,
> Whose spirit with divine ambition puff'd
> Makes mouths at the invisible event,
> Exposing what is mortal and unsure
> To all that fortune, death, and danger dare,
> Even for an egg-shell. Rightly to be great
> Is not to stir without great argument,
> But greatly to find quarrel in a straw
> When honour's at the stake.   (IV.iv.48–56)

The surface argument is contradicted by the detail. A spirit inflated with ambition—even when qualified with the epithet 'divine'—is guilty of the sin by which the angels fell, as Wolsey reminds us. The egg-shell and the straw underline the worthlessness of the prize; and the preceding dialogue makes it clear that honour is not at stake.

Hector's speeches in the debate in *Troilus and Cressida*[19] are devoted to showing that honour and justice should not be in opposing scales, and that 'fear of bad success in a bad cause' ought to qualify the desire for glory.

Hamlet admires Fortinbras as his opposite, but we are not meant to share his view which springs from despair and self-disgust. It is natural that when he is dying, his mind jogged by the news of the arrival of Fortinbras from his victorious campaign, he should prophecy the election to the throne of Denmark of the barbarous adventurer. His own disastrous failure made him choose as best for his country a man most unlike himself. Fortinbras is thus enabled to avenge his father's death, not merely regaining the territory he forfeited, but acquiring the whole country of Denmark.

The third avenger, Laertes, is even more obviously Hamlet's foil, as Hamlet himself recognises just before the final duel, and as he confesses to Horatio,

> by the image of my cause, I see
> The portraiture of his.

Laertes is not aware of the parallel. He does not know that Hamlet's father had been murdered by his successor, nor that Claudius had seduced Gertrude. He does know that Hamlet had killed Polonius—though it was not a deliberate murder; and he knows that his beloved sister had been driven mad and been drowned as a result of Hamlet's actions, and he thinks that Hamlet had tried to seduce her. They are both brilliant fencers. Here the resemblance ends. In almost every other way the two men are contrasted. In the first scene in which they appear, Hamlet wishes to return to the university at Wittenberg; Laertes wishes to return to Paris for extra-curricular activities. In his warning to Ophelia, Laertes assumes that Hamlet cannot marry her and that therefore his intentions are dishonourable. This view of the case is shown to be wrong when Gertrude, at Ophelia's graveside, mentions that she had hoped the girl would be Hamlet's bride. When Laertes hears of his father's death, he hurries home from Paris and raises a successful rebellion against the King. The ease with which he invades the palace suggests that Hamlet was not prevented from killing Claudius by external obstacles.

Laertes, in accepting his role as avenger, knows that he is violating the moral law:

> To hell, allegiance! vows, to the blackest devil!
> Conscience and grace, to the profoundest pit!
> I dare damnation: to this point I stand,
> That both the worlds I give to negligence,
> Let come what comes; only I'll be reveng'd
> Most throughly for my father.

Here, as elsewhere, Laertes is indulging in stock responses. He is behaving as he thinks other people would expect a bereaved son to behave. In the later scene where Claudius asks him what he would do to show himself his father's son, he answers: 'To cut his throat i' th' church.' This, as many critics have assumed, is an unconscious comment on Hamlet's conduct when he finds the King at his prayers, and fails to seize the opportunity. The King's reply to Laertes—

> No place indeed should murder sanctuarise—

implies that Hamlet's manslaughter of Polonius was a case of murder, while the murder of Hamlet in church would be a case of justifiable homicide. Later in the same scene Laertes enthusiastically seconds the treacherous scheme to kill Hamlet in a duel by the use of an unbated foil:

> he, being remiss,
> Most generous, and free from all contriving,
> Will not peruse the foils.

This tribute to Hamlet's character from his would-be murderer outweighs the denunciations of certain squeamish modern critics. Laertes agrees to the scheme and adds:

> And, for that purpose, I'll anoint my sword.
> I bought an unction of a mountebank,
> So mortal, that but dip a knife in it,
> Where it draws blood, no cataplasm so rare,
> Collected from all simples that have virtue
> Under the moon, can save the thing from death
> That is but scratched withal.   (IV.vii.141–6)

This reveals the full extent of Laertes' depravity—not merely because he is prepared to kill Hamlet treacherously, but because he purchased poison in case he might have occasion to use it.

Laertes appears on two other occasions. His leaping into Ophelia's grave and his ranting—what Hamlet calls 'the bravery of his grief'—provoke the confrontation between the two avengers and ensure that

Laertes will proceed with his treacherous plan. Just before the duel he promises to receive Hamlet's 'offered love, like love' and that he will not wrong it. Some qualms of conscience make him hesitate, but in the end he gives Hamlet the necessary scratch. Hamlet in turn wounds Laertes, and Laertes confesses that he is justly killed with his own treachery, and asks his 'noble' opponent to exchange forgiveness, though putting the blame on the King. Harold Jenkins protests[20] against the view that Laertes is 'some sort of villain', saying that Hamlet has more than his rank in mind when he calls him 'a very noble youth'. Of course, Laertes arouses some sympathy when he encounters Ophelia mad or hears of her drowning. But the general impression he makes is of a coarse-grained, insensitive figure, who is put into the play to exhibit the primitive avenger Hamlet is temperamentally unfitted to be.

These three avengers are all foils to Hamlet. They have lost their fathers, two in battle and one by manslaughter. None of them is faced with the task of avenging a brutal murder; nor is any of them spurred on by a supernatural command. Yet none of them is delayed or deterred by an inner conflict or by moral scruples. It is beside these, coarse-fibred as they are, that Shakespeare means us to consider his hero. That Hamlet calls Fortinbras 'a delicate and tender prince' and Laertes 'a very noble youth' tells us more about Hamlet than about his fellow-avengers, for we have just seen the evil aggression of the one and the treacherous designs of the other.

One other character is a foil to Hamlet, though Horatio's function as a chorus sometimes blurs the edges of his character. In the first scene he can instruct Bernardo and Marcellus about the preparations for war. In the second scene we learn that he came from Wittenberg for the funeral of Hamlet's father, but despite his friendship for the Prince he has not seen him during the six or seven weeks that have elapsed. In scene iv he seems to be ignorant of Danish customs, so that Hamlet has to instruct him. Thereafter he becomes Hamlet's only confidant, the only person to whom the Ghost's tidings are revealed. But he is absent from the stage for the whole of Act II and Act III scene i, so that Shakespeare can bring out Hamlet's essential isolation. He reappears as a witness of the play-scene; appears again, rather oddly, to urge the Queen to speak with Ophelia; receives the pirates; and is next seen with Hamlet at Ophelia's funeral. Oddly, again, he has not told Hamlet of the death of the girl he loved. The most significant

c

appearance of Horatio is just before the play-scene. Hamlet calls him
to ask him to watch Claudius during the performance; but he prefixes
this request with a tribute to his character:

> Horatio, thou art e'en as just a man
> As e'er my conversation cop'd withal . . .
>   Nay, do not think I flatter;
> For what advancement may I hope from thee,
> That no revenue hast but thy good spirits
> To feed and clothe thee? Why should the poor be flatter'd?
> No, let the candied tongue lick absurd pomp,
> And crook the pregnant hinges of the knee
> Where thrift may follow fawning. Dost thou hear?
> Since my dear soul was mistress of her choice
> And could of men distinguish her election,
> Sh'hath seal'd thee for herself; for thou hast been
> As one, in suff'ring all, that suffers nothing;
> A man that Fortune's buffets and rewards
> Hast ta'en with equal thanks; and blest are those
> Whose blood and judgment are so well comeddled
> That they are not a pipe for Fortune's finger
> To sound what stop she please. Give me that man
> That is not passion's slave, and I will wear him
> In my heart's core, ay, in my heart of heart,
> As I do thee.   (III.ii.52–72)

This eulogy of Horatio's character has to be taken in relation to
Hamlet's self-reproaches. All through the second act his frustration
and despair show through his pretence of madness. In the soliloquy at
the end of the act he calls himself a rogue, a peasant slave, and a
coward and compares himself to a drab and a stallion (or scullion).[21]
He can unpack his heart with words—use words as a safety-valve—
but is unable to avenge his father. He appears to be passion's slave. In
the soliloquy in III.i he suggests that people continue 'to grunt and
sweat under a weary life' only because they are afraid of what may
happen after death. In the closet scene he confesses to the Ghost that
he is 'lapsed in time and passion'. He contrasts himself implicitly with
Horatio, the man who reacts with equanimity to the changes and
chances of this mortal life.

Horatio has been compared[22] with Chapman's idealised hero,
Clermont D'Ambois, who is commanded by the Ghost of his brother
to do 'what corrupted law leaves unperform'd', and who finally kills
his enemy in fair fight. Guise, his friend, speaks of him much as
Hamlet speaks of Horatio:[23]

In his most gentle, and unwearied minde,
Rightly to vertue fram'd; . . .
In his contempt of riches and of greatnesse; . . .
His scorne of all things servile and ignoble,
Though they could gaine him never such advancement;
. . . the great rising,
And learning of his soule, so much the more
Against ill fortune . . .
In short, this Senecall man is found in him,
Hee may with heavens immortall powers compare,
To whom the day and fortune equall are,
Come faire or foule, what ever chance can fall,
Fixt in himselfe, hee still is one to all.

Horatio is the Senecal man—one who followed the precepts of
Seneca's essays—not one, as Chapman says elsewhere,[24] to

      reele and fall
Before the franticke pufs of blinde-born chance,
That pipes through emptie men, and makes them dance.

His self-control shows up Hamlet's apparent weakness. But to bear
patiently the whips and scorns of time and the oppressor's wrong is not
a satisfactory solution to the problem facing Hamlet. We should not
assume that Hamlet is passion's slave any more than we should believe
him morally inferior to Fortinbras. Indeed, the repetition of the
image of the pipe later in the same scene counteracts the impression
made by his speech to Horatio. ' 'Sblood,' he asks Guildenstern,[25] 'do
you think I am easier to be play'd on than a pipe?'

The parable of the recorders may be taken as a warning to commen-
tators and critics that they cannot pluck out the heart of Hamlet's
mystery by the use of some simple formula; and, although it is plainly
important to consider him in relation to his foils, this evidence is
mainly negative. It shows that the two extremes of criticism are both
wrong—that we could not really approve either of a Hamlet who
avenged his father without hesitation or compunction, or of one who
decided to let Claudius remain in possession of the fruits of his crime.

It is, perhaps, misleading to speak of approving or disapproving of
one of Shakespeare's heroes. We need, in the greatest tragedies, at
least to sympathise; and the kind of criticism which reads like a speech
by the public prosecutor, or—still worse—by the Grand Inquisitor,
has not proved very rewarding.

Hamlet is the only tragedy in which the audience watches the whole

action through the eyes of the hero. In *Julius Caesar* the point of view
is continually changing, as we have seen; and in *Othello* there are
scenes in which we are alienated from the Moor. But we watch Polonius, or Gertrude or Claudius, not as they see themselves but as
Hamlet sees them. We can, reading between the lines, deduce that
Claudius is an efficient ruler; but when Wilson Knight discovered in
him a 'host of good qualities' we may take leave to doubt.[26] Some
critics have supposed that in the prayer-scene Claudius shows himself
to be a better Christian than his nephew; but it is made clear that the
King has no intention of giving up the fruits of his crime and that he
is unable to pray:

> Words without thoughts never to heaven go.

Other critics have defended Rosencrantz and Guildenstern. As Leo
Kirschbaum argued,[27] they do not know that they are carrying Hamlet
to his execution. Horatio's comment—'So Rosencrantz and Guildenstern go to't'—could be taken as a criticism of Hamlet's complacency
at this point in the play; and Tom Stoppard's play was presumably
inspired by the thought that Shakespeare had been unjust to the two
men. But whatever defence is offered, Rosencrantz and Guildenstern
are to an audience faintly ridiculous time-servers, because this is how
Hamlet sees them. Even before Hamlet meets them, they are depicted
as nonentities, as indistinguishable as Tweedledum and Tweedledee:

> *King*   Thanks, Rosencrantz and gentle Guildenstern.
> *Queen* Thanks, Guildenstern and gentle Rosencrantz.   (II.ii.34–5)

Hamlet guesses they are sent to spy on him. It is to Guildenstern that
Hamlet reads the lesson of the recorders. Both Rosencrantz and
Guildenstern speak of Claudius's safety with 'holy and religious fear'.
Hamlet tells his mother that he will trust his school-fellows 'as I will
adders fang'd' and he tells Rosencrantz they are sponges.[28] The
audience is bound to accept Hamlet's view of them, and not to worry
unduly when he turns the tables on them. Beforehand he had declared
that they would marshal him to knavery:

> For 'tis the sport to have the engineer
> Hoist with his own petar; and't shall go hard
> But I will delve one yard below their mines
> And blow them at the moon.   (III.iv.206–9)

Afterwards he excuses himself to Horatio:

> Why, man, they did make love to their employment;
> They are not near my conscience; their defeat
> Does by their own insinuation grow:
> 'Tis dangerous when the baser nature comes
> Between the pass and fell incensed points
> Of mighty opposites.   (V.ii.57–62)

In both speeches the war imagery reminds us[29] that Hamlet and Claudius are engaged in a bitter struggle, in which some innocent and some guilty are bound to perish.

The Queen is another character we see almost entirely through Hamlet's eyes. In the First Quarto, which is probably contaminated with the earlier *Hamlet* play, the audience is left in no doubt about the Queen. She married 'within two months' of her first husband's death; she calls Hamlet 'boy'; she is informed that her first husband was 'Murdred, damnably murdred' by her second husband. She tells Hamlet

> as I have a soule, I sweare by heaven,
> I never knew of this most horride murder.

Hamlet replies by urging her to

> assist mee in revenge,
> And in his death your infamy shall die.

The Queen agrees:

> I vow by that maiesty,
> That knows our thoughts, and lookes into our hearts,
> I will conceale, consent, and doe my best,
> What stratagem soe're thou shalt devise.

On Hamlet's return from England, Horatio seeks out the Queen and tells her of the Prince's escape. Gertrude declares that Claudius's looks 'seem'd to sugar o're his villanie'!

> But I will soothe and please him for a time,
> For murderous mindes are always jealous.

She sends a message to her son by Horatio:

> bid him a while
> Be wary of his presence, lest that he
> Faile in that he goes about.

In the authentic text all these points are deliberately blurred.

Gertrude's remarriage is said by Hamlet to have taken place 'but two months' after his father's death, 'not two' months, and 'within a month'. In the closet scene, though Hamlet says

> almost as bad, good mother,
> As kill a king and marry with his brother;   (III.iv.28–9)

and later calls Claudius 'a murderer and a villain', the Ghost intervenes, presumably to spare Gertrude a full knowledge of Claudius's guilt. Gertrude does not protest her innocence; but she promises not to reveal that Hamlet is mad only in craft. She keeps her word and pretends that Hamlet is weeping for the death of Polonius.[30] It has been surmised, from Claudius's words to Laertes about the fading of love, that Gertrude has stopped going to her husband's bed, in accordance with Hamlet's advice.[31] The scene between Gertrude and Horatio is omitted.

Shakespeare leaves a good deal of licence to the individual director. He can—given the right Hamlet—make Gertrude still in her 'thirties. He can suggest that she repents of her infatuation by making her shrink from Claudius's touch. But, of course, there are other ways of interpreting the part and these will be largely determined by the way Hamlet is played.

III

Shakespeare stresses that the Hamlet we see in the second scene of the play—and, indeed, throughout the rest of the play—is not his normal self. Claudius calls it a transformation; Gertrude says that he is 'too much changed'; Hamlet confesses that he has lost all his mirth; but perhaps the best evidence is provided by Ophelia, who speaks of his noble mind,

> The courtier's, soldier's, scholar's, eye, tongue, sword;
> Th'expectancy and rose of the fair state,
> The glass of fashion and the mould of form,
> Th'observ'd of all observers . . .
> That unmatch'd form and feature of blown youth . . .   (III.i.151–9)

There is some evidence that Shakespeare had been reading Timothy Bright's *Treatise of Melancholy* and that he embodied in the character of his hero some traits of the melancholic man. But the cause of his melancholy is made apparent by the mourning he defiantly wears, by Claudius's appeal to him to 'throw to earth this unprevailing woe', and more precisely by the soliloquy which Hamlet speaks as soon as he is alone.

The soliloquy tells us what had been passing through Hamlet's mind during the preceding scene. It expresses a death-wish, a feeling that 'all the uses of this world' are 'weary, stale, flat and unprofitable', or as Hamlet is later to express it, the earth and the starry heavens seem to be 'a foul and pestilent congregation of vapours'. The cause of his disgust with life is his mother's hasty and incestuous re-marriage to his father's brother, so much inferior to the man she apparently loved. More terrible to him than the speed with which Gertrude posted 'to incestuous sheets', and his dislike of his stepfather, was the feeling either that her previous love might have been feigned or that the sexual appetite is profoundly corrupting. This leads him to the conclusion: 'Frailty, thy name is woman!'

Coleridge mentioned as one of Hamlet's characteristics 'the prevalence of the abstracting and generalising habit over the practical'.[32] It is doubtful whether this is particularly the vice of intellectuals, as other critics have suggested; but Hamlet's assumption that since his beloved mother had proved frail all women are equally sensual and inconstant contributes to his suicidal thoughts. The full significance of this is not revealed until the next scene when we learn that Hamlet has been courting Ophelia. T. S. Eliot was wrong to suggest that the real subject of the play was the effect of a mother's guilt on a son,[33] but he was right to see that this was an important clue to Hamlet's behaviour, particularly with regard to Ophelia, but also in his general attitude of world-weariness.

This soliloquy, as we have suggested, is a displaced aside, showing us what Hamlet had been thinking during the King's smooth speech from the throne, in which he implies that he has married Gertrude mainly for reasons of state. Nothing is said by Claudius, and nothing is said by Hamlet at this time, to suggest that there was anything unusual in the election. It is only later that we are given a number of hints that Hamlet would have been the normal successor to his father, and that Claudius had 'popped in between the election and' Hamlet's hopes.

Hamlet's first remark—after remaining silent for more than sixty lines—is an aside, punning on *kin* and *kind*, and referring to the

King's *cousin* and *son*. His next remark—this time aloud—is a quibble on *sun* and *son*, thus repudiating Claudius's claim to be his father. The only speech of any length spoken by Hamlet in this scene is his contrast between seeming and being. He admits that 'all forms, moods, shapes of grief' can be feigned,

> For they are actions that a man might play.

The speech links up with references and images in the play concerned with hypocrisy—Hamlet's realisation that one may smile and be a villain; Polonius's admission that 'devotion's visage/And pious action' may 'sugar o'er/The devil himself'; the King's mention of 'The harlot's cheek, beautied with plastering art' as a symbol of the contrast between his words and deeds; and Hamlet's attack on cosmetics both in his scene with Ophelia and in the graveyard where he tells Yorick: 'Now get you to my lady's chamber, and tell her, let her paint an inch thick, to this favour she must come.' But the speech is also linked with the discussion of the purpose of playing and the frequent stage imagery, as has been noted.[34]

One other thing should be noted about this scene. It is preceded by the scene on the battlements and the first two appearances of the Ghost. Horatio surmises that its appearance 'bodes some strange eruption to our state'; Bernardo thinks it has something to do with the threatened war; Horatio, again, compares it to the portents that heralded the assassination of Julius Caesar and asks if it is privy to its country's fate. So that while Claudius is speaking, the audience is aware that something is wrong and awaits the explanation of the haunting.

The Ghost is first referred to as 'this thing'. Horatio offends it by saying that it has usurped the form of the dead King; but this, which implies its genuineness, is partly discounted by the fact that when the cock crew

> it started like a guilty thing
> Upon a fearful summons.

Although the sceptical Horatio addresses it as 'Illusion', the audience is bound to assume it is either an evil spirit in the shape of Hamlet's father or his father's spirit indeed.

When Hamlet is informed of the appearance of the Ghost, he reveals for the first time the suspicions of his 'prophetic soul':

> My father's spirit in arms: all is not well.
> I doubt some foul play . . .
>   Foul deeds will rise,
> Though all the earth o'erwhelm them, to men's eyes.

Despite this assurance that it is his father's spirit, he is more cautious in speaking to Horatio:

> If it assume my noble father's person,
> I'll speak to it though hell itself should gape
> And bid me hold my peace.

This seems to imply the possibility that it is an evil spirit in the shape of his father.

This doubt is kept before the minds of the audience during the remaining scenes on the battlements. In Hamlet's first address to the Ghost he prays for protection, and then continues:

> Be thou a spirit of health or goblin damn'd,
> Bring with thee airs from heaven or blasts from hell,
> Be thy intents wicked or charitable . . .

The Ghost makes night hideous, but uses a 'courteous action' to invite Hamlet to follow him. Horatio is afraid the Ghost will drive the Prince mad, so that he kills himself; but Marcellus deduces from the appearance that 'Something is rotten in the state of Denmark'.

Our ambivalent attitude to the Ghost is continued throughout the following scene. Bernard Shaw spoke[35] of the weird music of the Ghost's speech 'which should be the spectral wail of a soul's bitter wrong crying from one world to another in the extremity of its torment'. The Ghost arouses our pity, as it does Hamlet's; and when he tells how he is

>   confin'd to fast in fires,
> Till the foul crimes done in [his] days of nature
> Are burnt and purg'd away,

we assume he is come not from hell, but from purgatory. His statement that virtue will never be moved

> Though lewdness court it in a shape of heaven;

his grief for Gertrude's fall; his horror at being suddenly killed with no opportunity of repentance,

> Unhous'led, disappointed, unanel'd;
> No reck'ning made, but sent to my account
> With all my imperfections on my head;

and his injunction to Hamlet:

> Taint not thy mind, nor let thy soul contrive
> Against thy mother aught; leave her to heaven,
> And to those thorns that in her bosom lodge
> To prick and sting her—

all these points incline us to the view that the Ghost's story is true and that he is indeed the spirit of the dead King, not a devil in his shape. Hamlet's swearing by St Patrick is thought by some critics to be a way of saying that the Ghost has come from purgatory. It is, as Hamlet tells his friends, 'an honest ghost'.

But immediately after this, when Hamlet has asked Horatio and Marcellus to swear never to reveal what they have seen, the Ghost under the stage seconds Hamlet's demand. Under the stage was the place from which devils normally came; and when Hamlet calls the Ghost 'truepenny', 'this fellow in the cellarage' and 'old mole' we are bound to wonder if the Ghost is not, after all, a devil in disguise. As we have seen, some recent critics have argued that the Ghost behaves like a devil because it is a devil. But other interpretations are possible. If the Ghost is Hamlet's father, he will be as anxious as a devil for secrecy, and anxious too that the secret of Hamlet's antic disposition should not be revealed. Hamlet himself could be using the voice under the stage as a means of throwing Marcellus off the scent. He tells Horatio the truth afterwards. The two men swear by Hamlet's sword— according to stage tradition by laying their hands on the hilt, which would be in the form of a cross: and the oath is a solemn and religious one—'So grace and mercy at your most need help you'.

Although, at the end of the scene, we should adhere to the belief that the Ghost is Hamlet's father's spirit, the strange events enable Hamlet afterwards to have doubts. He cannot, in any case, kill his uncle on the unsupported word of a Ghost, a word no other person has heard, not merely because he could not justify his action in the eyes of the world but because, being a man of scruple, he would wish for more objective evidence.

Two other points have often been noted about this scene. Hamlet's 'wild and whirling words' are an indication of how profoundly he is disturbed by the Ghost's terrible revelations and why he feels it necessary to put on an antic disposition. He could not otherwise keep secret from the King that he has received a shock other than his mother's hasty re-marriage. There is, indeed, a double shock—the murder his prophetic soul had suspected and (though this has been denied) his mother's adultery. This is the point of 'O most pernicious woman!'—the exclamation he makes before turning to curse Claudius. Not merely had Gertrude made a hasty and incestuous marriage—this Hamlet knew already—but she had been won to the shameful lust of Claudius during the life-time of her first husband.

The other point is equally important. Hamlet's aside, just before the end of the scene, contrasts with his words to the Ghost:

> Haste me to know't, that I, with wings as swift
> As meditation, or the thoughts of love,
> May sweep to my revenge.

After the Ghost's disappearance, he swears to remember him. Now he cries out against the burden of his mission:

> The time is out of joint; O cursed spite,
> That ever I was born to set it right!

Taken together these speeches clearly reveal the inner conflict which inevitably has a tragic outcome. Hamlet's determination to avenge his father and his reluctance to perform the necessary action are forces of almost equal strength; and it is the nature of that reluctance that divides the critics. Shakespeare could, if he had so wished, have allowed Hamlet himself, or some choric figure, to give a precise analysis of this reluctance. We must assume that it was neither incompetence nor carelessness on Shakespeare's part that made him refrain; but a discussion of his motives must be deferred to a later section of this chapter.

Before Hamlet encounters his destiny, we have been introduced to the Polonius family whose fortunes are inextricably linked with Hamlet's. It is noticeable that both Laertes and his father assume that Hamlet is trying to seduce Ophelia; but this is a better index to their own minds than it is to Hamlet's intentions or to Ophelia's frailty. Ophelia has a mild retort to her brother's sermon—

> Do not, as some ungracious pastors do,
> Show me the steep and thorny way to heaven,
> Whiles like a puff'd and reckless libertine,
> Himself the primrose path of dalliance treads
> And recks not his own rede— (I.iii.47–51)

and she has a little flash of resentment when Polonius slanders Hamlet with his obscenities:

My lord, he hath importun'd me with love
In honourable fashion . . .
And hath given countenance to his speech, my lord,
With almost all the holy vows of heaven.   (I.iii.110–4)

But in the end she dutifully agrees to break off relations with the
Prince.

IV

In the first scene of Act II we are given an opportunity of observing
Polonius's treatment of his other child. After the worldly advice which
accompanies his farewell blessing—so worldly that 'To thine own self
be true' hardly fits in—we are not unduly surprised when Polonius
instructs Reynaldo to spy on Laertes, obtaining a 'carp of truth' by a
'bait of falsehood'. It is worth mentioning that Polonius, who has
apparently spied on his daughter, is later to use her as a decoy while
he spies on her, and hides behind the arras to spy on Gertrude's inter-
view with her son, appropriately meets his death while engaged in this
occupation.

Ophelia's description of Hamlet's silent visit to her closet is a
passage which is interpreted in different ways. On the one hand it
appears to be the result of Ophelia's obedience to her father's command; and Hamlet seems to be reproaching Ophelia for repulsing him.
On the other hand, her description of his appearance,

As if he had been loosed out of hell
To speak of horrors

makes the audience imagine that Hamlet has just come from his inter-
view with the Ghost. It could be Hamlet's conviction that Frailty's
name is woman that leads him to behave in this way to Ophelia and
that he is not accusing her of her denial of his love; or Ophelia's
actions might seem to confirm what he had deduced from his mother's
conduct. Then there is the question of his appearance:

his doublet all unbrac'd,
No hat upon his head, his stockings foul'd,
Ungarter'd and down-gyved to his ankle.

Are we not liable to assume that this is the antic disposition Hamlet
said he might put on? And this raises the question of whether his
mime was deliberately designed to make people think that his 'mad-

ness' was caused by Ophelia's rejection of his love. It is not necessary to give definite answers to these questions at this stage. It may, indeed, be part of Shakespeare's method of presentation, as with the Ghost, to keep the options open.

The audience have heard the antic disposition proposed and described: in the remainder of Act II and in most of Act III we see it in action, and we see the various attempts made by the King to discover its cause. Gertrude ascribes it to the death of her first husband, and to her o'erhasty remarriage. Polonius is convinced that it is caused by disprized love. Rosencrantz and Guildenstern swallow Hamlet's bait that the cause is thwarted ambition—his feeling that he should have succeeded his father. Claudius, after watching the scene between Ophelia and Hamlet, concludes that love is not the cause and that his behaviour does not suggest that he is deranged. The last attempt to pierce Hamlet's secret is made by Gertrude. He confesses to her that he is mad in craft and calls her belief that he is mad indeed a flattering unction which will hinder her repentance. But by this time he has used insulting and threatening words to the King and killed Polonius so that, whatever she may think, Gertrude is compelled, for her son's own sake, to continue with the pretence that he is mad.

Hamlet does pretend he is mad in his encounters with Polonius. By harping on the subject of Ophelia, by calling her father a fishmonger and speaking of Jephthah's daughter, he lends countenance to the Polonius theory of his madness. But in his conversation with Rosencrantz and Guildenstern he seems to drop his pretence of madness. He engages in two wit-combats with his friends, makes them confess that they were sent for, and satirises their present attitude to Claudius, compared with what it had been in the previous reign. He is neither mad, nor pretending to be so: he displays a mind fully conscious of its powers, working at full pressure. He does, it is true, speak of Denmark as a prison—'one of the worst'—and confesses that he suffers from bad dreams:

O God, I could be bounded in a nutshell and count myself a king of infinite space, were it not that I have bad dreams.

But neither this nor his admission that the universe and man, 'the beauty of the world', can no longer give him any pleasure, do more than indicate that he is suffering from 'a severe depression' or a profound spiritual disillusionment.

His welcome of the Players, his comments on the Dido play, and his advice on acting show him as the courteous Prince, equally effective as a critic of acting and as a critic of drama, and able to quit himself well as an amateur actor. Whether princely amateurs should presume to instruct professionals, and whether Hamlet's minority taste in drama was really better than the general taste, do not greatly matter. The important thing to note is that Hamlet's critical views correspond to his views on human behaviour. A good play should be 'well-digested in the scenes, set down with as much modesty as cunning'. A good actor should not 'o'erstep the modesty of nature'. He must avoid rant and even in the whirlwind of passion 'acquire and beget a temperance'. The purpose of playing is 'to hold, as 'twere, the mirror up to nature', so that naturalness and restraint are the qualities to be aimed at. Hamlet, as we have seen, thinks of Horatio, who is not passion's slave, as his own opposite; and we can see why this should be so after the violent explosion of hatred against Claudius at the end of Act II, a verbal explosion which, as Hamlet half realises, is a substitute for action, and after the passionate invective of the nunnery scene.

The soliloquy with which Act II concludes is, like the one in the second scene of the play, a device to show us what has been passing through Hamlet's mind during the speeches about Pyrrhus and Hecuba. This can be seen from the fact that Hamlet has already asked the actors to stage a performance of 'The Murder of Gonzago' and yet, in the soliloquy, he apparently conceives the idea for the first time. Some months have elapsed since the Ghost's revelation and Hamlet has done nothing except to beweep all alone his outcast state. Now at last a plan presents itself to test the truth of the Ghost's story, to test indeed whether the Ghost was a devil or his father's spirit, to 'catch the conscience of the King'.

The conscience of the King is caught in the very next scene, not by a performance of a play but by some casual moralising by Polonius:

> With devotion's visage
> And pious action we do sugar o'er
> The devil himself.   (III.i.47–9)

When Claudius murmurs to himself, 'How smart a lash that speech doth give my conscience!' the audience is certain for the first time that the Ghost's story is true. The smiling, carousing, amorous, diplomatic monarch is revealed as a secret poisoner and adulterer.

The thought of conscience is the climax of Hamlet's next soliloquy. The critics, it need hardly be said, disagree among themselves about the meaning of the whole speech. To some it is a discussion on suicide, to others it is concerned with the question of killing the King. Some have been puzzled by the reference to the bourn 'from which no traveller returns', since Hamlet has seen his father's spirit. There have been at least three explanations of the difficulty: that the soliloquy was originally spoken in the second scene of the play where 'O that this too too sullied flesh' now is, and that Hamlet had not then encountered the Ghost; that the phrase indicates that Hamlet now supposes that the Ghost was the devil in disguise; and that the appearance of an apparition is not the same thing as returning from the underworld as Lazarus or Alcestis did. One recent critic, Mr W. G. Bebbington, has ingeniously argued[36] that Hamlet was not thinking aloud but reading from a book, 'a series of aphoristic, even platitudinous meditations on life, death and suicide', with occasional interpolated comments by Hamlet himself, such as 'Ay, there's the rub'. There are several objections to this theory. There is no indication in the text that Hamlet is reading; it does not give the impression of extracts from a book; and it is concerned too plainly with Hamlet's personal dilemma for it to be part of a treatise.

In the opening lines of the soliloquy Hamlet is not discussing whether to kill himself or not. On his last appearance he has decided to test the truth of the Ghost's story by the King's behaviour at the performance of the play. He has little doubt that Claudius's guilt will unkennel itself. Then, for the first time, he will be compelled to make up his mind—whether to kill the King or 'suffer the slings and arrows of outrageous fortune', which would mean in effect to endure the rule of the murderous usurper. The choice is not as straightforward as this because the King is bound to realise at the performance of the play that Hamlet has somehow guessed his guilty secret; and this means that if Hamlet does not strike first he will be the King's second victim. Whether Hamlet fully realises this or not—and why should he not?— he certainly thinks that the killing of the King may involve his own death. He therefore proceeds without a break to consider the felicity of dying, and so of escaping from

> the thousand natural shocks
> That flesh is heir to.

Then he thinks of what may happen after death. It may not be felicity after all. His father, although a good king and a good man, was being tortured in purgatory for the foul crimes he committed in his lifetime. The secrets of his prison-house were too horrible to be revealed. No wonder then that men prefer to endure the miseries of life—the calamity of a long life—than to escape by suicide, a sin which will ensure worse miseries in a future life. At this point in his meditation, as critics have noted, Hamlet is thinking of mankind in general, as the list of human miseries proves:

> Th'oppressor's wrong, the proud man's contumely,
> The pangs of dispriz'd love, the law's delay,
> The insolence of office, and the spurns
> That patient merit of th'unworthy takes.

One is reminded of Shakespeare's own reasons for thinking of death as felicity:[37]

> Tir'd with all these for restful death I cry:
> As, to behold desert a beggar born,
> And needy nothing trimm'd in jollity,
> And purest faith unhappily forsworn,
> And gilded honour shamefully misplac'd,
> And maiden virtue rudely strumpeted,
> And right perfection wrongfully disgrac'd,
> And strength by limping sway disabled,
> And art made tongue-tied by authority,
> And folly, doctor-like, controlling skill,
> And simple truth miscall'd simplicity,
> And captive good attending captain ill.

But man decides to go on living, either because of human affection, as in Shakespeare's case, or because of 'the dread of something after death', the pains of purgatory or hell. 'To be honest as this world goes', Hamlet had said earlier, 'is to be one man picked out of ten thousand.' And soon he was to tell Ophelia:

I am myself indifferent honest, but yet I could accuse me of such things that it were better my mother had not borne me. I am very proud, revengeful, ambitious ... What should such fellows as I do crawling between earth and heaven?   (III.i.122–8)

Even if we assume that he was here concerned with the general corruption of humanity, and the mistake of breeding yet more sinners, his very consciousness of original sin was enough to make him afraid of death and judgement. Knowing, therefore, that his enterprise against the King may well involve his own death, Hamlet naturally hesitates—not because he is an exception to the common run of humanity, but simply because he is a man:

> Thus conscience does make cowards of us all,
> And thus the native hue of resolution
> Is sicklied o'er with the pale cast of thought.

The word *conscience* does not mean 'consciousness' or 'awareness', as some have suggested: it is used in the ordinary modern sense of the word, as in the last words of Act II, 'the conscience of the King'. There is some resemblance between these lines and the words Hamlet uses in his last soliloquy—

> some craven scruple
> Of thinking too precisely on th'event.

But 'the pale cast of thought' is the consideration of his own fate after death, while the 'craven scruple' is apparently the realisation that in a complex situation we cannot be sure of the results of our actions. The question Hamlet asks himself at the beginning of the soliloquy— whether it is nobler to kill the King or to suffer patiently—he answers implicitly that the former course is nobler but that, even when the King's guilt has been proved, he may refrain from action because of the dread of something after death.

V

The Nunnery scene which follows has likewise given rise to a number of different interpretations. It has been suggested that Hamlet knows all the time that he is being spied on, or that he notices a movement of the arras just before he asks Ophelia where her father is, or that he does not know at all.

Professor Jenkins has rightly pointed out[38] that Hamlet's injunction to Ophelia to enter a nunnery, five times repeated with increasing emphasis, are a continuation of his warnings to her father:

Let her not walk i' th' sun. Conception is a blessing. But as your daughter may conceive—friend, look to't.   (II.ii.184)

Jephthah's daughter, to whom he later compares Ophelia, died a virgin. He may be satirising Polonius's fear that Hamlet will seduce Ophelia, which makes him order her to break with Hamlet, or he may be generalising from his mother's faithlessness, so that Ophelia's rejection merely confirms his belief in the frailty of women.

It has often been noticed that Ophelia speaks as one who has been rejected by Hamlet, although she has rejected him:

> Rich gifts wax poor when givers prove unkind.

We should not take this as a sign of Ophelia's duplicity, but rather as a sign of her realisation that Hamlet has fallen out of love. Perhaps, encouraged by the Queen's hint that a marriage might be arranged despite the assumption of Laertes and Polonius that it would be politically impossible, Ophelia hopes to win Hamlet again. But Hamlet denies that he gave her any presents, admits that he did love her once, confirms the cynical attitude of her father by saying 'you should not have believed me'. He implies that because of original sin his love is tainted, 'for virtue cannot so inoculate our old stock but we shall relish of it'. Immediately afterwards Hamlet urges Ophelia to enter a nunnery to avoid being a breeder of sinners. As Harold Jenkins observes, it is of his own sins that he speaks first—he is 'very proud, revengeful and ambitious'. But men in general 'are arrant knaves, all', 'crawling between earth and heaven'. Then he asks Ophelia where her father is and her reply 'At home, my lord' leads to a change of tone. Up to this point Hamlet has said nothing which Ophelia could regard as a symptom of madness. He changes his mind, he has a cynical and degraded view of sex, he exaggerates his own depravity, but there is no sign of an antic disposition. But after the words 'Let the doors be shut upon him, that he may play the fool nowhere but in's own house', Ophelia prays, 'O help him, you sweet heavens!' Actors generally, and surely rightly, speak the next two speeches much more wildly than the rest of the scene. Women in general—not specifically Ophelia—are accused of using cosmetics, of adopting sexually alluring postures, of obscene conversation among themselves, of pretended innocence, and of being unfaithful to their husbands. As men and women are equally vile, Hamlet wishes marriage and breeding to be stopped. 'Those that are married already, *all but one*, shall live.' These wild and whirling words are a threat to the eavesdropping King, either because Hamlet knows or suspects he is being spied on—a slight hesitation in Ophelia's reply to his question about her father would be enough—or because Shakespeare wishes to indulge in dramatic irony. Because Polonius plays the fool outside his own house, and again behind the arras, he meets his end; and the King hears Hamlet's threat to his own marriage. As Harold Jenkins says,[39] 'What the play requires is not that Hamlet shall know, but that we shall know, that the King is there to hear it.' He continues:

The opportunity for such dramatic piquancies was far too good for an accomplished dramatist to miss. But as Shakespeare's art exploits it, there is more than a brief thrill. The situation of Ophelia at the moment of her crisis is combined and involved with the other situations out of which Hamlet's tragedy develops. While Hamlet is announcing to Ophelia her fate, he fore-shadows the fates of Polonius and the King; while he is bidding her to the nunnery, he reminds us of his duty of revenge. And the marriage that will not now take place is linked with one that has taken place already.

As in the Helpmann ballet, Hamlet's love for Ophelia is contaminated by Gertrude's second marriage which

> takes off the rose
> From the fair forehead of an innocent love
> And sets a blister there.

In a similar way Laertes thinks his mother would be branded as a harlot if he were calmly to accept the murder of his father.

Ophelia, left alone, is much more concerned with the overthrowing of Hamlet's noble mind than she is with her own plight. It is characteristic of her selflessness; and it is characteristic of her innocence that she should take Hamlet's railings against sex and marriage to be signs of a diseased mind. The view that Ophelia is sophisticated and Hamlet's cast-off mistress, as revealed by her understanding of his obscenities and by her mad songs, conflicts with too much evidence for it to be acceptable. The 'rose of May', whose 'innocent love' is contrasted with the corrupted love of the Queen, is allowed, even by the churlish priest, 'her virgin crants' and 'her maiden strewments'. Her flesh, Laertes tells us, is unpolluted.

At the performance of 'The Murder of Gonzago', Hamlet, with his head on Ophelia's lap, grossly insults her before the assembled Court. She rebukes him gently, ascribing his indecencies to his madness; and it may be that Hamlet behaves as he does to support the Polonius theory of his madness. But lying against the woman he loved, he comments to her on the inconstancy of one queen, watched by another equally inconstant.

This is the last time we see Hamlet and Ophelia together, for Hamlet is dispatched to England on the following morning. In the next act it is made apparent that Ophelia's madness has been caused partly by thwarted love—as Hamlet's was supposed to have been—and partly by her father's death, especially because her lover was responsible for it. Her death is accidental—to judge by the Queen's report of it—and it is therefore surprising that we should be told in the graveyard scene that her death was 'doubtful'. Mr J. M. Nosworthy has provided[40] us with a probable explanation of the discrepancy—that the Queen's account of the drowning was an afterthought. Presumably Shakespeare wished to round off the plot to murder Hamlet with an incident that would make us more sympathetic to Laertes. The Queen's beautiful description is clumsily introduced. Laertes has to ask 'Drowned? O, where?' to provide the Queen with the opportunity of saying her piece.

On the evidence of the Queen the only proper verdict for the coroner's jury was accidental death, as the jury who sat on Katherine Hamlet, who was drowned in the Avon in Shakespeare's youth, had decided.[41] Presumably Shakespeare did not notice that the Queen's account conflicted with the references to Ophelia's death in the next scene, unless he meant us to deduce that the lyrical account was a polite fiction to conceal from Laertes the more brutal truth that she had taken her own life. There is, in any case, as Harold Jenkins observes, an added poignancy in the fact that the account is put into the mouth of the woman who was associated with Ophelia in Hamlet's mind.[42]

Here, as elsewhere, Shakespeare sacrifices probability to a dramatic point. Another example occurs in the graveyard scene. It is incredible that Horatio would not have informed Hamlet of Ophelia's death, but Shakespeare asks us to accept this so that we can witness Hamlet's reactions to the funeral for which he is completely unprepared. It is this shock and Laertes' theatrical exhibition of his grief that enables Hamlet to confess, what he had denied in the Nunnery scene:

> I lov'd Ophelia; forty thousand brothers
> Could not with all their quantity of love
> Make up my sum.

But here again there is an area of ambiguity. Is Hamlet aware of his

indirect responsibility for the girl's madness and death, by forcibly
involving her in his problems, or by repudiating her love because of
his mother's guilt, and by killing her father? Does he make no mention
of it because he does not feel it or because the wound is too great? Is
his rant at the graveside a camouflage of his sense of guilt? Shakespeare
leaves the actor and the audience to decide.

VI

By means of the performance of 'The Murder of Gonzago' Hamlet
convinces himself and Horatio that the Ghost's story was true; but the
choice of the play informs Claudius that Hamlet has stumbled on his
secret, and Hamlet's insulting behaviour is so reckless that one can
only assume that he knows that he will have to kill Claudius soon or
be murdered by him. His manic behaviour after the King's departure
makes the audience suppose that he is about to sweep to his revenge.
But the double message from the Queen, brought first by Rosencrantz
and then by Polonius, deflects Hamlet's mind to the other duty
imposed on him by the Ghost—to contrive nothing against Gertrude,
but rather leave her to heaven and the stings of conscience. Hamlet's
soliloquy at the end of the scene begins with the hatred and violence
of a conventional avenger. He appears to be working himself up to a
state of excitement in which he can kill the King:

> 'Tis now the very witching time of night,
> When churchyards yawn, and hell itself breathes out
> Contagion to this world. Now could I drink hot blood,
> And do such bitter business as the day
> Would quake to look on.   (III.ii.378ff.)

Then he remembers that he has to visit his mother and cautions himself
against the use of violence:

> O heart, lose not thy nature; let not ever
> The soul of Nero enter this firm bosom.
> Let me be cruel, not unnatural:
> I will speak daggers to her, but use none.

Nero did not merely murder Agrippina, he committed incest with her.
Hamlet has to caution himself against committing matricide; and the
words have been used to support the theory that Hamlet is in love with

his mother and jealous of Claudius. But the reference to Nero may have been suggested by the name of Claudius; for the Emperor Claudius, whom Agrippina incestuously married, was murdered by her so that Nero could be Emperor. The story seems to have been in the mind of whichever dramatist was responsible for the renaming of Feng as Claudius.[43]

Immediately afterwards Hamlet is given his first opportunity of avenging his father. The performance of 'The Murder of Gonzago' has proved Claudius's guilt; Hamlet has lashed himself into a violent mood; and he stumbles on the King, unguarded and defenceless. Instead of seizing the opportunity, he spares him, ostensibly because a man killed at his prayers would go to heaven instead of to the hell he deserved. Shakespeare reveals that the King, unknown to Hamlet, was unable to pray.

This is one of the crucial episodes in the play and our interpretation of Hamlet's character depends to a considerable extent on the way we interpret Hamlet's speech, 'Now might I do it pat'.

Do we take Hamlet's reasons for not killing the King at their face value, and shall we then be as much revolted by them as Johnson was? Or shall we assume, with Coleridge and Bradley, that the wish to send Claudius to hell was an afterthought, offered by Hamlet to excuse his own failure to act? Such critics can point to the tell-tale *might* in the first line or to the 'craven scruple' of which Hamlet speaks as he embarks for England. Or shall we suppose that Hamlet has an instinctive revulsion from killing a defenceless man at the foot of an altar—unlike Laertes and Pyrrhus—and then, revolting against his own revulsion, works himself up into a passion of hatred which provides him with a substitute for action? The desire to damn one's enemy, body and soul, is characteristic of the revenge play; but Shakespeare may be using a commonplace for more sophisticated purposes.[44]

Whichever interpretation is followed, we are driven to the conclusion that Hamlet hates the man he has to kill. He cannot kill in cold blood; but if he kills in rage his action will be the expression of revenge rather than of justice.

In the scene with his mother, Hamlet is able to stab the rat behind the arras, believing it to be the King. No spectator has thought this strange because it is an instinctive and natural reaction. So too is his cool and callous dispatch of Rosencrantz and Guildenstern to their doom—it was their life or his.

It has been argued by some critics that in his upbraiding of his mother, Hamlet is fascinated by what he condemns . . . And it is because of the impurity and indiscriminateness of his rejections that, brief moments of friendship and respite apart, he takes refuge in postures.[45]

He is, we are told, complacent and self-righteous, as when he asks Gertrude to forgive him his virtue. Freudians go further and declare that

It is an unavoidable psychological conclusion that the torrent of erotic pictures which Hamlet hurls at his mother indicate unconscious fantasies on his own part in which he is not only the accusing spectator, but also the active participant.[46]

The self-righteousness apparently shown in some speeches is offset by Hamlet's former condemnation of himself as a miserable sinner crawling between earth and heaven; and the violent attack on his mother's sin is mingled, not surely with incestuous feelings, but with filial affection for the sinner. Hamlet, in accordance with his plan, is speaking daggers to her, so as to arouse her sluggish conscience. This goes beyond the Ghost's injunction of leaving her to heaven and the pricking of conscience. Hamlet's method is to hold up a mirror in which the Queen can see herself and her 'inmost part', by describing with brutal realism the significance of her adultery at an age when 'the heyday in the blood is tame', and by showing her 'The counterfeit presentment of two brothers'—the godlike and the bestial. Hamlet's plan is justified by its success. His words like daggers enter Gertrude's ears and she repents: she sees the black spots in her soul. The Ghost appears at the height of Hamlet's denunciation of Claudius, not surely to prevent the Queen's repentance, but to save her from the knowledge that her first husband had been murdered by her second.

But despite his success with his mother, Hamlet is in a desperate position. He has revealed to his uncle that he knows his secret crime; he has passed over the one opportunity he has had of avenging his father; and, by killing Polonius, he has raised up an avenger, driven Ophelia mad, and given Claudius a good excuse for taking strong action against him. It is no wonder that, after the death of Polonius, Hamlet should wonder whether he is God's minister, called upon to execute justice on a sinner who would otherwise escape punishment, or a scourge of God, a wicked man who is used by God to punish sinners, but at the expense of damning himself.[47]

In the soliloquy he speaks just before sailing to England, Hamlet is

faced with the complete failure of his mission, and he cannot understand why he has not carried out the Ghost's commands.

> whether it be
> Bestial oblivion or some craven scruple
> Of thinking too precisely on th'event—
> A thought which, quarter'd, hath but one part wisdom
> And ever three parts coward—I do not know
> Why yet I live to say 'This thing's to do'.   (IV.iv.39–44)

Oblivion it obviously is not; ordinary cowardice it cannot be; but it
may be, as Coleridge thought, that Hamlet thought 'too precisely on
th'event', or that he was deterred by 'some craven scruple'. It is a
curious paradox that the one intellectual among Shakespeare's tragic
heroes should be least able to know why he acts or fails to act.

On the voyage, as we have noted, Hamlet does act, spontaneously,
ruthlessly and bravely; and on his return he is greatly changed, medi-
tating gravely but without bitterness on man's mortality, and no
longer agonising about his failure to carry out the Ghost's command.
The reasons for the change are not revealed until the final scene. His
escape from death by means of the forged warrant and the providential
attack by the pirates convince him that

> Our indiscretion sometime serves us well
> When our deep plots do pall; and that should learn us
> There's a divinity that shapes our ends,
> Rough-hew them how we will.   (V.ii.8–11)

Then, as Horatio immediately recognises, news would soon arrive of
the execution of Rosencrantz and Guildenstern and therefore if
Hamlet did not act quickly it would be too late. On this Hamlet
remarks calmly, 'The interim is mine'. But he also has a premonition
of his own death and a quiet acceptance of it which differs considerably
from his previous death-wish:

There is a special providence in the fall of a sparrow. If it be now, 'tis not to
come; if it be not to come, it will be now; if it be not now, yet it will come—
the readiness is all.   (V.ii.212ff.)

After detailing the sins and crimes of Claudius, culminating in the
attempt on his own life, Hamlet asks Horatio:

> Is't not perfect conscience
> To quit him with this arm? And is't not to be damn'd
> To let this canker of our nature come
> In further evil?   (V.ii.67–70)

The contraction of the time available, the certainty of the justice of his cause, and the conviction that providence is watching over him and that he will be provided with an opportunity for executing the King, combine in Hamlet's mind—and critics may combine them in different proportions. What they should not do is to ignore the hints given by Shakespeare in the text and to misread the tone of those passages as despair or the resignation of defeat.

As soon as the Queen falls dead and he learns from Laertes that he himself is dying, Hamlet slays the King without hesitation. Not, surely, as the Freudians would have it, because he and the King are no longer rivals; nor because the King, to prevent his own exposure, has allowed the Queen to drink from the poisoned cup; nor because Hamlet is the supreme egotist who can avenge himself but not his father. Some of the reasons for the lifting of the inhibition which prevents Hamlet from acting have already been discussed—the change of heart apparent since his return to Denmark, his determination to wait for the right, providential opportunity, his conviction that he need have no scruple about killing the King, the knowledge that time is running short. The death of the Queen and Laertes' accusation of Claudius provide the opportunity for which Hamlet has been waiting: he can kill the King in such a way that the action will be seen as just; on the spur of the moment, so that he will not be able to think too precisely on the event; after Gertrude's death so that he will not cause her either shame or grief by the revelation of Claudius's crimes; and, of course, his own death-wound makes immediate action necessary.

In his last moments Hamlet is concerned for the state of Denmark and gives his vote to Fortinbras—a concern which Dame Rebecca West, despite her dislike of Hamlet, has brought herself to applaud.[48] But he is also concerned lest his name should be vilified by people ignorant of the true facts. He therefore urges Horatio not to drink the poison:

> Absent thee from felicity awhile,
> And in this harsh world draw thy breath in pain
> To tell my story.

Shakespeare, too, is concerned to defend Hamlet from his detractors.

His repentant killer, Laertes, calls him noble and exchanges forgiveness. Fortinbras gives him a soldier's funeral and pronounces that he would have made an excellent king. Horatio, to whom his death makes life intolerable despite his ability to endure fortune's buffets, gives him a tender valediction:

> Good night, sweet prince,
> And flights of angels sing thee to thy rest!

We are plainly not meant to regard Hamlet with the disapproval several recent critics have expressed.

Horatio tells us of the woe and wonder—the admiration and commiseration—that is the appropriate reaction and summarises the action of the play:

> So shall you hear
> Of carnal, bloody, and unnatural acts;
> Of accidental judgments, casual slaughters;
> Of deaths put on by cunning and forc'd cause;
> And, in this upshot, purposes mistook
> Fall'n on th'inventors' heads.

VII

It will be apparent what conclusions follow from the line of argument we have been pursuing. As the Ghost was the authentic spirit of Hamlet's father and not the devil in his shape, one must accept the fact that, in the world of the play, it was Hamlet's bounden duty to avenge the murder. In the situation in which he was placed, Hamlet had to establish the honesty of the Ghost; he had to convince others that he was not killing the King because he had been cheated of the throne; and he had to avoid exposing his mother's adultery and incest. But in addition to these practical reasons for delay, there seems little doubt that Hamlet had scruples about the ethics of revenge. In Lascelles Abercrombie's phrase,[49] Hamlet exhibited 'the heroism of moral vacillation'. If he had refused altogether to execute justice on the King, on the grounds that a Christian should not resist evil, we should feel that he had failed in his duty. If, on the other hand, he had swept to his revenge without hesitation, we should regard him as insensitive and barbarous. Although he never directly questions the morality of revenge, Hamlet's soliloquies would convey to an Elizabethan audience (as Professor Lawlor has cogently argued)[50] that he was being deterred

by precisely this. Living in a rotten society he could not be guided by
its moral code—he had to construct his own: and on his actions
depended the future of his country. His agonised self-communings
show how he was wrung by the anguish of choice. The tragedy is
caused partly by the situation—the usurpation by an incestuous
murderer—and partly by the character of the man called upon to set
right the disjointed society. The deaths of Polonius, Ophelia, Laertes,
Rosencrantz, Guildenstern and Gertrude are directly or indirectly due
to Hamlet's failure to strike the King at his prayers.

As I have said[51] elsewhere, what Shakespeare did

was to imagine a 'noble' and 'sweet' Prince, sensitive, sophisticated and
intelligent, placed in a situation where his acknowledged duty could only be
repugnant—as it would be to Hamlet's critics if they were unfortunate
enough to find themselves in his position—and where his intelligence made
his duty all the more difficult.

It is, of course, necessary not to minimise Hamlet's sins and shortcomings. We have to remember that we catch only glimpses of the
Prince as he was before the two-fold shock he sustained by the sudden
death of his father and the hasty remarriage of his mother to the uncle
he disliked. To this double shock which plunged Hamlet into acute
melancholia, there were added three more—the knowledge that his
father had been murdered, the knowledge that his mother had committed adultery, and the desertion of Ophelia. His consciousness of the
evil power of sexual desire colours his outlook so that he believes that
reason panders will, that beauty transforms honesty to a bawd, and
that mankind is utterly corrupt. He might have used Newman's words:
'Since there is a God, the human race is implicated in some terrible
aboriginal calamity.'

Hamlet is aware in general terms of his own morbidity, and his own
sinfulness. But he sometimes seems blind on particular occasions to the
evil in himself. It was inevitable that he should hate Claudius, and
natural that as a substitute for action he should lash himself into rages
against his enemy, but it is a hatred that interferes with the successful
accomplishment of his task. It was natural that he should kill Polonius,
but wrong that his repentance should be so perfunctory; it was necessary to send Rosencrantz and Guildenstern to their deaths, but wrong
to disclaim any scruples about them, and he is bitterly cruel to the
woman he loved. He says nothing about his responsibility for Ophelia's

death, but Shakespeare may have decided that this would have inter-
fered with the effect he was aiming at in the last act of the play.

Hamlet, then, is by no means an ideal figure. But his faults are largely
caused by the situation in which he finds himself and by the distasteful
task he is called upon to perform. Like many avengers, he becomes the
deed's creature. But he purges himself of some of his morbidity about
sex, by disgorging it in the closet scene; and he recovers calm and
dignity in the final scene. No audience feels that it was inappropriate of
Horatio to pray for flights of angels as his friend dies.

5

OTHELLO

Man can endure earthquake, epidemic, dreadful disease, every form of spiritual torment; but the most dreadful tragedy that can befall him is, and will remain, the tragedy of the bedroom.[1]   (Tolstoy)

After Hamlet, Shakespeare wrote a play which critics have found hard to characterise. *Troilus and Cressida* has been called a comedy, a tragedy, a comical satire, a tragical satire, a black comedy, and a case can be made out for any one of these labels. Most readers would agree that the play satirises the glamour attached to war and sex. All the argument, as Thersites says, is a whore and a cuckold. The Trojans act in defiance of the moral laws of nature and of nations in refusing to restore Helen to the Greeks. The Greeks themselves are at best Machiavellian, at worst barbarians, boors and thugs. In the love-plot Chaucer's delightful heroine is transformed into a daughter of the game, and Troilus's frame of order is destroyed by the disillusionment that follows his absurd idealisation of Cressida. But despite the presence of Thersites in the scene where Troilus observes Cressida's betrayal of his love, the intensity of his feeling, conveyed to us by the splendour of the poetry, makes it impossible for us to regard it satirically:

> If beauty have a soul, this is not she;
> If souls guide vows, if vows be sanctimonies,
> If sanctimony be the gods' delight,
> If there be rule in unity itself,
> This was not she. O madness of discourse,
> That cause sets up with and against itself!
> Bifold authority! Where reason can revolt
> Without perdition, and loss assume all reason
> Without revolt: this is, and is not, Cressid.
> Within my soul there doth conduce a fight
> Of this strange nature, that a thing inseparate
> Divides more wider than the sky and earth;

> And yet the spacious breadth of this division
> Admits no orifex for a point as subtle
> As Ariachne's broken woof to enter.   (V.ii.136ff.)

The tempest in his soul is shown, as I. A. Richards suggested,[2] by his conflation of Ariadne and Arachne. In the other plot the murder of Hector, brought on by his involvement in the Trojan guilt, is also tragic.

A subsidiary theme in *Hamlet*, expressed in the words 'Frailty, thy name is woman!' becomes the dominant theme of *Troilus and Cressida*, with Cressida and Helen as exemplars. But it should be noticed that Troilus, at the very moment of disillusionment, is anxious that stubborn critics (or satirists) should not 'square the general sex by Cressid's rule'.[3]

The play itself provides no evidence that Troilus is being satirised as a sophisticated sensualist. The mirror scene where the lovers and Pandarus make their vows, not as characters in the play but as the types they were to become in literature and legend, shows clearly that Shakespeare is depicted as a faithful lover, not as an 'Italianate roué'.[4]

The tone of *Othello* is obviously very different, but there are links between the two plays. The Moor, like Troilus, is made to believe that he has been betrayed by the woman he loves, and the supposed betrayal destroys for him the very meaning of existence. In his case reason cannot revolt without perdition. Just before his happiness is destroyed he says of Desdemona:

> Perdition catch my soul
> But I do love thee; and when I love thee not
> Chaos is come again.   (III.iii.91–3)

The irony here is that chaos does not come because he ceases to love Desdemona, but because he continues to love her after he thinks he has lost her love—after he believes her to be a Cressid.

There is another important link between the two plays. The debate about the restoration of Helen becomes a debate on objective and subjective value in which Troilus takes the line that the beauty of Helen outweighs every other consideration and that value is subjective, while Hector shows that it is mad idolatry

> To make the service greater than the god;
> And the will dotes that is attributive
> To what infectiously itself affects,
> Without some image of th'affected merit.   (II.ii.57–60)

In another significant scene Ulysses tells Achilles

> That no man is the lord of anything,
> Though in and of him there be much consisting,
> Till he communicate his parts to others;
> Nor doth he of himself know them for aught
> Till he behold them formed in th'applause
> Where th'are extended. (III.iii.115–20)

The relationship between virtue and reputation, value and opinion, seems to have been much in Shakespeare's mind about this time. Duke Vincentio, when he preaches on the text of 'Let your light so shine before men' in the first scene of *Measure for Measure*, tells Angelo:

> Thyself and thy belongings
> Are not thine own so proper as to waste
> Thyself upon thy virtues, they on thee.
> Heaven doth with us as we with torches do,
> Not light them for themselves; for if our virtues
> Did not go forth of us, 'twere all alike
> As if we had them not. Spirits are not finely touch'd
> But to fine issues; nor Nature never lends
> The smallest scruple of her excellence,
> But, like a thrifty goddess, she determines
> Herself the glory of a creditor,
> Both thanks and use. (I.i.30ff.)

Vincentio is appropriately using the scriptural argument of the parable of the talents, that faith without works is vain: he is not pretending, as Ulysses does, that a man's virtue depends on what people think of him.

In *Othello* the villain takes both sides in the debate on reputation. He tells the Moor that good name in man and woman

> Is the immediate jewel of their souls.

But to Cassio, who thinks of reputation as the immortal part of himself, he declares that 'Reputation is an idle and most false imposition; oft got without merit, and lost without deserving'. Brabantio thinks his reputation is irreparably tarnished by his daughter's elopement. Several of Shakespeare's tragic heroes are anxious not to leave a wounded name behind them but Othello is unique in his concern from the first act to the last with his reputation.

One other link with previous plays is worth mentioning. Iago extracts money from Roderigo by holding out hopes of Desdemona's hand in the same way as Sir Toby Belch milks Sir Andrew Aguecheek by encouraging his suit with Olivia. It has even been argued—though not very plausibly—that Iago's subsequent actions are motivated by his wish to continue using his fool as his purse.[5]

Shakespeare found the plot of *Othello* in the collection of stories by Cinthio which also contained a variant of the *Measure for Measure* plot. The story which ends with the murder of Desdemona by a stocking filled with sand in the hands of the Ensign is not at first sight particularly promising as dramatic material. But there were three points about it that seem to have kindled Shakespeare's imagination. After the murder, we are told, the Moor mourned for the loss of his wife, because he had loved her more than his very eyes. Equally significant was Cinthio's description of the villain as

a man of very fine appearance but of the most depraved nature that ever a man had in the world . . . Although he was a most detestable character, nevertheless with imposing words and his presence, he concealed the malice he bore in his heart, in such a way that he showed himself outwardly like another Hector or Achilles.

Then, thirdly, the virtuous white woman falls in love with a Moor. The consummate hypocrite, the mixed marriage, and the murderer who loves his victim are the triple foundation of the tragedy. They provided Shakespeare with opportunities of contrast, irony and paradox, which he exploited to the full. Did the audience at the Globe expect the Moor to be a lecherous villain, like Aaron in *Titus Andronicus* or Ithamore in *The Jew of Malta*? They were presented with a picture of a baptised Moor, much esteemed by the senators of Venice. Did the Globe audience suppose that a white woman who takes the initiative in wooing a coloured man was certainly perverse and probably sensual? Shakespeare was careful to establish in the account of the wooing that Desdemona loved Othello's visage in his mind; and that Othello is more anxious to be free and bounteous to Desdemona's mind than to please the palate of his appetite. Did the Globe patrons, since the Devil himself was depicted as black, expect Othello to be devilish? But the demi-devil of the play is white. Did they suppose, as Rymer supposed later in the century, that soldiers in plays should be depicted as honest? Shakespeare depicted an Iago exploiting this superstition for his own ends.[6] Did they expect Moors to be violently jealous? In this Shakespeare appears to have satisfied their expectations, though some of the best critics have denied that Othello was jealous.

In *The Brothers Karamazov* (VIII.3) there is a discussion of Mitya's jealousy. Dostoevsky distinguishes between this and Othello's feelings:

'Othello was not jealous, he was trustful,' observed Pushkin. And that remark alone is enough to show the deep insight of our great poet. Othello's soul was shattered and his whole outlook clouded simply because *his ideal was destroyed.* But Othello did not begin hiding, spying, peeping. He was trustful, on the contrary. He had to be led up, pushed on, excited with great difficulty before he could entertain the idea of deceit. The truly jealous man is not like that. It is impossible to picture to oneself the shame and moral degradation to which the jealous man can descend without a qualm of conscience ... Othello was incapable of making up his mind to faithlessness —not incapable of forgiving it, but of making up his mind to it—though his soul was as innocent and free from malice as a babe's. It is not so with the really jealous man.

Unknown to Pushkin, and probably unknown to Dostoevsky, Coleridge had expressed similar views about Othello. Jealousy, he declared, was not the point of his passion:[7]

I take it to be rather an agony that the creature, whom he had believed angelic, with whom he had garnered up his heart, and whom he could not help still loving, should be proved impure and worthless. It was the struggle *not* to love her. It was a moral indignation and regret that virtue should so fall.

Bradley similarly declared that Othello's[8]

tragedy lies in this—that his whole nature was indisposed to jealousy, and yet was such that he was unusually open to deception, and, if once wrought to passion, likely to act with little reflection, with no delay, and in the most decisive manner conceivable.

The Coleridge–Pushkin interpretation is often followed by actors. Stanislavsky argued that Othello was childlike, gentle and pure in heart;[9] Alexander Ostuzhev, who played the part in 1936, assumed that jealousy was not the theme of the play; and in all but one of the seventy-eight productions of the play in the Soviet Union between 1945 and 1957, the same interpretation was followed.

The weight of this tradition should not prevent us from questioning it. The first known critic of the play, Leonard Digges, Shakespeare's neighbour, spoke of 'the jealous Moor';[10] and Othello speaks of himself

D

as 'not easily jealous'—not denying that he was jealous. We may allow that the shattering of an ideal by Desdemona's supposed adultery, so that (in Troilus's phrase) 'the bonds of heaven are slipped, dissolv'd and loos'd', is an essential part of the tragedy, but that Othello is desperately jealous it would be idle to deny.

There are, of course, several different kinds of jealousy, from irrational suspicion to unwilling conviction, from spiritual horror to animal possessiveness. One can appreciate that Coleridge would wish to distinguish Othello's jealousy from some of these. But the very characteristics of jealousy listed by him to show that Othello is free of it seem rather to prove the opposite. An 'eagerness to snatch at proofs' is displayed by him several times in the crucial temptation scene—the story of Cassio's dream is told by Iago when Othello demands 'a living reason' that Desdemona is disloyal, and he snatches at the 'proof' provided by the handkerchief. 'A disposition to degrade the object of his passion by sensual fancies and images' could be illustrated from almost any scene from the central acts of the play:

> I had been happy if the general camp,
> Pioners and all, had tasted her sweet body . . .   (III.iii.349–50)

> It is not words that shakes me thus—
> pish!—noses, ears, and lips.   (IV.i.41–2)

> The fountain from the which my current runs,
> Or else dries up—to be discarded thence!
> Or keep it as a cistern for foul toads
> To knot and gender in!   (IV.ii.60–3)

> Goats and monkeys!   (IV.i.260)

'Catching occasions to ease the mind by ambiguities' is apparent in the brothel scene; 'a dread of vulgar ridicule' can be seen, for example in Othello's reference to the 'forked plague'; and 'a spirit of selfish vindictiveness' is reflected in his invocation of 'black vengeance', in 'O, I see that nose of yours, but not that dog I shall throw't to' and in 'I'll chop her into messes!'

It is strange that Coleridge failed to notice such passages, or failed to see that they conflicted with his conception of Othello. It was easy for Edgar Elmer Stoll[11] to demonstrate that Coleridge was mistaken and that Othello was clearly jealous; but he went further and argued that it was impossible to reconcile the jealous maniac of Act IV with the noble self-controlled character depicted in Act I. Shakespeare's character portrayal in Stoll's view was based on a specious and unreal psychology and he sacrificed consistency of characterisation to theatrical effect. To make Othello accept Iago's slanders rather than trust Desdemona is to Stoll absurd, especially as Iago's temptation is unconvincing:[12]

An honest man who undertakes to tell you that your wife and your dearest friend have played you false makes a clean breast of it, without flourish or ado. He does not twist and turn, tease and tantalize, furtively cast forth the slime of slander and ostentatiously lick it up again . . . Shakespeare, in his neglect of plausibility, would have us labour under the delusion that the manners of honesty and dishonesty are almost one and the same.

But the temptation scene can be defended in various ways—by the fact that an irresolute friend might behave not very differently from Iago; that Elizabethan views of human behaviour differ in some respects from ours; that Othello did not have the advantage of Shakespeare's readers or audience of knowing that Iago was a villain; that every character in the play is deceived by Iago; and that a dramatic poet does not attempt to give a naturalistic, 'photographic' picture of human behaviour, provided that he can convince an audience of his truth to life. Audiences do in fact accept Iago's temptation of Othello as a true representation of how a villain pretending to be an honest man would behave and they accept Othello's behaviour as the natural reaction of a noble, but credulous, Moor.

Of course the temptation scene is telescoped: and those critics who think they can estimate Othello's proneness to jealousy by demonstrating that between the beginning of the temptation and the fall represented by the words 'Set on thy wife to observe' is less than a hundred and fifty lines are absurdly prosaic.[13] When Othello at the end of the play declares that he was not easily jealous, Shakespeare means us to believe him, at least in the sense that he was not of a jealous temperament. He would not have suspected Desdemona if he had not been deceived by the villain.

This is not the view of two of the best critics of our day, T. S. Eliot and Dr F. R. Leavis, and of their numerous disciples. Eliot in a famous essay[14] stigmatised Othello for his boyaryism, declaring that in his final long speech he was cheering himself up and escaping from reality into illusion, by blaming fate and the Ancient. As I have tried to show elsewhere, such an interpretation is incompatible with the text

of the final scene. Othello regrets the murder before Desdemona's
name is cleared:

> I have no wife.
> O, insupportable! O heavy hour!

He implies to Emilia that he has been driven mad, by the fact that the
moon

> comes more nearer earth than she was wont,
> And makes men mad.

He admits that if he had not proceeded upon just grounds he would be
'damned beneath all depth in hell'. When he learns the truth, he
naturally tries to kill Iago, though he knows that he himself has
reached his journey's end. Although he asks 'Who can control his
fate?' he does not disclaim his own responsibility. He knows that he
is damned, that his soul will be snatched by fiends, and that he will be
tortured for ever. At last he executes justice on himself, believing that
his suicide would seal his damnation.

Is he really 'cheering himself up' in the speech which ends with his
suicide?

> Soft you; a word or two before you go.
> I have done the state some service and they know't:
> No more of that. I pray you in your letters
> When you shall these unlucky deeds relate
> Speak of me as I am: nothing extenuate
> Nor set down aught in malice. Then must you speak
> Of one that loved not wisely, but too well;
> Of one not easily jealous, but, being wrought,
> Perplexed in the extreme; of one whose hand
> Like the base Indian threw a pearl away
> Richer than all his tribe; of one whose subdued eyes,
> Albeit unused to the melting mood,
> Drop tears as fast as the Arabian trees
> Their med'cinable gum. Set you down this:
> And say, besides, that in Aleppo once
> Where a malignant and a turbaned Turk
> Beat a Venetian and traduced the state,
> I took by th'throat the circumcised dog
> And smote him thus.

That Othello in such circumstances refers to his services to Venice has
been regarded as a sign of egotism. An Elizabethan audience would
have seen it rather as the natural expression of proper pride. Othello,

like Hamlet, does not wish to leave a wounded name behind him. He does not wish anyone to extenuate his guilt despite the phrase 'unlucky deeds'. The key phrase in his apologia is that he had loved 'not wisely, but too well'. To some critics this reflects his self-deceit. If he had loved Desdemona better, he would have forgiven her supposed adultery. How much better, we are told, the hero of *A Woman Killed by Kindness* behaves! But tragic heroes are seldom or never patterns of right conduct. What Othello means by saying he loved too well is that his whole life had been transformed by his love. His total commitment meant that if he believed he had lost Desdemona's love, life would become a desert. His tears express his grief and his repentance and the medcinable gum may hint at atonement. The final anecdote is not merely to distract attention so that his auditors cannot prevent his suicide: he also reminds us of a time when he was a champion of Christian civilisation and implies by his fatal blow that he is killing the pagan in himself.

But, we are told by Dr Leavis, 'A habit of self-approving self-dramatization is an essential element in Othello's make-up',[15] even in this final apologia. At best it is 'the impressive manifestation of a noble egotism'. The Othello music of which Wilson Knight has written[16] so eloquently conveys 'romantic glamour'. Othello's attitude to emotion is essentially sentimental. His love for Desdemona 'is composed very largely of ignorance of self as well as ignorance of her' and 'an essential condition of the tragedy' is that his 'romantic idealising love' is 'dubiously grounded on reality'.[17] Leo Kirschbaum is another critic who complains that Othello refuses to look squarely at his crime,[18] that he indulges in self-idealisation, that he 'loves not Desdemona but his *image of her*'. Such an Othello hardly needs a demi-devil to bring about his ruin. As Dr Leavis says, 'the tragedy may fairly be said to be Othello's character in action'.[19]

It must be admitted that these critics have some grains of truth in their remarks. It is true that Othello's previous experience as a soldier has left him singularly ignorant of women, especially of women of a different race, and his own awareness of this makes it difficult for him to argue rationally with Iago. There is irony, too, in the fact that his initial, unsophisticated idea of Desdemona was true, while his sophisticated idea of her, after he has been Iago's pupil, is totally false. It is therefore not true to suggest that his love is based on ignorance. It is based on intuitive, but quite genuine, knowledge—a knowledge which

Iago undermines. In the same way, Desdemona's love is based on intuitive knowledge. She sees Othello's visage in his mind; she loves him not merely for the dangers he has undergone, but for the noble simplicity of character which shines through his autobiography and makes his colour basically irrelevant. Irrelevant to her, but not to the scheme of the play; for Iago plays on Othello's ignorance of Venetian women and undermines his instinctive trust. The difference of race makes him particularly vulnerable. As Professor Eldred Jones says, *Othello* 'is a complex story of how a noble and upright but isolated *man* is subjected to temptation in the area of his being where he is most vulnerable—his difference in race'.[20] It could be argued that Othello is deluded when he plays down the erotic aspect of the marriage—'the young effects in [him] defunct'; but he is a general anxious to persuade the Senate to agree to Desdemona's plea to be allowed to accompany her husband on active service, and he naturally argues that her presence will not interfere with his efficiency.

Those who see Othello as a braggart soldier are surely mistaken. He has a proper pride in his vocation; he is aware of his military achievements, his service to the state, his personal bravery. If anything he is guilty of understatement, and no Jacobean spectator would have found anything blameworthy in his awareness of his own merits. Nor can it be said that the 'Othello music' is somehow a symptom of egotism or of self-dramatisation. Shakespeare had to find an idiom and vocabulary which distinguished him from the Europeans; which was supremely eloquent at the same time as it enabled Othello to regard his speech as rude and unsophisticated. If we think that his account of his wooing shows that he had bragged and told fantastical lies, we are of the demi-devil's party without knowing it. The Duke directs our responses:

> I think this tale would win my daughter too.

We need not go beyond the first scene in which Othello appears (I.ii) to see the distinction between his true nobility and the hollow egotistical 'nobility' with which he is credited. Iago warns him that Brabantio will prevent his marriage from being consummated. Othello replies—quite truly, as it turns out—that his services to the state will out-tongue Brabantio's complaints, that he comes of royal ancestors, and that his merits make him worthy of Desdemona. Iago urges him to go in, but Othello refuses:

> My parts, my title, and my perfect soul
> Shall manifest me rightly.

And when Brabantio arrives to arrest him, Othello averts a fight with a line which shows him to be a man of natural authority:

> Keep up your bright swords, for the dew will rust them.

This scene shows that Othello is not without pride; but it also displays a man of nobility and self-control rather than an egotist.

Another example of self-dramatisation adduced by Dr Leavis is afforded by the lines in the final scene of the play:

> Behold, I have a weapon:
> A better never did itself sustain
> Upon a soldier's thigh.

The lines are a surprise to Gratiano, who believes Othello's statement that he is unarmed is true; but it is not at all a surprise to the audience who have seen Othello looking for the sword, tempered in the ice-brook, in his chamber, and have heard him describe it. His other sword, with which he had wounded Iago, has been taken from him, so that it is assumed that the aged Gratiano is an adequate guard. The audience will imagine for a moment that Othello is going to try to escape; and perhaps the Moor, who would not put himself in circumscription and confine for the sea's worth, intends at first to do this. But, if so, he soon realises that he has come to the end of the road. This is an example of dramatisation by Shakespeare, not of self-dramatisation by Othello; for the audience, having seen him discard a second sword, is more likely to be surprised by his suicide. Indeed, Cassio, who is best acquainted with Othello's character, half expected him to commit suicide, 'but thought he had no weapon'. From the dramatic point of view it is necessary to show that Othello deliberately throws away his chance of escaping and equally to make his suicide seem both inevitable and surprising.

It looks as though a prejudice against the theatre and a failure to realise the necessities of the stage have led Dr Leavis into confusing dramatisation with its necessary projection of character and the self-dramatisation of characters in real life. In his essay on the sentimentalist's Othello he was not merely disagreeing with Bradley but with three hundred years of stage tradition.

If one examines what the other characters in the play say about

Othello, the impression we derive from his own speeches is strengthened. We expect the Senate to pay tribute to his military prowess and for Montano to speak of him as a worthy governor. But Cassio's admiration and affection is apparent all through the play. Even after the death of Desdemona Cassio speaks of him as 'Dear General' and as great of heart. Othello claims that Brabantio loved him, even though he did not want him as a son-in-law. Lodovico, after seeing Othello strike his wife, asks:

> Is this the noble Moor, whom our full senate
> Call all-in-all sufficient? Is this the nature
> Whom passion could not shake? Whose solid virtue
> The shot of accident nor dart of chance
> Could neither graze nor pierce?   (IV.i.261–5)

In the last scene he addresses him as

> O, thou Othello, that wast once so good.

But the strongest testimony to the Moor's virtues comes from his bitterest enemy. Although in talking to others Iago makes derogatory remarks about him, complaining of his bombast, his bragging, his lies and his lasciviousness, in soliloquy and even in dialogue he reveals that the Moor is a great and valiant soldier and that, although he hates him, he has a 'constant, loving, noble nature',

> a free and open nature
> That thinks men honest that but seem to be so.

It is surely difficult to argue that everyone in the play is mistaken about the Moor and that in defiance of their estimate of his character we must accept the diagnosis of two or three modern critics that he is a self-deceiving egotist, bombastic and naturally jealous. Even Iago knew better than that. He knew that Othello's fatal flaw was his credulity, which enabled him to be led by the nose. Like Chapman's hero,[21]

> He would believe, since he would be believed:
> Your noblest natures are most credulous.

We are liable at times to agree with Iago that Othello is 'egregiously an ass' for believing his wife has played him false on the slender evidence provided—the story of Cassio's dream and the handkerchief in the hands of a harlot. Even in the theatre we may be tempted to sympathise with the spectator who is said to have shouted out during the temptation scene 'You black fool, can't you see?' Certainly when Emilia after the murder of Desdemona exclaims

> O gull! O dolt!
> As ignorant as dirt!

she expresses the feelings of the audience at this moment of the play. But credulous as Othello is, we do not ultimately regard him as stupid. We are prevented from doing so by the fact that Iago imposes on everyone, and particularly by the convincing nature of the temptation scene in the theatre. The epithet applied to Iago until just before the end is 'honest'. Roderigo is convinced that the Ancient is devoted to his interests; Cassio believes him to be his friend; even Emilia, who knows him best, does not suspect that he hates Othello and Cassio. We are told by Milton, after Satan has slipped into paradise unrecognised by the angelic sentry, that Hypocrisy is

> the onely evil that walks
> Invisible, except to God alone.[22]

Shakespeare seems to have shared Milton's opinion on this matter, as we can see from his obsessional treatment of the theme of seeming.

The Leavis view that Iago 'is not much more than a necessary piece of dramatic mechanism'[23] may be a necessary retort to those who exaggerate his intellectual superiority; and it may be true, in a certain sense, 'that he represents something that is in Othello'.[24] But this kind of emphasis immeasurably impoverishes the metaphysical content of the play. It is difficult not to accept S. L. Bethell's view that Shakespeare introduced sixty-four 'diabolic' images into the play to show 'Othello and Iago as exemplifying and participating in the age-long warfare of Good and Evil'.[25] Iago, who refers to hell and damnation eight times in the course of the first act, brings it to an end with the hatching of his plot:

> I have't. It is engender'd. Hell and night
> Must bring this monstrous birth to the world's light.

The second act ends with Iago considering his satanic theology—the divinity of hell—and identifying himself as a devil.

> When devils will the blackest sins put on,
> They do suggest at first with heavenly shows
> As I do now.

He boasts that he is going to make out of Desdemona's goodness a net
to enmesh her, Othello and Cassio. In the last act Othello attacks Iago
with the words

> If that thou be'st a devil, I cannot kill thee.

A little later he calls him a demi-devil. These references—they are not,
properly speaking, images—cannot be brushed aside as peripheral.
Those critics who see Iago as a descendant of the Vice of the Moralities
can point to a number of characteristics they have in common; but he
resembles more closely the traditional stage devil. On one level,
therefore, the play can be seen as the temptation of a good man by a
devil to commit mortal sin.

This fits in with Coleridge's belief that Iago's soliloquies show 'the
motive-hunting of a motiveless malignity' if not with Hazlitt's brilliant
analysis of the character:[26]

Some persons, more nice than wise, have thought this whole character
unnatural, because his villainy is without a sufficient motive. Shakespeare,
who was as good a philosopher as he was a poet, thought otherwise. He
knew that the love of power, which is another name for the love of mischief,
is natural to man . . . Iago in fact belongs to a class of character, common to
Shakespeare and at the same time peculiar to him; whose heads are as acute
and active as their hearts are hard and callous. Iago is to be sure an extreme
instance of the kind; that is to say, of diseased intellectual activity, with the
most perfect indifference to moral good or evil, or rather with a decided
preference for the latter, because it falls more readily in with his favourite
propensity, gives greater zest to his thoughts and scope to his actions. He is
quite or nearly as indifferent to his own fate as to that of others; he runs all
risks for a trifling and doubtful advantage; and is himself the dupe and
victim of his ruling passion—an insatiable craving after action of the most
difficult and dangerous kind. . . . [He] plots the ruin of his friends as an
exercise for his ingenuity, and stabs men in the dark to prevent *ennui*. His
gaiety, such as it is, arises from the success of his treachery; his ease from the
torture he has inflicted on others. He is an amateur of tragedy in real life;
and instead of employing his invention on imaginary characters, or long-
forgotten incidents, he takes the bolder and more desperate course of getting
up his plot at home, casts the principal parts among his nearest friends and
connections, and rehearses it in downright earnest, with steady nerves and
unabated resolution.

There are some details about this analysis which are questionable. It
can hardly be maintained that Othello and Cassio are Iago's 'friends';
there is no mention of his hatred of the Moor; and Hazlitt substitutes
the love of power for the divinity of hell. The passage is perhaps

intended as an answer to Coleridge for Hazlitt regards the love of power as a sufficient motive for Iago's actions. But it may be observed that he ignores all Iago's avowed motives.

Hazlitt's description of Iago as an amateur of tragedy in real life was taken up by Swinburne who called him 'a contriving artist in real life';[27] by Bradley, who pointed out a 'curious analogy between the early stages of dramatic composition' and the soliloquies in which Iago conceives his plot;[28] and by Granville-Barker who argued that the Ancient was endowed with the intuition of the artist and that he loved evil for its own sake, 'pursued with the artist's unscrupulous passion',[29] but that he was an actor rather than a dramatist. It is certainly true that in creating the character Shakespeare was able to make use of his personal knowledge of the psychology of an actor-dramatist, though it looks as though Granville-Barker were influenced by Shaw's eloquent statement on the unscrupulousness of the artist, expressed through the mouth of Jack Tanner.

Coleridge's view of Iago's motivelessness was also taken up by Charles Lamb in his account of Bensley in the part, in which he also stresses the impenetrability of hypocrisy:[30]

No spectator, from his action, could divine more of his artifice than Othello was supposed to do. His confessions in soliloquy alone put you in possession of the mystery. There were no by-intimations to make the audience fancy their own discernment so much greater than that of the Moor. The Iago of Bensley did not go to work so grossly. There was a triumphant tone about the character, natural to a general consciousness of power; but none of that petty vanity which chuckles and cannot contain itself upon any little successful stroke of its knavery—as is common with your small villains, and green probationers in mischief. It did not clap or crow before its time. It was not a man setting his wits at a child, and winking all the while at other children, who are mightily pleased at being let into the secret; but a consummate villain entrapping a noble nature into toils against which no discernment was available, where the manner was as fathomless as the purpose seemed dark, and without motive.

Booth similarly advised any actor playing Iago to try to impress even the audience with his sincerity. 'Iago should appear to be what all but the audience believe he is.'[31] Bensley and Booth were surely right because an obvious villain would lower one's opinion of Othello's intelligence and the play is much more serious than it would be if played as a melodramatic villain entrapping a credulous fool.

The last two words of Lamb's remarks have been accepted by most critics as true and the view was powerfully restated by Lytton Strachey.[32] Shakespeare, he declared,

determined that Iago should have no motive at all. He conceived of a monster, whose wickedness should lie far deeper than anything that could be explained by a motive—the very essence of whose being should express itself in the machinations of malignity . . . and, when the moment of revelation came, the horror that burst upon the hero would be as inexplicably awful as evil itself.

From what was said above, it will be apparent that the Satanic Iago who hates good simply because it is good is one level on which the character must be interpreted; and, on a lower level, he can be regarded, as Stoll continually argued, as a stage villain. But an exclusive emphasis on these two sides of Iago's role ignores or distorts the significance of the motives the villain himself puts forward for his plot against the Moor, and to these we must now devote some attention.

Cinthio's villain has a single, uncomplicated motive. His love for Desdemona is turned into the bitterest hatred by his lack of success and he blames the Captain for it. His plot is directed mainly against Desdemona and his hatred of the Captain is caused by sexual jealousy, not by professional envy. Shakespeare apparently discards this motive, except for the very curious confession in one of Iago's soliloquies:

> Now, I do love her too;
> Not out of absolute lust—though peradventure
> I stand accountant for as great a sin—
> But partly led to diet my revenge.   (II.i.285–8)

He wishes to feed his revenge, seducing Desdemona partly to spite Othello, and partly (one supposes) for a more direct sensual pleasure. This is the first we have heard of Iago's 'love', but it is possible that these lines throw a retrospective light on earlier scenes. In the first scene of the play, it might be argued, Iago is surprised and upset by Othello's marriage, not merely because he is in danger of losing Roderigo's subsidies, but because he is envious of Othello's good fortune. The vivid language he uses to inflame Brabantio's anger—the black ram, the barbary horse, the beast with two backs—may also reflect sexual envy and racial prejudice. In Act II, when Cassio is talking with Desdemona, Iago's envy is even more apparent:

> Ay, smile upon her, do. I will gyve thee in thine own courtship . . . Very good: well kissed . . . Yet again your fingers to your lips? Would they were clyster-pipes for your sake!   (II.i.169–77)

In the scene on the same evening after Othello and Desdemona have retired to bed, there is an obvious contrast between Cassio's respect for Desdemona and Iago's insinuations:

Iago He hath not yet made wanton the night with her; and she is sport for Jove.
Cassio She is a most exquisite lady.
Iago And, I'll warrant her, full of game.
Cassio Indeed, she is a most fresh and delicate creature.
Iago What an eye she has! Methinks it sounds a parley to provocation.
Cassio An inviting eye, and yet methinks right modest.
Iago And when she speaks, is it not an alarum to love.
Cassio She is indeed perfection.   (II.iii.15-25)

But although the motive of the source may exist as a residue in Shakespeare's tragedy, colouring Iago's thoughts, it is plainly not the main motive for his actions. In the opening scene of the play Iago tells Roderigo that he hates Othello for promoting Cassio over his head, despite his long service and the intervention of 'three great ones of the city'. He complains of the way promotion is obtained by influence, although he had been pulling strings himself. We need not suppose that Iago is necessarily telling the truth to Roderigo, and there is no reason to believe that he is telling the whole truth. He has merely to convince Roderigo that he hates Othello by giving a plausible reason. It may be argued that in the opening scene of a play it is important not to mislead the audience and that therefore we should accept what Iago says as true. But we can deduce that he is a malcontent and that he hates Othello, without necessarily supposing that we know precisely why; and when in the second scene we find that Othello is quite different from the picture we have been given and observe Iago carrying out his policy of deceit, we are bound to revise our opinions. An arch-hypocrite who, on his own confession, is animated entirely by self-interest, cannot long deceive the audience. The Moor's commendation of him in the third scene as a man of honesty and trust already appears as a stroke of irony. But it is not until the end of the act that Iago, after promising Roderigo that he shall enjoy Desdemona, is allowed to soliloquise. We must doubt everything Iago says to every other person in the play since we know that he is manipulating them all; but we ought to accept everything he says in soliloquy, since he has no reason to lie to himself. This first soliloquy, therefore, tells the audience what has been passing through his mind during the first act

of the play: that he is using Roderigo as his purse; that he hates
Othello; and that he covets Cassio's job. The precise words he uses
are significant:

> I hate the Moor,
> And it is thought abroad that 'twixt my sheets
> He's done my office. I know not if't be true
> But I, for mere suspicion in that kind,
> Will do as if for surety. He holds me well:
> The better shall my purpose work on him.
> Cassio's a proper man: let me see now;
> To get his place and to plume up my will
> In double knavery. How? How? Let's see.
> After some time, to abuse Othello's ear
> That he is too familiar with his wife;
> He hath a person and a smooth dispose
> To be suspected, framed to make women false.   (I.iii.38off.)

Several things emerge from this speech. As critics have noted, Iago
does not say he hates the Moor, because it is thought he has been
cuckolded by him. The conjunction *And*, as Bernard Spivack has said,
represents[33] 'the seam between the drama of allegory and the drama of
nature'. In other words the evil Iago hates Othello precisely because he
is good; but since Shakespeare was writing for a secular audience and
dramatising an almost contemporary story he provides Iago with a
plausible psychological motive, not so much the fear that Emilia has
been unfaithful as the fear that other people think she has. Since
Coleridge's day this has generally been dismissed as motive-hunting:
Iago, evil as he is, has to look for an excuse for his conduct. There have
been a few critics, however, who have gone to the other extreme, and
assumed that Iago was justified in his suspicions. D. J. Snider declared
that 'the family of Iago has been ruined by Othello; now Iago, in his
turn, will ruin the family of the destroyer of his domestic life';[34] and
Tannenbaum in an article entitled 'The wronged Iago' made[35] the
same point, arguing that there is nothing improbable in the supposition
that Othello had seduced Emilia who is 'depicted as a lewd and filthy-
speaking harlot'. His proof of Emilia's adultery is based on total misunderstanding of a crucial passage in the 'brothel' scene. He thinks
that 'This is a subtle whore' refers to Emilia and that the fact that he
had 'seen her kneel and pray' was proof of his intimacy. In fact Othello
had referred to Emilia as a bawd in the previous line, but it is Desdemona he calls whore. Why Mr Tannenbaum imagines that seeing a

woman at her prayers is a proof that he has been to bed with her is not easy to understand.

It is not, then, suggested that Iago had any grounds for his suspicions; but Shakespeare makes it clear to us that these suspicions were not fabricated on the spur of the moment to excuse his villainy by making Emilia refer to them in a later scene:

> Some such squire he was
> That turned your wit the seamy side without
> And made you to suspect me with the Moor.   (IV.ii.146–8)

The argument that, if Iago really suspected his wife, he would have mentioned it before, is flimsy. Since he is afraid of being an object of ridicule it was not a matter on which he could speak to anyone, much less to Roderigo. Injured merit, according to the way of the world, is a more respectable, and less ludicrous, grievance. As Snider rightly says, 'the true motive for Iago's hate is given . . . nowhere in his conversation with others, since he would not be likely to announce his own shame, or herald his self-degrading suspicions'.[36]

Iago's desire to get Cassio's place, to which he also refers in this soliloquy, links up with the resentment he mentions to Roderigo. But it is not unreasonable to suggest that Cassio's promotion rankled so much because of his sexual fears of Othello and (as we hear later) of Cassio. The 'double knavery' of which he speaks is to revenge himself on both his enemies at once by making one jealous of the other.

In the first scene in Cyprus, Booth when he played the part of Iago winced when Cassio kisses Emilia;[37] and this prepares the way for the soliloquy at the end of the scene in which Iago confesses that he fears Cassio with his nightcap too. But the same soliloquy reveals his perverted love for Desdemona and underlines his suspicion of Othello, that

> the lusty Moor
> Hath leaped into my seat, the thought whereof
> Doth, like a poisonous mineral, gnaw my inwards,
> And nothing can, or shall, content my soul
> Till I am evened with him, wife for wife;
> Or failing so, yet that I put the Moor
> At least into a jealousy so strong
> That judgement cannot cure.   (II.i.289–96)

The image of the poisonous mineral is difficult to brush aside as motive-

hunting. As Kittredge said,[38] Iago's jealousy is 'a raging torment'; and
if he cannot revenge himself by seducing Desdemona, which he must
realise is impossible, he is determined to make Othello suffer from the
torments of jealousy, the green-eyed monster he knows from personal
experience. He does not at this stage foresee the consequences of his
plot, that he will himself be exposed unless Desdemona, Cassio and
Roderigo are all killed.

In the last scene of the play Othello, who cannot bring himself to
address Iago directly, asks Cassio or Lodovico:

> Will you, I pray, demand that demi-devil
> Why he hath thus ensnared my soul and body?

Iago replies:

> Demand me nothing; what you know, you know:
> From this time forth I never will speak word.

He has already confessed his deeds, but he refuses to say anything
about his motives. Some critics believe that the motives he has produced during the course of the play are mere rationalisations in which
he doesn't himself believe and that he can hardly say that he has acted
from an irrational hatred of Othello, or that, being evil, he hates good
and wishes to do evil. But if, as we have suggested, the motives are
real, then it is easy to see why even after his fall Iago should not wish
to confess himself an object of ridicule, a cuckold.

This argument—that Iago was the jealous man of the play—
depends on the assumption that his soliloquies reveal his thoughts, but
that we ought not to accept as true anything he tells other people. His
soliloquies are, in fact, displaced asides. Just as Hamlet's soliloquies in
the first two acts tell us what has been passing through his mind during
the immediately preceding scenes, so Iago's soliloquies, though longer
delayed, remove the mask for a moment or two. Novelists sometimes
employ a similar device. In *The Portrait of a Lady* we are kept in the
dark about the failure of Isabel's marriage until the chapter, of which
James was justifiably proud, in which we are let into the secret of what
Isabel has been thinking.[39]

Iago's refusal to speak leaves the audience feeling that there is
something left unexplained and mysterious—that he represents the
mystery of iniquity. So many motives have been mentioned that we
don't know which is the dominant one: his hatred of Othello which
precedes any real cause, the promotion of Cassio and the desire to get

his place, thwarted love of Desdemona, racial prejudice, sexual jealousy of Othello and Cassio, his fear that Roderigo will stop supplying him with money. There is one other motive which has not yet been mentioned. When Iago is discussing the advantages of getting Roderigo to attack Cassio, he shows that if Roderigo survives he will demand the restitution of his gold and jewels; and

> If Cassio do remain
> He hath a daily beauty in his life
> That makes me ugly.   (V.i.18–20)

This may refer to Cassio's relative handsomeness, for Iago, unlike Cinthio's villain, is not spoken of as handsome; or it may rather refer to the fact that Cassio, in spite of getting drunk and having a mistress, is morally superior to Iago. Iago wishes to plume up his will in double knavery because he is as much aware of his moral inferiority as of his cleverness.

Lily B. Campbell has rightly said[40] that with Iago 'jealousy is but one phase of envy' and the multifarious motives for his actions are all branches of the same attitude. It is natural for him to envy Othello's success with Desdemona, to resent Cassio's promotion, and to suspect all men of sleeping with his wife. Bacon's description of envy might almost be an analysis of Iago's character:[41]

There be none of the *Affections*, which have been noted to fascinate, or bewitch, but *Love*, and *Envy*. They both have vehement wishes; They frame themselves readily into Imaginations, and Suggestions; ... A man, that hath no vertue in himselfe, ever *envieth* Vertue in others. For Mens Mindes will either feed upon their owne Good, or upon others Evill; And who wanteth the one, will prey upon the other; And who so is out of Hope to attaine to anothers Vertue, will seeke to come at even hand, by Depressing anothers Fortune. .... It is also the vilest Affection, and the most depraved; For which cause, it is the proper Attribute of the Devill, who is called; *The Envious Man, that soweth tares amongst the wheat by night*. As it always commeth to passe, that *Envy* worketh subtilly, and in the darke; And to the prejudice of good things, such as is the *Wheat*.

It may have been the association of envy with the Devil that led Shakespeare to stress Iago's diabolic nature.

The interpretation of the play which has been outlined above is supported by two other considerations. Just as in *Hamlet* there are, as we have seen, a number of contrasted avengers, so in *Othello* there are a number of different kinds of jealousy. Bianca is jealous of her supposed rival in Cassio's affections; Roderigo, the 'gulled gentleman', begins as

an absurd but honourable lover, and under the influence of jealousy
ends as a potential murderer; and, as we have seen, both the villain
and the hero are jealous.

The other consideration concerns the imagery. Every critic who has
analysed the imagery of the play has been struck by the way it is used
to differentiate character.[42] Iago's trade of war is a vocation to Othello;
his prosaic images of seamanship are contrasted with Othello's romantic
ones; his images from money are contrasted with Othello's pearl and
crysolite. But what is more significant is the way Iago's hold over
Othello's mind is shown by the transfer from villain to hero both of
the diabolic images and also of the repellant animal images. There
could not be a more effective way of showing that Iago infects Othello
with his own jealousy.

Another group of images is concerned with magic and witchcraft,
many of them relating to Brabantio's charge that Desdemona had been
bewitched. But the most impressive use of the theme of magic is
contained in the scene in which Othello demands to see the lost
handkerchief:

>   That handkerchief
> Did an Egyptian to my mother give:
> She was a charmer and could almost read
> The thoughts of people. She told her, while she kept it,
> 'Twould make her amiable and subdue my father
> Entirely to her love; but, if she lost it
> Or made a gift of it, my father's eye
> Should hold her loathed, and his spirits should hunt
> After new fancies. She, dying, gave it me,
> And bid me when my fate would have me wive,
> To give it her. I did so; and take heed on't:
> Make it a darling, like your precious eye.
> To lose or give't away were such perdition
> As nothing else could match . . .
> 'Tis true: there's magic in the web of it.
> A sibyl, that had numbered in the world
> The sun to course two hundred compasses,
> In her prophetic fury sewed the work:
> The worms were hallowed that did breed the silk,
> And it was dyed in mummy, which the skilful
> Conserved of maidens' hearts.   (III.iv.55–75)

The handkerchief, of course, symbolises love; but the magic in the
web of it, in which Othello believes wholly and Desdemona partially,

suggests that Othello's christianity has not entirely eradicated a residue of superstition and that it symbolises too the fate that makes and destroys his marriage. The magic in the web leads Desdemona into her fearful and foolish lie which Othello takes as a proof of her guilt.

Some critics have also found her guilty, not of adultery but of misbehaviour. Professor Bonnard argued[43] that the original audience would have regarded her elopement as a crime and that all their sympathies would have been with her father. John Adams thought she was 'coarse and unnatural in her tastes, bold and undutiful in her elopement, and obviously destined to come to grief through her marriage'. Professor Allardyce Nicoll argued[44] that 'she is introduced to us as practising deceit'; she lies about the handkerchief; and she ends her life on a lie, when she tells Emilia that she has killed herself:

It is a pitiful lie; but all our pity for her should not blind us to the fact that this is entirely characteristic of her—her lack of self-respect, her tendency towards concealing of truth by prevarication.

But, of course, the lie demonstrates her love and loyalty more effectively than the truth could have done. Shakespeare cannot have meant us to agree with Othello that 'like a liar' she had 'gone to burning hell' for it is a lie that shakes his belief in her guilt.

Not that she is entirely faultless. She intervenes unwisely on Cassio's behalf and her threat to importune Othello, though a natural result of her innocence and generosity, as Iago calculates, is nevertheless a tactless intrusion into affairs which do not properly concern her. Although Iago hints to Roderigo and even to Othello that her sexual tastes are perverted, he admits in soliloquy that the success of his plot depends on her innocence and goodness.

Rymer complained[45] that the play violated our sense of poetic justice, with the innocent Desdemona murdered, Brabantio dying of a broken heart, Cassio maimed, and Othello slaying himself after he has been degraded to Iago's level. Better critics than Rymer have expressed a vague disquiet. Bradley thought the play produced feelings of oppression, and Granville-Barker was equally distressed by it.[46] To Rymer's indignant question, 'If this be our end, what boots it to be virtuous?' we can retort that no philosophy or religion is able to protect us from disaster. To those critics who imagine that Othello is brought down to Iago's level, we can point to his recovery just before the end, and (as has been said) 'the ultimate defeat of Iago'. Those who regard a claustrophobic domestic tragedy as necessarily on a lower level than *King Lear* or *Macbeth* may be reminded that to Tolstoy 'the tragedy of the bedroom' is the most dreadful tragedy that can befall man; that the Turkish danger, reminding a Jacobean audience of Lepanto,[47] would make them think of Othello as the champion of Christendom; that as Landor said,[48] 'Othello was loftier than the citadel of Troy; and what a Paradise fell before him!'; and that the age-long struggle between good and evil cannot be said to lack a metaphysical dimension.

It has been argued that the play is flawed for us—as many tragedies of the Golden Age of Spanish drama are flawed—by conceptions of honour which we have outgrown. But it is possible that when Shakespeare makes Othello call himself, with bitter irony, 'an honourable murderer', he was criticising 'the aberrations of an accepted code'.[49]

In one respect Dr Leavis is right. Othello is betrayed by what is false within, projected into the figure of the villain. For Iago is the intellect divorced from the imagination, the acid which eats away love and trust. So we do not merely watch a perfect marriage destroyed by a demi-devil; we watch our 'own divided heart'.

6

KING LEAR

high and excellent Tragedie . . . that with sturring the affects of Admiration and Comiseration, teacheth the uncertaintie of this world, and uppon how weak foundations guilden roofes are builded; . . .

(Sidney)

I

When André Gide had nearly reached the age of Lear when he divided his kingdom he went to see Laurence Olivier in the part and recorded in his journal:[1]

Yesterday's production strengthens my opinion. I am almost on the point of considering the play execrable, of all Shakespeare's tragedies the least good, and by far. I constantly thought: How Hugo must have liked it! All his enormous faults are evident in it: constant antitheses, devices, arbitrary motives; barely, from time to time, some glimmer of a sincere human emotion. I cannot even very well grasp what is considered the difficulty of interpretation of the first scene: difficulty of getting the public to accept the King's naive stupidity; for all the rest is in keeping: the entire play from one end to the other is absurd. Only through pity does one become interested in the tribulations of that old dotard, a victim of his fatuousness, his senile smugness, and his stupidity. He moves us only at the rare moments of pity that he himself shows for Edgar and for his sweet fool . . . Nothing that is not intentional, arbitrary, forced; and the crudest means are employed to seize us by the guts. It has ceased to be human and become enormous; Hugo himself never imagined anything more gigantically artificial, more false. The last act ends with a gloomy hecatomb in which good and evil are mingled in death . . . Art triumphs. One has only to applaud.

'Art triumphs.' In some contexts this could be regarded as praise, but Gide believed that in *King Lear* the triumph was at the expense of life. Yet he was a genuine admirer of Shakespeare and an admirable translator, so that his imperfect sympathies cannot be due to the fact that *King Lear* is the play of Shakespeare's that is least like Racine's. Gide's view of the play was shared by John Middleton Murry who argued[2] that, unlike *Coriolanus*, it was 'cold and inhuman'; that, despite the great pains Shakespeare took in its composition, it remains an artefact; and he seems to have been spurring his imagination, 'which in consequence was something less than imagination'.

The reason for Murry's dislike of the play can be seen from some of his other comments. He complained of Shakespeare's 'uncontrollable despair' and of his 'terrible primitive revulsion against sex'. In such a state silence would have been 'more wholesome and more natural'. Shakespeare was making 'a tremendous effort towards control': the play was 'Shakespeare's deliberate prophylactic against his own incoherence'. Murry would have liked to think that the play was too horrible to be true, as he once averted his eyes from the Crucifixion. Something of the same attitude is to be seen in Samuel Johnson's comments on the play. He found the death of Cordelia so painful and so contrary to poetic justice that he confessed that he preferred Tate's happy ending in which Lear is restored to the throne and Cordelia is married to her rescuer, Edgar. Whatever we may think of this preference, Johnson was mistaken on one point. He asserted that, in allowing Cordelia to be sacrificed, Shakespeare ignored the testimony of the chronicles. He omitted to mention the tragic sequel: Cordelia is deposed by her nephews and commits suicide in prison. Such an ending, besides being structurally weak, would have been much more painful than Shakespeare's.

The most powerful attack on *King Lear* was made by Tolstoy,[3] perhaps the greatest writer since Shakespeare. He accused it of being unnatural in its style and characterisation and he professed to prefer the source play, *King Leir*. A number of previous Russian critics had questioned Shakespeare's supremacy[4] and in Tolstoy's case there may have been a number of unconscious motives for his attack: he wished to show that he himself was greater than Shakespeare; he deplored the lack in Shakespeare's plays of positive religious convictions; and perhaps the octogenarian King was too much like the sage of Yasnaya Polyana for the portrait to be relished.

King Lear, then, has been criticised as an artefact, for its falseness, and for its pessimism; but it has also been condemned for its 'loose, episodic structure'[5] and the carelessness of its workmanship. This last criticism is hard to understand. Anyone who has studied the way in which Shakespeare drew on a play, a prose romance, a chronicle, two poems and a satirical pamphlet on exorcism must have been struck by the infinite pains taken by the dramatist, whatever his measure of success; and the parallelism of character, situation, ideas and images proves that the structure is very carefully organised. One must assume that those critics who complain of Shakespeare's bad workmanship in this particular play were applying the standards of a more naturalistic theatre. Certainly Bradley, who thought it was unsatisfactory as a stage play, was misled by Lamb's proclamation that it could not be acted. Lamb, of course, had seen only Tate's adaptation; and if Bradley ever saw a stage performance it would have been adapted and victorianised.

Yet Bradley declared that *King Lear* was Shakespeare's greatest work and this appears to be the view of most competent critics today. Professor Nicholas Brooke, for example, declares that it is 'supreme, even among tragedies'[6] and Professor L. C. Knights regards it as 'the great central masterpiece, the great exploratory allegory'.[7]

II

It is difficult to understand how any critic could regard the construction of the play as loose and episodic, for every incident contributes to the design of the whole. Both Lear and Gloucester reward their evil children and cast out the good. In the second act we see the results of these errors in the ingratitude of the favoured children, which leads in the third act to the blinding of Gloucester and the madness of Lear. In the fourth act Gloucester is saved from suicide and Lear is cured of his madness by the ministrations of the ill-treated children, who repay good for evil; but the evil passions unleashed by the initial mistakes of Lear and Gloucester bring about the catastrophe in the last act. Lear and his daughters, Gloucester and Edmund die: only Edgar, of the two families, survives.

The underplot is linked with the main plot in various ways. Edgar's feigned madness is the thing which finally overturns Lear's sanity; and his killing of Oswald provides him with the evidence to expose Goneril's murderous designs against her husband. Gloucester is betrayed by Edmund for helping Lear; and it is Edmund who orders the death of Lear and Cordelia. The rivalry between the evil sisters for the hand of Edmund leads Goneril to poison Regan.

In constructing his play Shakespeare had to ensure that it ended with the death of the hero, and that before he died he would be fully aware

of the results of his actions. This meant that Cordelia had to die first
and not, as in the chronicles, commit suicide many years later. He had
to ensure, too, that Goneril and Regan should also die, or the feelings
of the audience would be outraged. In the old play Leir is restored to
his throne by the help of a French army. Shakespeare was able to bring
about the necessary catastrophe by making the British army victorious
and so putting Lear and Cordelia in the power of the wicked sisters.
From the later suicide of Cordelia in his sources, Shakespeare took
Edmund's plan to publish a statement that she fordid herself from
despair. Edmund's motive is simple: he is aiming at the throne. Lear
is saved long enough to lament Cordelia's death. Regan is poisoned by
Goneril who is determined to marry Edmund herself; and Goneril
commits suicide when her plot to murder Albany is revealed.

The character of Albany is largely determined by the plot.[8] He has
to be in love with Goneril in the first half of the play until he recognises
her true nature. He has to be willing to repel a foreign invader, though
sympathising with Lear; and in his denunciation of Goneril he has to
wield a genuine moral authority. Even quite minor characters are
nicely designed to conform to the requirements of the plot. Oswald,
for example, has to be effeminate, greedy, a go-between and a flatterer;
but he is also faithful to his mistress, his last thought being of the
delivery of her letter to Edmund. It is this redeeming trait in Oswald
which leads Edgar to discover the damning evidence against Goneril
and Edmund. Another character, so minor that he is not even given a
name, is the servant of Cornwall who turns on his master. His action
is the turning point of the play. The killing of Cornwall brings into
the open the sex-rivalry of Goneril and Regan and so leads to their
destruction and to that of their lover.

Not merely are the plots inextricably interwoven, so that events in
one plot either influence or are parallel to events in the other, but
Edgar, besides being an actor, serves as a commentator on events in
both. He is one of the judges in the mock trial of Goneril and Regan
and a spectator at the meeting of Lear and Gloucester in Act IV. These
two scenes, which might seem to be unnecessary to the plot, are essential to our understanding of Lear's development; and, indeed, the
meeting of the blind Gloucester with the mad Lear could be regarded as
the thematic climax of the play. The parallel paradoxes—that Gloucester
attains insight in blindness and Lear wisdom in madness—take us to
the heart of the play.

Professor R. B. Heilman sub-titled[9] his book on the imagery of the play 'Image and Structure in *King Lear*'; and few of his readers would wish to deny that the imagery was used by Shakespeare to reinforce the tightly-knit structure. Bradley long before had commented on the significance of the animal imagery:[10]

> As we read the souls of all the beasts in turn seem to have entered the bodies of these mortals; horrible in their venom, savagery, lust, deceitfulness, sloth, cruelty, filthiness; miserable in their feebleness, nakedness, defencelessness, blindness.

Poor Tom uses animals as symbols of the seven deadly sins, as Harsnett had done. More significantly Albany speaks of the breakdown of order through the violation of the moral law in terms of animal imagery:

> If that the heavens do not their visible spirits
> Send quickly down to tame these vile offences,
> It will come:
> Humanity must perforce prey on itself
> Like monsters of the deep.   (IV.ii.46–50)

But the most important use of animal imagery is to define the nature of man. Lear asks: 'Who is it can tell me who I am?' In the storm scene, seeing the naked Bedlam beggar, he asks:

> Is man no more than this? Consider him well. Thou ow'st the worm no silk; the beast, no hide; the sheep, no wool; the cat, no perfume. Ha? here's three on's are sophisticated. Thou art the thing itself; unaccommodated man is no more but such a poor, bare, forked animal as thou art.
>
> (III.iv.102–7)

Montaigne, not long before, had made similar comparisons between man and the other animals. When he considered 'man all naked, . . . his natural subjection and manifold imperfections' he was not surprised that we borrowed clothes from the other animals. He declared that we had sophisticated nature and that whereas animals were supplied with armour and weapons and learnt instinctively how to survive,

> man only (oh silly wretched man) can neither go, nor speak, nor shift, nor feed himself, unless it be to whine and weep only, except he be taught.[11]

So in *King Lear*, from the first scene to the last, we have a continual repetition of the contrast between man and his clothes. The naked beggar, a symbol of man reduced to his essence, is contrasted with the fashionable lady:

> If only to go warm were gorgeous,
> Why, nature needs not what thou gorgeous wear'st,
> Which scarcely keeps thee warm.   (II.iv.267–9)

In the mad scenes Lear harps on the way clothes, symbolising distinctions of class and wealth, pervert justice:

> Through tatter'd clothes small vices do appear;
> Robes and furr'd gowns hide all. Plate sin with gold,
> And the strong lance of justice hurtless breaks;
> Arm it in rags, a pigmy's straw does pierce it.   (IV.vi.164–7)

Important as the imagery relating to animals and clothes undoubtedly is, Caroline Spurgeon showed[12] earlier that the iterative image of the play, the one most frequent in occurrence, is that of

a human body in anguished movement, tugged, wrenched, beaten, pierced, stung, scourged, dislocated, flayed, gashed, scalded, tortured, and finally broken on the rack.

Death, in the world of the play, is a release from torture, as Kent declares when Lear is dying:

> O, let him pass! he hates him
> That would upon the rack of this tough world
> Stretch him out longer.   (V.iii.312–14)

One image, indeed, seems to suggest that the torture will be continued after death. When Lear thinks he has died he cries to Cordelia:

> Thou art a soul in bliss; but I am bound
> Upon a wheel of fire, that mine own tears
> Do scald like molten lead.   (IV.vii.46–8)

Another group of images is concerned with sight and blindness. As Professor Heilman has shown, there are examples of this imagery in nearly every scene, some of it comparatively casual, as when Gloucester says to Edmund 'If it be nothing, I shall not need spectacles', or when the Fool sings:

> Fathers that wear rags
> Do make their children blind.

The blinding scene has often been criticised as an unnecessary piece of horror brought in to please the groundlings: but, as Raleigh wisely remarked,[13]

In nothing is Shakespeare's greatness more apparent than in his concessions to the requirements of the Elizabethan theatre . . . yet transmuted in the giving, so that what might have been a mere connivance in baseness becomes a miracle of expressive art.

The blinding provides the audience with a concrete illustration of the imagery of sight and blindness; and, as Mr J. I. M. Stewart suggests, it represents 'a sort of crystallising of the element of physical outrage' which is held in suspension by the imagery. By staging the blinding, rather than having it reported, Shakespeare achieved

the powerful effect of a suddenly realised imagery: the oppressive atmosphere of the play here condensing in a ghastly dew.[14]

One of the central, and paradoxical, ideas of the play is expressed by this imagery. Gloucester confesses: 'I stumbled when I saw.' He sees the truth only after he has lost his eyes. In the last scene of the play Edgar speaks of the conceiving of the bastard as an act of spiritual blindness which was the ultimate cause of his father's being blinded:

> The dark and vicious place where thee he got
> Cost him his eyes.

The ubiquity of this imagery, in both plots, can be illustrated from Lear's threat to pluck out his eyes, and from 'the impetuous blasts, with eyeless rage' of the storm-scene.

III

There is no madness in the old play of *King Leir*, none in the story of Lear as told by Holinshed, Spenser, or in any other version before Shakespeare's time, and none in Sidney's story which provided the basis for the underplot. If the madness was suggested by the true story[15] of Brian Annesley and his three daughters—the older ones being harsh and the youngest, Cordell, kind—we may be sure that it was not merely the desire for topicality that made Shakespeare take the suggestion as a cat laps milk. Maeterlinck believed[16] that Shakespeare deliberately unsettled the reason of his protagonists, and thus opened

the dike that held captive the swollen lyrical flood. Henceforward, he speaks freely by their mouths; and beauty invades the stage without fearing lest it be told that it is out of place.

It seems probable that Maeterlinck was influenced by the dominance of prose in the theatre of his time, against which his own plays were an unsuccessful protest. Orwell, on the other hand, regarded Lear's madness as a protective device to enable Shakespeare to utter dangerous thoughts. Shakespeare, he says,[17] is

> noticeably cautious, not to say cowardly, in his manner of uttering unpopular opinions. Almost never does he put a subversive or sceptical remark into the mouth of a character likely to be identified with himself. Throughout his plays the acute social critics, the people who are not taken in by accepted fallacies, are buffoons, villains, lunatics or persons who are shamming insanity or are in a state of violent hysteria. *Lear* is a play in which this tendency is particularly well marked. It contains a great deal of veiled social criticism . . . but it is all uttered by the Fool, by Edgar when he is pretending to be mad, or by Lear during his bouts of madness. In his sane moments Lear hardly ever makes an intelligent remark. And yet the very fact that Shakespeare had to use these subterfuges shows how widely his thoughts ranged.

Against this view of Shakespeare as the subversive sceptic without the courage of his own convictions it must be pointed out that none of his characters should be taken as his own mouthpiece. Ulysses' views on order are shared by Rosencrantz, whom Shakespeare treats with scant sympathy, and considerably modified by the King in *All's Well That Ends Well*. We cannot deduce from the plays whether Shakespeare was a cowardly sceptic or a natural conformist. His acceptance of the establishment and his criticism of it are equally in character. This is not to say that no point of view emerges from each play and from his collected works; but the point of view is complex, subsuming both the anarchical and the conformist. The Shakespearian dialectic is not a reflection of the poet's timidity but of his negative capability. In the dialogue with Gloucester in Act IV, Lear's invective has a double target—the hypocrisy of the simpering dame and the hypocrisy of the law. There is no evidence to show that Shakespeare was hiding behind a mask. The attack on lechery can be paralleled in the diatribes of Timon, and the attack on authority and law is no more extreme than that of the eminently sane Isabella or that of the praying Claudius[18] who knew that

> In the corrupted currents of this world
> Offence's gilded hand may shove by justice,
> And oft 'tis seen the wicked prize itself
> Buys out the law.

Lest the audience should be tempted to dismiss what Lear says as mere raving, Shakespeare provides a choric comment through the mouth of Edgar:

> O, matter and impertinency mix'd!
> Reason in madness! (IV.vi.175–6)

Lear's mad speeches, moreover, have substantial links with other passages in the play. The revulsion against sex, besides being a well-known symptom of certain forms of madness, is linked with Lear's earlier suspicion that the mother of his evil daughters must be an adulteress, with Gloucester's pleasant vices which led to the birth of Edmund, and with Edmund's use of his sexual attractiveness as a step to the throne. The attack on the imperfect instruments of justice, themselves guilty of the sins they condemn in others, is merely a reinforcement of Lear's speech in the storm, before he crossed the borders of madness:

> Let the great gods,
> That keep this dreadful pother o'er our heads,
> Find out their enemies now. Tremble, thou wretch,
> That hast within thee undivulged crimes,
> Unwhipp'd of justice: hide thee, thou bloody hand;
> Thou perjur'd, and thou simular man of virtue
> That art incestuous: caitiff, to pieces shake,
> That under covert and convenient seeming
> Hast practis'd on man's life: close pent-up guilts,
> Rive your concealing continents, and cry
> These dreadful summoners grace. (III.ii.49ff.)

Here, as in the mad scene, the justice of the gods, from whom no secrets are hid, is contrasted with the imperfections of earthly justice.

One of Lear's first speeches after his wits begin to turn consists of a prayer to houseless poverty:

> Poor naked wretches, whereso'er you are,
> That bide the pelting of this pitiless storm,
> How shall your houseless heads and unfed sides,
> Your loop'd and window'd raggedness, defend you
> From seasons such as these? O, I have ta'en
> Too little care of this! Take physic, pomp;
> Expose thyself to feel what wretches feel,
> That thou mayst shake the superflux to them,
> And show the heavens more just. (III.iv.28ff.)

It has not escaped notice that Gloucester expresses similar sentiments
when he hands his purse to Poor Tom:

> heavens, deal so still!
> Let the superfluous and lust-dieted man
> That slaves your ordinance, that will not see
> Because he does not feel, feel your power quickly:
> So distribution should undo excess,
> And each man have enough.   (IV.i.67ff.)

This repetition is of some importance since Schücking argued[19] that
it is not really consistent with Shakespeare's philosophy to see in the
play a gradual purification of Lear's character. Shakespeare, he declared,
nowhere associates compassion for the poor 'with a higher moral
standpoint'. The point is not whether Lear's pity was intended to
arouse the audience's sympathy for him, nor even whether Shakespeare himself agreed with Lear's sentiments—though one would hate
to think he did not—but whether the audience would understand that
his newly aroused concern for the poor was a sign of moral improve-
ment. Here, surely, there can be no doubt. Shakespeare's audience was
not so cut off from the Christian tradition as not to know that charity
was a virtue; and the fact that similar sentiments are put into Gloucester's mouth is a reinforcement of Lear's words. If Lear were mad at
this point—and he has not yet crossed the frontier—he would be
expressing reason in madness. Even Schücking is constrained to admit
that Lear's later criticisms of society show profound insight; but he
claims that this does not exhibit a development of Lear's character
because it is dependent on a state of mental derangement. The Lear
who welcomes prison with Cordelia

is not a purified Lear from whose character the flame of unhappiness has
burnt away the ignoble dross, but a nature completely transformed, whose
extraordinary vital forces are extinguished, or about to be extinguished.

But, as I have pointed out elsewhere,[20] the three moments in the play
crucial to Bradley's theory of Lear's development—his recognition of
error, his awakening compassion for the poor, and the conquest of his
pride as he kneels to Cordelia—occur either before or after his madness; and Schücking seems insufficiently aware of the 'reason in
madness' theme so essential to the play's meaning. Shakespeare was
only following tradition in making fool and madman the vehicle for
unpopular truths; and Lear's Fool fades from the scene at the moment

when his master, as madman, can carry on the Fool's role. But whereas the Fool's criticism is mostly directed against Lear himself, Lear's is directed against the hypocrisies and injustices of society.

The Fool, we are told,[21] labours to out-jest the heart-struck injuries of his master and this no doubt is his intention; but it is arguable that the way he harps on Lear's treatment of his daughters and his resentment at Cordelia's banishment have the effect of intensifying, rather than of relieving, Lear's mental disturbance. On the other hand, it could be argued that it is better to face the causes of disturbance rather than attempt to forget them.

It is sometimes asserted that Shakespeare and Webster were the only two dramatists of the period to treat madness as other than matter for mirth. But there are scenes in *The Spanish Tragedy*, especially the anonymous Painter scene, which are quite serious in intention; and though the mad scene in *The Honest Whore*, Part 1, may have aroused some laughter, as indeed the mad scenes of *King Lear* may have done, Dekker was careful to demand a more sympathetic reaction on the part of the audience. Anselmo remarks:[22]

> Tho 'twould greeue a soule, to see Gods image
> So blemisht and defac'd, yet do they act
> Such anticke and such pretty lunacies,
> That spite of sorrow they will make you smile.

Later in the same scene the First Madman rebukes the visitors for their laughter:

> Do you laugh at Gods creatures? Do you mock old age you roagues?

But neither Kyd nor Dekker, nor even Webster, use madness for any fundamental criticism of society; but in Lear's case, as Bucknill pointed out,[23]

It is only when all the barriers of conventional restraint are broken down, that the native and naked force of the soul displays itself. The display arises from the absence of restraint, and not from the stimulus of disease.

The steps of Lear's descent into madness are clearly marked by Shakespeare. When, after Cordelia's banishment, Kent tells the King:

> Be Kent unmannerly
> When Lear is mad . . .

it is obvious that Kent does not regard his master as insane; and when

Goneril and Regan discuss their father at the end of the scene, they complain that his age is full of changes, that he has shown poor judgement in casting off Cordelia, that even in his prime 'he hath ever but slenderly known himself' and that they must expect from him 'not alone the imperfections of long-engraffed condition, but therewithal the unruly waywardness that infirm and choleric years bring with them'. In other words, they accuse him of senility, but not of madness.

Lear is driven insane by a series of shocks. First, there is the rebuff by Cordelia. Then there is the attack by Goneril which makes him pretend not to know her, and not to know himself; but at this point it is still pretence:

> Doth any here know me? This is not Lear:
> Doth Lear walk thus? speak thus? Where are his eyes?
> Either his notion weakens, or his discernings
> Are lethargied—Ha! waking? 'Tis not so.—
> Who is it that can tell me who I am?   (I.iv.225ff.)

He is reduced, as the Fool tells him, to Lear's shadow. Later in the same scene he begins to realise that he has wronged Cordelia:

> O most small fault,
> How ugly didst thou in Cordelia show! . . .
> O Lear, Lear, Lear!
> Beat at this gate, that let thy folly in,
> And thy dear judgement out!   (I.iv.266–71)

In the next scene he comes to a full recognition of his folly—though some critics suppose he is thinking of Goneril: 'I did her wrong.' At the end of the act he has his first serious premonition of insanity:

> O, let me not be mad, not mad, sweet heaven!
> Keep me in temper: I would not be mad!   (I.v.42–3)

The third great shock comes when Lear finds Kent in the stocks. This insult to the royal dignity causes the first physical symptoms of hysteria, 'racing heart' and 'rising blood pressure', or as Elizabethans called it, 'the suffocation of the mother':

> O, how this mother swells up toward my heart!
> Hysterica passio, down, thou climbing sorrow.
> Thy element's below . . .
> O me, my heart, my rising heart! but, down!   (II.iv.55–7,119)

The fourth shock, the rejection by Regan, follows immediately. Lear prays for patience. He threatens revenges—the terrors of the earth—

on the two daughters. His refusal to ease his heart by weeping is accompanied by the first rumblings of the storm which is a projection on the macrocosm of the tempest in the microcosm. He knows from the thunder that what he most feared will come to pass: 'O fool, I *shall* go mad!' Exposure to the storm completes what ingratitude began.

Lear's identification with the storm is both a means of presenting it on the stage and a sign that his reason has been overthrown by his passions. He contends 'with the fretful elements':

> tears his white hair,
> Which the impetuous blasts, with eyeless rage,
> Catch in their fury, and make nothing of;
> Strives in his little world of man to out-storm
> The to-and-fro-conflicting wind and rain.   (III.i.7–11)

But when Lear makes his next appearance, invoking the storm to destroy the seeds of matter, urging the gods to find out their hidden enemies, or addressing the poor naked wretches, he is not yet wholly mad, though he admits that his wits are beginning to turn. What finally pushes him over the borderline is the sudden appearance of Poor Tom who is both a living embodiment of naked poverty and one who is apparently what Lear had feared to become. Edgar, in acting madness, precipitates Lear's.

> What! have his daughters brought him to this pass?
> Could'st thou save nothing? Didst thou give 'em all? . . .
> Is it the fashion, that discarded fathers
> Should have thus little mercy on their flesh?
> Judicious punishment! 'twas this flesh begot
> Those pelican daughters.   (III.iv.63–74)

The Fool comments that 'This cold night will turn us all to fools and madmen'. It is in fact the exposure and the physical exhaustion which prevents Lear's recovery from the shocks he has received. He is soon trying to identify himself with unaccommodated man by tearing off his clothes.

The madness of the elements, the professional 'madness' of the Fool, the feigned madness of Edgar, and the madness of the King himself together exemplify the break-up of society and the threat to the universe itself under the impact of ingratitude and treachery. When Gloucester appears, confessing that he is almost mad and that grief for his son's treachery has crazed his wits, only Kent is left wholly sane.

E

Poor Tom compares himself with emblematic animals and Lear, as
we have seen, contrasts the naked Bedlam, who does not borrow from
the animals, with the civilised people who do. Man in essence is 'a poor,
bare, forked animal', as man without reason is no more than a beast.
Yet the mad Lear is anxious to discuss abstruse questions with the man
he takes to be a learned Theban. His first question, 'What is the cause
of thunder?' had been a stock one since the days of Pythagoras, who
had taught[24]

> The first foundations of the world: the cause of every thing:
> What nature was: and what was God: whence snow and lyghtning
>   spring:
> And whether *Jove* or else the wynds in breaking cloudes doo thunder.

The question is suggested to Lear by the storm.

Just as Ophelia is obsessed by her father's death and by the warnings
she has received about preserving her virginity, so Lear returns again
and again to the thing which had driven him mad—his daughters'
ingratitude. He asks if Poor Tom's daughters have brought him to this
pass and exclaims:

> Now all the plagues that in the pendulous air
> Hang fated o'er men's faults light on thy daughters.   (III.iv.67–8)

He declares that nothing but his unkind daughters 'could have subdu'd
nature / To such a lowness' and he inveighs against the flesh which
'begot / Those pelican daughters'.

Just before he was driven out into the storm Lear had declared that
he would avenge himself on his daughters:

> I will have such revenges on you both
> That all the world shall—I will do such things,—
> What they are, yet I know not; but they shall be
> The terrors of the earth.   (II.iv.281–4)

Now, in the refuge provided by Gloucester, Lear begins to brood on
his revenge. In the lines—echoed from Harsnett[25]—

> To have a thousand with red burning spits
> Come hissing in upon 'em—

Lear seems to be thinking of his daughters being tortured in hell; but
if he is thinking rather of punishing them in this world, he suddenly

decides to bring them to trial first. Poor Tom in his blanket and the Fool in his motley suggest to his disordered mind two robed men of justice, and he imagines that he sees Goneril and Regan. This is his first actual illusion. When we remember Lear's later attacks on the operations of justice because the judges are as guilty as the criminals they try, the justices in the mock trial of Goneril and Regan—a Bedlam beggar, a Fool, and a serving-man—are at least as likely to deal justly as a properly constituted bench, even though Lear accuses them of corruption in allowing the criminals to escape.

Shakespeare hits on two characteristics of certain kinds of mental derangement—the substitution of a symbolic offence for a real one ('she kick'd the poor King her father') and the obsession with a visual image. Lear thinks of the 'warped looks' of Regan, though in an earlier scene he had spoken of her 'tender-hefted nature' and of her eyes which, unlike Goneril's, 'do comfort and not burn'. It was the contrast between her beauty and her behaviour when she, like Goneril, put on a frowning countenance, that impressed Lear with her warped looks; and the same contrast makes him ask: 'Is there any cause in nature that makes these hard hearts?' The question is an appropriate introduction to the next scene in which we see the tender-hefted Regan assisting at the blinding of Gloucester.

When the imaginary curtains are drawn on the sleeping Lear we do not see him again for nearly 500 lines—about half an hour's playing time—but we are prepared for the development of his lunacy by the two short scenes in the middle of the fourth Act. In one of these Kent reveals that Lear refuses to see Cordelia:

> A sovereign shame so elbows him: his own unkindness,
> That stripp'd her from his benediction, turn'd her
> To foreign casualties, gave her dear rights
> To his dog-hearted daughters, these things sting
> His mind so venomously, that burning shame
> Detains him from Cordelia.   (IV.iii.42–7)

It is significant that after the admission at the end of Act I 'I did her wrong', Lear makes no further reference to Cordelia until he recovers his wits at the end of Act IV. The reason for this is partly, no doubt, that the ingratitude of Goneril and Regan drives everything else from his mind; but we may suspect, too, that Lear's sovereign shame prevents him from confronting his own guilt. In the other short scene (IV.iv) Cordelia describes her father,

> singing aloud;
> Crown'd with rank fumiter and furrow weeds,
> With burdocks, hemlock, nettles, cuckoo-flowers,
> Darnel, and all the idle weeds that grow
> In our sustaining corn.   (IV.iv.2–6)

The significance of this picture is that Lear has reverted to his child-
hood. The doctor prescribes rest:

> Our foster-nurse of nature is repose,
> The which he lacks; that to provoke in him
> Are many simples operative, whose power
> Will close the eye of anguish.   (IV.iv.12–15)

His colleague at Dunsinane holds out no such hopes for Lady
Macbeth. The perilous stuff which weighs upon her heart cannot be
cleansed from her bosom. The doctor cannot minister to her diseased
mind, because the disease is caused by mortal sin. 'More needs she the
divine than the physician.' Timothy Bright, who was both physician
and divine, distinguished clearly between feelings of guilt caused by
neurosis and those caused by sin:[26]

> whatsoever molestation riseth directly as a proper object of the mind, that
> in that respect is not melancholicke, but hath a farther ground then fancie,
> and riseth from conscience, condemning the guiltie soule of those ingrauen
> lawes of nature, which no man is voide of, be he never so barbarous. This is
> it, that hath caused the prophane poets to have fained Hecates Eumenides,
> and the infernall furies; which although they be but fained persons, yet the
> matter which is shewed under their maske, is serious, true, and of wofull
> experience.

In the scene in which the mad Lear meets the blinded Gloucester,
there is a wonderful blend of 'matter and impertinency'. Even the
impertinency has the kind of free association which is often found in
the utterances of some types of lunatics; and precisely because he is
mad Lear is freed from the conventional attitudes of society. He is able,
at moments, to see more clearly and piercingly than the sane, because
the sane buy their peace of mind by adjusting themselves to the
received ideas of society. Lear recognises the way he has been shielded
from reality by flattery. He also sees the hypocritical pretensions of
society with regard to sex and with regard to its treatment of criminals.
And, finally, he sees that human life is inescapably tragic:

> Thou must be patient; we came crying hither;
> Thou know'st the first time that we smell the air,

> We wawl and cry . . .
> When we are born, we cry that we are come
> To this great stage of fools.   (IV.vi.179–84)

When we next see Lear he is awakening from a drugged sleep. The Doctor has given him the repose he needs. The second part of the cure consists of music which, as later with Pericles, was a means of winding up the untuned and jarring senses. The third part of the cure is Cordelia's love. It is characteristic of her that she is eloquent so long as Lear is asleep, and that she falls back into her natural reticence when he awakens. The cure is completed when he kneels to the daughter he has wronged and begs her forgiveness.

The difference between Lear's madness and Ophelia's illustrates Shakespeare's extraordinary insight into different kinds of mental illness; and, moreover, the feigned madness of Edgar is quite different from the feigned madness of Hamlet, suitable both to the character and to the situation, though neither would be mistaken by a competent doctor for real insanity. Many of Shakespeare's contemporaries believed that madness was often, if not always, the result of possession; but he himself treated only mistaken or feigned madness in this way. Antipholus is thought to be possessed; Malvolio, although known to be sane, is treated by Feste as though he were possessed; and Edgar pretends that he has been possessed. A reader of Harsnett's *Declaration*, which Shakespeare used for the details of Poor Tom's chatter, would probably be sceptical of demoniac possession. At least it may be asserted that the mental illness of Lear has nothing supernatural about it.

IV

Edgar, describing his father's death, said that it was caused by the joy of reconciliation coming on top of his dreadful experiences:

>   his flaw'd heart,—
> Alack, too weak the conflict to support!—
> 'Twixt two extremes of passion, joy and grief,
> Burst smilingly.   (V.iii.196–9)

So the Paphlagonian King 'with many teares (both of joy and sorrow) . . . even in a moment died . . . his hart broken with unkindnes and affliction, stretched so farre beyond his limits with this excesse of comfort, as it was able no longer to keep safe his roial spirits'. It can hardly be doubted that Shakespeare's account of Gloucester's death was based on these phrases in the *Arcadia* and there is an obvious parallel with Lear's death:

> Pray you, undo this button: thank you, sir.
> Do you see this? Look on her, look, her lips,
> Look there, look there!   (V.iii.308–10)

Bradley commented that Lear dies of joy, believing Cordelia to be alive; and this interpretation is supported by Sidney's words. Lear's 'heart had been broken with unkindness and affliction' and was now 'stretched so far beyond his limits with this excesse of comfort'. A few recent critics have oddly regarded this interpretation as sentimental, as though it were softening the harsh realities of the situation. The audience, of course, knows that Cordelia is dead; and their knowledge that Lear is deluded is a final twist of the knife.

Bradley's interpretation—his demand that the actor at this point should express 'unbearable joy'—has been rendered suspect by more recent critics who, with various degrees of assurance, have suggested that Lear's delusion is intended to foreshadow an after-life. His earlier delusion, that the living Cordelia was 'a soul in bliss', implies a belief in a future life; but any such consolation is excluded from the ending of the play. Lear's death, as mediated to the audience by Kent, is merely a cessation of the agonies of existence:

> He hates him
> That would upon the rack of this tough world
> Stretch him out longer.   (V.iii.313–15)

Hamlet's death is accompanied by a prayer for flights of angels, Othello's and Macbeth's by an assurance of a judgement after death; but Lear's is merely an escape into oblivion. This tells us nothing about Shakespeare's personal beliefs at the time he wrote the play for, unlike the three tragedies mentioned, *King Lear* is set in a pagan world.

Is it, as Professor J. C. Maxwell once asserted, 'a Christian play about a pagan world'?[28] This question is largely one of definition, as we shall see. All the major characters in the play refer to the gods, often in contradictory ways. Lear himself swears by

> the sacred radiance of the sun,
> The mysteries of Hecate and the night;

he prays later to Nature to make Goneril barren; he prays to the gods
not to let him be mad; during the storm, for which he thinks the gods
are responsible, he blames them for joining his daughters and urges
them to find out hidden sinners. In the last scene he tells Cordelia that
'Upon such sacrifices . . . The Gods themselves throw incense'; but
after her death he makes no more references to the gods. There is a
similar ambiguity about Gloucester's religious views. At the beginning
of the play he is superstitious, though his belief in astrology is not in
itself that; Kent asks the gods to reward Gloucester's kindness in
providing shelter for Lear and the reward given him by Cornwall and
Regan, if not by the gods, is to gouge out his eyes. Even after he has
been blinded Gloucester prays to the 'kind gods' to forgive his treatment of Edgar; yet in the next scene he exclaims bitterly:

> As flies to wanton boys, are we to th' Gods;
> They kill us for their sport.

This is an understandable remark from one in his situation, though he
has been betrayed by men and not by the gods; but it is worth noting
that it is the expression of only a momentary mood. When he gives
his purse to Poor Tom a few lines later, he implies that the gods
approve of a just distribution of the world's goods. 'Heavens, deal so
still!' When he tries to commit suicide he prays to the gods:

> This world I do renounce, and in your sights
> Shake patiently my great affliction off;
> If I could bear it longer, and not fall
> To quarrel with your great opposeless wills,
> My snuff and loathed part of nature should
> Burn itself out. If Edgar live, O, bless him!   (IV.vi.35ff.)

After the 'miracle' he decides to wait patiently for death and eventually
agrees with his son's words:

> Men must endure
> Their going hence, even as their coming hither:
> Ripeness is all.   (V.ii.9–11)

If in Gloucester we see a gradual development from superstition to
religious resignation, in Edgar we watch a development from a laugh-
able credulity to a virtue that has been tested in the fires of adversity.
It was argued by the late Leo Kirschbaum that Edgar is not so much a
character as a series of roles: Bedlam beggar, well-spoken Kentishman,
dialect-speaking rustic, knightly champion, and choric commentator.

It may be said, however, that there is more consistency in the character than Kirschbaum allowed. He learns from his experiences as Poor Tom and the asides he is given do not merely serve as a choric commentary on the action: they show that he has the power of forgetting his own sufferings in those of the King:

> My tears begin to take his part so much
> They mar my counterfeiting.

Watching Lear makes it easier for him to bear his own danger and suffering:

> When we our betters see bearing our woes,
> We scarcely think our miseries our foes . . .
> How light and portable my pain seems now,
> When that which makes me bend makes the king bow.   (III.vi.102–9)

He has, by this time, overheard his father's confession of love—'I lov'd him, friend, / No father his son dearer'—and this prepares the way for his immediate forgiveness when he meets him after the blinding. He has just congratulated himself on the fact that any change must be for the best; but on seeing his blinded father, he murmurs:

> O Gods! Who is't can say 'I am at the worst'?
> I am worse than e'er I was.

With love and patience he cures Gloucester of despair, defends him from Oswald, and is a spectator of his meeting with Lear. He pretends to Gloucester that he has been saved by the intervention of 'the clearest gods who make them honours / Of men's impossibilities', a piece of deceit which parallels Edmund's earlier deception of Gloucester. He tells his father that he is

>   a most poor man,
> Who, by the art of known and feeling sorrows,
> Am pregnant to good pity.   (IV.vi.223–5)

But in spite of the love he displays for the father who has wronged him, Edgar is without sentimentality. After defeating Edmund he offers to exchange forgiveness with him.

>   Let's exchange charity . . .
> The Gods are just, and of our pleasant vices
> Make instruments to plague us:
> The dark and vicious place where thee he got
> Cost him his eyes.   (V.iii.166–72)

It has been suggested[29] by William R. Elton that the harshness of these words about Gloucester's adultery is an attempt by Edgar to ease Edmund's last moments by using the only language he can understand. As Edgar elsewhere shows pity and sympathy for his father, Professor Elton thinks it unlikely that these words express his true opinion or that he imagines that the justice of the gods is manifested in Gloucester's blinding. Perhaps it would be better to take the words as a reminder to the audience that the ultimate cause of the evil committed by Edmund was the act of adultery committed by Gloucester years before. It is another example of the necessity of considering remarks about the gods in relation to the speaker and to the precise moment of the action.

Albany is another character who rises in moral stature during the course of the play as he becomes disillusioned with his wife. His three significant references to the gods all come in the last two acts of the play. The first of these has been quoted above as an illustration of the animal imagery. If the heavens do not punish those who have driven Lear mad by sending down spirits in visible form, Albany declares,

> Humanity must perforce prey on itself,
> Like monsters of the deep.

A few lines later it seems that the heavens have responded, if not by sending down visible spirits, by using an earthly instrument to slay Cornwall; and Albany exclaims:

> This shows you are above,
> You justicers, that these our nether crimes
> So speedily can venge!

Albany's third reference to the gods makes us doubt whether there are justicers above concerned with human affairs. When he hears that Edmund has ordered the murder of Lear and Cordelia, he cries 'The Gods defend her!' Immediately afterwards Lear enters with the murdered Cordelia. The gods have not defended her.

The juxtaposition of the prayer and the entrance of Lear is clearly intentional, but the intentions are ambiguous. It has been taken to imply that there are no gods, or that if there are any they cannot be understood by human beings; but other critics would say merely that the gods do not always answer prayers, that they do not always intervene to save men from the consequences of their sins and follies. It is worth observing that it is only the evil characters who appear to be atheists and that the characters discussed above all express views or exhibit attitudes to the gods which are appropriate to the changing situation. Professor Elton, indeed, allows[30] that Edgar and Cordelia represent *Prisca Theologia*, Goneril, Regan and Edmund, pagan atheism, and Gloucester pagan superstition; but his final conclusion is that the play is not a Christian play, 'a drama of meaningful suffering and redemption, within a just universe ruled by providential higher powers'. He argues that those critics who follow Bradley in asserting that the theme of the play is the redemption of Lear ignore the events of the last act; that there are many passages which appear to repudiate any idea that the gods answer prayers; that the direction of the tragedy is 'annihilation of faith in poetic justice and, within the confines of a grim, pagan universe, annihilation of faith in divine justice'.[31] Many spectators would doubtless assume that as Shakespeare's play was set in a pagan world, the reactions of the characters to their gods had no relevance to Christianity; but Professor Elton believes that the more thoughtful members of the audience would regard the play as the expression of a sceptical attitude to Christian dogmas. Professor Brooke goes further and suggests that we are 'forced by the remorseless process of *King Lear* to face the fact of its ending without any support from systems of moral or artistic belief at all'.[32]

It is certainly true that Shakespeare deliberately detached his play from the naively Christian world of *King Leir*, and this was doubtless to give himself greater room for manœuvre. It is also true that he rejected the simple notions of poetic justice, of which the better poets have always been sceptical. Shakespeare does not seem to have subscribed to the view of one of his contemporaries that 'when the bad bleed then is the tragedy good'. The bad do bleed in his tragedies; but in most of them the innocent also suffer, from Lavinia and the Princes in the Tower to Ophelia, Desdemona, Cordelia, Duncan, Lady Macduff and her children. A dramatist who pretended that only the wicked suffer in this life would be immoral because he would know that his picture of life was a false one. It may be mentioned that, although Rymer thought that plays which depicted the suffering of the good would shake our belief in providence, the central tenet of his faith was the Crucifixion, and this he did not regard as incompatible with the providential government of the universe.

Shakespeare in his tragedies depicts a world in which evil is generally triumphant, but in his comedies and tragi-comedies evil is converted

or confounded. It would be hazardous to suppose that only the tragedies are a reflection of his actual beliefs. It is, moreover, important to
note that in *King Lear* there are as many good characters as evil ones,
that some of them become wiser and better in the course of the play,
and that Edmund, at the end, attempts to avert the murder of Cordelia.
We are made to feel that, whatever her fate, it is better to be Cordelia
than Goneril or Regan. We are made to recognise, as Nicholas Brooke
says, 'the perpetual vitality of the most vulnerable virtues'.[33] It is
obvious that the virtue which is its own reward, virtue for its own sake,
has more value than the honesty which is the best policy. It may therefore be suggested that Shakespeare gave his tragedy a pagan setting,
not to express sceptical views about the government of the world, but
rather to free himself from dogmatic assumptions in order to consider
man in his essence. A Christian tragedy is liable to involve its author
in difficulties, quite apart from censorship. If the suffering innocent is
rewarded in another world and the triumphant villain is delivered over
to an eternity of torment, we are left feeling that all is for the best and
that the end is not properly tragic. In *King Lear* we are denied the
comfort of Christian hope: there is no promise of a future life for Lear
and Cordelia, for when Lear imagines she is a soul in bliss, she is really
alive, and when he imagines that her lips move, she is dead. There is
nothing to encourage belief in a special providence: all prayers are
given a dusty answer; and the one 'miracle' we see is the trick played
by Edgar on his father.

There is, nevertheless, a sense in which *King Lear* can be regarded
as a Christian play. We are asked to imagine a world in which there is
no knowledge of Christian teaching, in which there is a savage
struggle for survival, in which men like ravenous fishes feed on one
another; and we are driven to realise that man needs neither wealth,
nor power, but patience, fortitude, love and mutual forgiveness. The
Christian virtues prove to be necessities; and from the development
of the virtuous characters and such flawed characters as Gloucester,
Albany and Lear himself, the world appears, as in Keats's famous
parable, to be a vale of soul-making.[34]

This is not to suggest that *King Lear* is a morality play, or even that
it is directly didactic. The evil characters all come to a violent end, but
so do most of the good characters. Shakespeare is not showing a
particular Providence 'protecting the Good and chastising the Bad';
nor, despite Washington Irving, was he 'the bard who gilded the dull

realities of life with innocent illusions'.[35] His tragic view demanded more than a look at the worst; and 'worst there is none' than the final scene with Lear's howls of agony and his realisation that Cordelia is dead:

> No, no, no life!
> Why should a dog, a horse, a rat, have life
> And thou no breath at all? Thou'lt come no more,
> Never, never, never, never, never.   (V.iii.305–8)

V

Sidney's account of the Paphlagonian King was 'worthy to be remembered for the unused examples therein, as well of true natural goodness, as of wretched ungratefulness'. There are equally good examples of these contrary qualities in the Lear story. Although the play is not an allegory, it is obvious that many of the characters are deliberately simplified; and although they cannot be written off as personified virtues or vices, they have less complexity than the characters in the other mature tragedies. On the one side are Cordelia, Edgar, Kent, the Fool and the King of France; and on the other side are Goneril, Regan, Edmund, Cornwall and Oswald. Albany, whose marriage to the beautiful Goneril makes him at first of the devil's party without knowing it, deserts that party as soon as he realises the truth.

The simplified characterisation, together with a number of scriptural echoes, have lent some colour to allegorical interpretations of the play, with Cordelia as a Christ figure and Edgar conducting his father up the purgatorial ascent. Yet it is, perhaps, the love-test which makes it plain that Shakespeare is writing about a world which is not merely pagan and prehistoric, but one in which actions are symbolic rather than psychologically plausible. Lear is not simply a king who wishes for incompatible things—abdication and power; he is also any old man who looks on his children resentfully as his hated successors, and hopefully as those who would care for him in his last years; and he is any man who is brought to wonder if there is 'any cause in nature that makes these hard hearts' and to doubt, because of man's inhumanity to man, whether the gods are just, whether, indeed, there are any gods. The play could not have been written in the ages of faith, but neither could it have been written in an age of unbelief or an age of reason. At the beginning of the seventeenth century the right conditions existed:

a universal Christian society, but with some of its basic tenets called in question by intellectuals; a realisation that the qualities which make for success are not the basic Christian virtues; and the beginnings of a conflict between science and faith.

King Lear is generally regarded as the most pessimistic, the most 'tragic' of all Shakespeare's tragedies. In *Hamlet* both the innocent and the guilty die, and the court at Elsinore is evil, but no fundamental belief is called in question. In *Othello* the hero is degraded to the level of the villain, and Desdemona is murdered, but Othello recovers his faith and his nobility before the end. Macbeth damns himself by his own actions and the play as a whole has no trace of scepticism. All three are affirmations of a divinely ordered universe. In *King Lear* Shakespeare seems to be considering the possibility that the world is not providentially governed and to be asking 'What then?' The answer he gives is that whether there are gods or not, whether there is an after-life or not in which the wicked are punished and the good rewarded, is almost irrelevant to the question of how we should behave or to the principles on which society should be founded.

MACBETH

high and excellent Tragedie . . . that maketh Kings feare to be Tyrants,
and Tyrants manifest their tyrannical humours . . . that maketh vs know,
Qui scæptra saeuus duro imperio regit,
Timet timentes, metus in authorem redit.

(Sidney)

I

It has been suggested that *Othello* was coloured with thoughts of the battle of Lepanto, about which James I had written his best-known poem, that *Measure for Measure* embodied some of his characteristics in the portrait of Vincentio, and that *King Lear* was concerned with the dangers of a disunited kingdom at the time when James was urging the union of England and Scotland.[1] Whatever we may think of these suggestions, *Macbeth* was a more obvious attempt to study the interests of the royal patron of Shakespeare's company. The promise of an empire without end to Banquo's descendants had been the subject of the Latin playlet performed before the gratified King when he visited Oxford in the summer of 1605; demonology was the subject of one of his books; and the discovery of the Gunpowder Plot and the subsequent trials were matters in which he, along with his subjects, was vitally interested.[2] There is therefore no reason to doubt that Shakespeare, both in his choice of subject and in his treatment of it, took some pains to write what would please the King. In particular he took care to whitewash Banquo who had actually been involved in the assassination of Duncan. But it is important not to exaggerate the extent to which Shakespeare was restricted by his desire to satisfy a royal command or royal prejudices. It could be maintained that once the poet had decided to dramatise the story in the autumn of 1605, his treatment was determined by purely dramatic considerations. Even the miraculous powers of Edward the Confessor, the introduction of which has been blamed as a disgracefully irrelevant compliment to King James, can be dramatically justified on three separate grounds: it provides a necessary interval during which Macduff can come to believe in Malcolm's integrity—which would otherwise be too abrupt; it is a means of characterising the English Court without having to bring in the King himself; and it provides a good supernatural to offset the evil supernatural of the Weird Sisters. It is true that James was beginning to touch for the King's Evil; but he was doing it with reluctance and repugnance, and he always insisted that it was prayer, rather than the royal touch, which was efficacious.

Even if James had not claimed Banquo as an ancestor, the character would have had to be whitewashed, both as a means of concentrating the attention of the audience on the tragic hero and as a means of showing that Macbeth's will was free. Moreover, as soon as Shakespeare abandoned the idea of an open conspiracy by fusing the stories of Donwald and Macbeth, he could dispense with Banquo as an accomplice. The murder of their guest and their king by Macbeth and his wife was infinitely more effective.

The Weird Sisters could be depicted as Fates or, as Holinshed said, 'the goddesses of destinie, or else some nymphs or feiries, indued with knowledge of prophesie by their necromanticall science', so that Shakespeare could play on these diverse theories. The Weird Sisters could be taken by the audience as witches, as their beards suggested, or as devils disguised as witches. Shakespeare had read the sceptical writings of Reginald Scot and Samuel Harsnett; but, as we can tell from various echoes, he had also read James's *Daemonologie*. It was dramatically convenient for him to allow members of the audience to hold different theories about the Weird Sisters, as they might differ about the ghost of Hamlet's father. The Gunpowder Plot provided Shakespeare with an opportunity, which he seized with avidity, of bringing home to the audience the relevance of his central theme of king-killing. His historical plays, both English and Roman, were never concerned merely with the past. Like Tudor chroniclers and historians, he believed that the function of history was not primarily to establish what really happened, but rather to offer a moral lesson for his own contemporaries. The testing of Macduff by Malcolm, detailed not merely by Holinshed but by other chroniclers, is a case in point. Although Shakespeare took rather more liberties with historical fact in *Macbeth* and *King Lear* than he had done in *Richard II* and *Julius Caesar*, the results were different in degree rather than in kind.

II

Professor L. C. Knights' provocative title—*How Many Children Had Lady Macbeth?*—was a useful way of drawing attention to one limitation of Bradley's method; and his declaration that the play was 'a statement of evil' reminded his readers that an analysis of the characters was not the most fruitful introduction to a poetic drama. Yet even a poetic drama, though it may sometimes deal with abstractions, is commonly a play about people, written to be performed by living actors. In his later writings Knights has partially retracted his views on character, but one suspects that he would rather read Shakespeare's tragedies than see them performed.

Macbeth, indeed, to judge from a fairly wide experience of the play in the theatre, is more difficult to perform than *King Lear*. This is partly due to the decline of belief in witchcraft and the consequent danger that the Weird Sisters will appear comic; partly to the union in Macbeth's character of characteristics which seldom co-exist, so that critics as diverse as Bridges and Shaw could deny that the man could ever have committed a series of murders; and partly to the fact that Macbeth, as depicted by most actors, loses the sympathy of the audience in the second half of the play. The applause which invariably greets Macduff at the end of Act IV, when he vows to avenge the murder of his wife and children, is a manifestation of relief that their dramatic sympathies and their moral sense are not pulling in opposite directions.

It has often been pointed out that Shakespeare intensifies the guilt of his hero. He omits altogether the years during which the historical Macbeth ruled wisely and well. The whole of his reign in the play is a reign of terror. The murder of Duncan in the *Chronicles* is carried out by an open conspiracy in which Banquo too was involved. By combining the stories of Macbeth and Donwald, Shakespeare was able to protect the reputation of Banquo, at the same time as he increased, by isolating it, the guilt of Macbeth and his wife. Duncan is Macbeth's sovereign and liege lord and a guest in his castle; and, unlike the historical Duncan, he is old and saintly. He is murdered while he sleeps; and Macbeth's initial crime is followed by many more. Hamlet is responsible for several deaths and Othello murders his wife, but one has to go back to Richard III to find a criminal record as black as Macbeth's. Although we may repudiate the epitaph, 'this dead butcher' it summarises his deeds, if not his character.

Yet Macbeth differs in kind from Richard. The early hero deliberately chooses evil, and, except in sleep, does not suffer from remorse; the later hero is potentially noble and he drifts into evil. The one is the villain as hero; in the other we see the hero become a villain. But the incompatibility between Macbeth's character and his actual deeds led Bernard Shaw to declare that his 'ferocious murders and treacheries and brutalities' could not be squared with 'the humane and reflective temperament of the nervous literary gentleman whom Shakespear thrust into his galligaskins'. This is, of course, absurd; for it was precisely the contrast between the man and the deed which was the spur to Shakespeare's imagination: but if his method was to imagine himself in the situation of his characters, it is not surprising that he endowed Macbeth with a conscience and an imagination. Not, as Bradley argued, a conscienceless imagination, for the imagery used by Macbeth expresses the torture of the conscience—the agenbite of inwit—and also the revulsion of his imagination against the deed he is contemplating. His 'single state of man' is shaken by the 'horrid image' of the temptation of murder; and though in the crucial soliloquy in I.vii he argues from strictly prudential reasons that the game is not worth the candle, the apocalyptic imagery of

> Pity, like a naked new-born babe
> Striding the blast, or heaven's Cherubins, hors'd
> Upon the sightless couriers of the air

reveals that it is not such reasons alone that make him decide, as he does, not to murder Duncan. Sixty lines later he has been persuaded to do the deed, although he loathes it before, during its commission, and afterwards.

It is Lady Macbeth who confesses that her husband is

> too full of the milk of human kindness,

and without the 'illness' which should attend ambition. He seems, as Shaw complained, to be a most unlikely person to commit a murder: but few people watching the play, or even reading it, are unable to suspend their disbelief. Shakespeare uses several methods to convince us. In the battle Macbeth is described as bathing in reeking wounds, making 'strange images of death', his sword smoking 'with bloody execution', unseaming the rebel 'from the nave to th'chaps'. Although he is loyally fighting for Duncan, the emphasis on the carnage prepares our minds for his later deeds of blood.

Then Shakespeare employs several kinds of irony. After the description of the execution of the Thane of Cawdor, Duncan declares that

> There's no art
> To find the mind's construction in the face:
> He was a gentleman on whom I built
> An absolute trust—   (I.iv.11–14)

He breaks off to welcome the new Thane of Cawdor whom we have just seen wrestling with the temptation to murder Duncan. Before the end of the scene he is again assailed by temptation. He had previously decided to wait for the crown to come to him on the natural death of the aged Duncan, but the proclamation of Malcolm as Prince of Cumberland meant that he could no longer hope to succeed to the throne. At the same moment, Duncan's announcement that he was to be the guest of Macbeth at Inverness seemed to provide a hell-sent opportunity which might never recur.

Yet, by the time Macbeth arrives in Inverness, his determination has weakened. It is only after his wife has used all the arts of persuasion that he finally consents. The irony here is that Lady Macbeth's ambitions are not at all for herself, but entirely for her husband. She lashes him into murder, and thus into ruin, because she believes he is desperately anxious for the crown. Macbeth, for his part, commits the murder, against which his whole being revolts, to satisfy his wife.

Lady Macbeth's tactics are masterly. She deliberately evades questions of morality and concentrates on four main points. First, that at some unspecified time in the past, before they knew Duncan was to be their guest, Macbeth had suggested the murder. Whether this was true or a tactical distortion of a less definite hint Shakespeare leaves unsettled:

> Nor time, nor place,
> Did then adhere, and yet you would make both:
> They have made themselves, and that their fitness now
> Does unmake you.   (I.vii.51–4)

Secondly, Lady Macbeth makes the commission of the murder a test of her husband's love. When he tries to wriggle out of it she says scornfully:

> From this time
> Such I account thy love.

Thirdly, she accuses the famous warrior, who has proved his courage
as Bellona's bridegroom in hand-to-hand fighting, of being a coward:

> Art thou afeard . . . ?
> Would'st thou have that
> Which thou esteem'st the ornament of life,
> And live a coward in thine own esteem . . . ?

If he does not commit the murder he will show that he lacks manliness,
though Macbeth claims that he dares 'do all that may become a man'.
Then, fourthly, Lady Macbeth steers the discussion away from questions of principle to questions of method. She produces a plausible
practical plan which will enable them to avoid detection and Macbeth,
because he has not based his opposition on a moral objection, is won
over.

It has been pointed out by more than one critic that after the initial
moment of temptation when Macbeth refers to the murder by its
right name, both the murderers use euphemistic terms—'This night's
great business', 'my intent', 'this business', 'this enterprise', 'our great
quell', and 'this terrible feat'. It is something which requires courage
and resolution and is therefore something to be admired. Macbeth,
indeed, admires the 'undaunted mettle' of his wife.

The disparity between the rational arguments against the murder
used by Macbeth and his horror and repugnance revealed by the
imagery is one indication of the success of Lady Macbeth's strategy.
She manœuvres her husband into a position where it seems that a
refusal to kill the king will show that he is inconsistent, cowardly,
lacking in 'manliness' and, above all, lacking in love for her. He therefore commits the deed almost, as Bradley said, as a horrible duty.

Throughout the first three acts we are continually reminded of the
horror Macbeth is experiencing, and in the final act he summarises his
life since the first temptation in the words: 'I have supped full with
horrors'. Before his fall he declares that 'present fears are less than
horrible imaginings'. The horror of regicide, the worse horror of
violating the laws of hospitality, and, worst of all, the horror of
murdering a saintly old man are apparent in Macbeth's soliloquy in the
last scene of Act I. When he sees the imaginary dagger which leads him
to Duncan's chamber—an hallucination for which the powers of darkness are doubtless responsible—he fears that the stones will cry out
and 'take the present horror from the time'. The murder is carried out
while Macbeth appears to be in a trance-like state in which he thinks he

hears a voice pronouncing on him the doom of everlasting sleepless-
ness, as though in killing the sleeping king he had murdered sleep itself.
The climax of horror comes when Lady Macbeth has to take back the
daggers to the chamber of the murdered King and Macbeth looks at his
blood-stained hands which he hardly recognises as his own:

> What hands are here? Ha! They pluck out mine eyes.

It is almost as though he thinks the hands are as much an hallucination
as the dagger he sees before the murder, as though his hands had an
independent existence and he had been involuntarily damned because
of the deed committed by them.

The knocking at the gate, which heralds the discovery of the
murder, acts on Macbeth's conscience and completes the destruction of
his nerve. A few moments later the Porter's acting out of the role of
the Porter of Hell Gate and his imaginary colloquies with three of the
damned, not only prevent us from regarding the events of the play as
merely historical, but also suggest that the castle at Inverness has been
turned into hell because of the hellish deed enacted there. When the
murder is revealed Macbeth attempts, as his wife had suggested, to
make his 'griefs and clamour roar' upon Duncan's death. He begins a
hypocritical speech to express his horror at the regicide, but, as he
speaks, the words intended to deceive become a precise account of his
real feelings:

> Had I but died an hour before this chance,
> I had lived a blessed time; for from this instant
> There's nothing serious in mortality:
> All is but toys: renown and grace is dead;
> The wine of life is drawn, and the mere lees
> Is left this vault to brag of.   (II.iii.89–94)

Notwithstanding this realisation, Macbeth begins to plan the murder
of Banquo, half deluding himself into the belief that 'the tortures of
the mind' on which he lies 'in restless ecstasy' are due not to remorse
but to the knowledge that Banquo and Fleance live. His fear of
Banquo is not primarily because he may reveal his knowledge of the
Weird Sisters' prophecy, though this may underlie the lines at the
beginning of Macbeth's soliloquy:

> Our fears in Banquo stick deep;
> And in his royalty of nature reigns
> That which would be fear'd: 'tis much he dares,

> And, to that dauntless temper of his mind,
> He hath a wisdom that doth guide his valour
> To act in safety. There is none but he
> Whose being I do fear: and under him
> My Genius is rebuk'd, as it is said
> Mark Antony's was by Caesar.   (III.i)

Macbeth may fear Banquo's revelation, or that just as he assassinated Duncan, so Banquo will assassinate him so that his descendants will become kings; but it is also clear that stronger motives for the murder of Banquo are the contrast of his own 'barren sceptre' and the line of kings promised to Banquo, and above all the royalty and integrity which are a standing rebuke to his own treachery and disloyalty. He does not realise that the murder of Banquo will not restore his peace of mind since the death of his victim merely perpetuates the rebuke.

Macbeth is deluded in yet another way. He hopes to avoid the mental torture he experienced after Duncan's murder by employing others to murder Banquo and Fleance and he hopes to spare his wife by not informing her of his plans. But when he has told her to praise Banquo at the banquet, confessed that his mind is full of scorpions because Banquo and Fleance live, comforted himself with the reflection that they are assailable, and spoken of the 'deed of dreadful note' which will be committed before nightfall, she would be stupid if she did not guess the nature of the deed. Macbeth's invocation of night and his reference to its black agents remind the audience of his wife's invocation of the powers of darkness. He does not protect his wife and he does not save himself from the terrors of guilt. The double appearance of Banquo's ghost, first as a blood-stained corpse and then apparently as a skeleton with marrowless bones, is clearly the result of hallucination since it is seen by Macbeth alone. (Although when Simon Forman saw a performance of the play in 1610 the Ghost entered and sat in Macbeth's place, and although the Folio stage-direction confirms this, it would be more effective for the Ghost not to appear in this scene.) As Lady Macbeth says, the hallucination is called up by his guilty fear:

> This is the very painting of your fear:
> This is the air-drawn dagger which, you said,
> Led you to Duncan.   (III.iv.61–3)

His use of murderers does not enable him to evade a sense of guilt and his behaviour at the banquet makes his throne more, and not less, precarious. In spite of which, the only moral he draws from the experience is that his hallucination was caused by

> the initiate fear that wants hard use:
> We are yet but young in deed.

He imagines that when he has committed a few more murders they will cease to trouble him and before the end of the scene he has decided to wade further into blood. In a sense he is right. The murder of Macduff's family and the reign of terror to which it is a prelude leave Macbeth comparatively unperturbed, so that, as he declares:

> I have almost forgot the taste of fears . . .
>   I have supp'd full with horrors;
> Direness, familiar to my slaughterous thoughts,
> Cannot once start me.   (V.iv.9–15)

This state of insensibility is a sign that Macbeth has succeeded in deadening his conscience. His fears had continued as long as he was wrestling with evil and critics who think of him as going beyond good and evil have distorted the meaning of the last act of the play. Macbeth's freedom from fear is also a freedom from feeling. This can be seen from his reception of the news of his wife's death. 'She should have died hereafter' is the only epitaph he can utter on the woman for whose sake he killed Duncan; and in the lines that follow he expresses the conviction that life is meaningless—

>   a tale,
> Told by an idiot, full of sound and fury
> Signifying nothing.

Bernard Shaw and others have absurdly argued that Shakespeare was here using Macbeth as his mouthpiece and that the poet too imagined that life was absurd, a blood-and-thunder melodrama written by a madman and performed by an incompetent actor. More plausibly, Lascelles Abercrombie suggested that Macbeth triumphed by facing and expressing so superbly the fact that life is without a meaning.[3] Even this will not do. The superb expression is the poet's, not his creature's. In their context the lines reveal that Macbeth believes that life is meaningless because he has damned himself by his crimes. He knows he has forfeited the things 'which should accompany old age' and it is significant that as he fights for his life he should compare himself to a bear tied to a stake. He has proved the truth of his own warning:

> I dare do all that may become a man:
> Who dares do more is none.

In spite of his crimes and the moral deterioration he undergoes in the course of the play Macbeth is not initially or inherently evil. Hecate, though possibly un-Shakespearian, rightly calls him 'a wayward son' who

> Loves for his own ends, not for you.

It is Lady Macbeth, stigmatised at the end as 'fiend-like Queen', who is more positive and conscious in her choice of evil. When she hears that Duncan is coming to Inverness, she invokes the ministers of darkness to take possession of her:

>   Come, you spirits
> That tend on mortal thoughts, unsex me here,
> And fill me, from the crown to the toe, top-full
> Of direst cruelty! make thick my blood
> Stop up th' access and passage to remorse,
> That no compunctious visitings of nature
> Shake my fell purpose, nor keep peace between
> Th' effect and it! Come to my woman's breasts
> And take my milk for gall, you murdering ministers,
> Wherever in your sightless substances
> You wait on nature's mischief! Come, thick night,
> And pall thee in the dunnest smoke of hell,
> That my keen knife see not the wound it makes
> Nor heaven peep through the blanket of the dark,
> To cry 'Hold, hold!'   (I.v.37–50)

Shakespeare's personal views on demoniacal possession are not certainly known. His reading of Samuel Harsnett and Reginald Scot may indicate that he was sceptical on the subject: but just as he gave the Weird Sisters supernatural powers since this was the kernel of the Macbeth story, so, we must assume, he makes Lady Macbeth a demoniac.[4] She believes that evil spirits can and do take possession of human beings. Shakespeare does not require his audience to believe this too. They can suppose that Lady Macbeth is deluded but not that she is speaking metaphorically. It is worth mentioning that the most effective of all actresses in the part, Mrs Siddons, assumed that Lady Macbeth was possessed.

Some critics have thought that Lady Macbeth's mention of her 'keen knife' implies that at this point in the play she intended to do the actual murder, presumably because she feared that her husband's scruples would prevent him from screwing up his courage to the sticking-point. She says afterwards that if the sleeping Duncan had not resembled her father she would have killed him. Nevertheless, there is no reason to think that a scene has been cut. In her possessed state Lady Macbeth thinks of the murder weapon as hers, even when wielded by her husband, because he is acting as her instrument.

Lady Macbeth's usual mode of speech differs considerably from the lines quoted above. It is normally down-to-earth and prosaic. She never indulges in the soaring metaphorical language used by her husband. She uses proverbial phrases to clinch her arguments.

> Letting 'I dare not' wait upon 'I would',
> Like the poor cat in the adage.

> The sleeping and the dead are but as pictures.

> You lack the season of all natures, sleep.

>   Things without all remedy
> Should be without regard: what's done is done.

When she is informed that the King has been murdered her comment reveals her commonplace mind:

>   Woe, alas!
> What, in our house?

Some of her sayings are ironically contrasted with those of Macbeth. He can ask:

> Will all great Neptune's ocean wash this blood
> Clean from my hand? No; this my hand will rather
> The multitudinous seas incarnadine,
> Making the green one red.   (II.ii.60–3)

Lady Macbeth, in the very next speech, declares flatly:

> A little water clears us of this deed.

Shakespeare cannot devote much time to Lady Macbeth's later development; but her weariness and despair are apparent in Act III. She realises that the possession of the crown has not given Macbeth happiness or peace of mind. She confesses in soliloquy that 'Nought's had, all's spent'; and she does not deny that she too is shaken nightly by terrible dreams. She tries to comfort her husband but she is no longer the dominant partner, no longer even in his confidence. She makes a great effort in the Banquet scene to save the situation resulting from her husband's terror; but from this point in the play Macbeth's guilt is freely discussed by the choric figure of Lennox.

Lady Macbeth makes only one more appearance. In the sleep-walking scene she reveals the breakdown of her iron self-control and perhaps her abandonment by the spirits she had invoked. She reverts again and again to the three chief murders of which her husband is guilty—of Duncan, Banquo, Lady Macduff; she is obsessed by the need to prevent him from revealing his guilt and to calm his terrors; and the symbolic action of washing her hands is a fitting answer to her boast that a little water would clear them of the murder. Most of her speeches in this scene refer back to earlier actions or speeches. The words used in Act III to persuade her husband not to brood on the past—'What's done is done'—are changed into the despairing: 'What's done cannot be undone.' Her confident invocation of the powers of evil is answered by her grim recognition that 'Hell is murky'. Her severely practical assurance that they cannot be accused of murder if only they wash off the blood leads to the recognition that 'All the perfumes of Arabia will not sweeten this little hand'.

One other thing may be noted about this scene. Apart from the sentence just quoted, Lady Macbeth speaks in a remarkably simple style, with a preponderance of monosyllables:

Out, damned spot! out, I say! One: two: why, then 'tis time to do't. Hell is murky. Fie, my lord, fie! . . . what need we fear who knows it, when none can call our power to account? Yet who would have thought the old man to have had so much blood in him? The thane of Fife had a wife; where is she now? What, will these hands ne'er be clean? No more o'that, my lord, no more o' that: you mar all with this starting.   (V.i.34ff.)

More than nine out of ten of the words she uses in this scene are mono-syllables. Her childish vocabulary is reinforced by the nursery jingle: 'The thane of Fife had a wife'.

III

The scene in England was once criticised for the improbability of Malcolm's self-accusation and the irrelevance of the King's Evil passage. We have already seen the justifications which may be offered for the King's Evil episode. The long dialogue between Malcolm and Macduff is the only scene of the play in which Shakespeare closely echoed Holinshed's words. It is, in fact, the only substantial passage of dialogue in this part of the *Chronicles* and a similar conversation appears in several earlier versions. Although it cannot be regarded as historical, the testing of Macduff impressed poets and historians as a story containing a useful lesson. It shows how tyranny leads to the growth of suspicion, until no one can be trusted. During the years of Nazi rule the scene no longer appeared the improbable fiction it had seemed to some earlier critics, but painfully true.

The historical Macbeth was for most of his reign a good ruler; but Shakespeare for dramatic reasons had to ignore this fact. He had to show his hero's swift disintegration and the miserable state of Scotland 'under a hand accursed', so that the rebellion against his rule could be abundantly justified. It was dramatically necessary to build up the character of Macduff who was fated to be Macbeth's executioner. Macduff had briefly appeared in Act II; he had been mentioned once or twice in Act III; but he first assumes dramatic importance in the first scene of Act IV when the Weird Sisters warn Macbeth against the Thane of Fife and we hear a few minutes later that he has fled to England. In the next scene Lady Macduff complains to Ross of her husband's flight and Ross replies that she does not know 'Whether it was his wisdom or his fear'. Her doubts seem to be justified when she and her children are murdered, so that it is natural that Malcolm should be suspicious of Macduff when he arrives at the English court and that he should test him as he does. At the end Macduff convinces Malcolm— and, incidentally, the audience—of his integrity.

Among Macbeth's sins Malcolm lists two of which he would seem to be innocent—lechery and avarice. But these and the voluptuousness, avarice and hatred of peace of which he accuses himself are a means of contrasting the evils of tyranny with the king-becoming graces:[5]

> justice, verity, temperance, stableness,
> Bounty, perseverance, mercy, lowliness,
> Devotion, patience, courage, fortitude.   (IV.iii.92–4)

Amongst other things *Macbeth* is a mirror for magistrates with Duncan, Edward the Confessor and Malcolm serving as *exempla* of the good ruler, and Macbeth himself of the tyrant. One of the functions of tragedy, as Sidney argued, was to make kings fear to be tyrants; and James I, in a book which Shakespeare may well have read, contrasted the characteristics and fate of the good king with those of the bad.[6]

As in several other tragedies, Shakespeare keeps his hero off stage for much of Act IV. We do not see Macbeth again until the third scene of Act V. This was partly, no doubt, to give the actor a rest. But Shakespeare uses the period to switch our sympathies away from Macbeth. Despite his crimes, he does not entirely lose our admiration or alienate our sympathies until the end of Act III. During Act IV his complete identification with evil and chaos in the cauldron scene, the savage butchery of Macduff's family, the picture we are given of the state of Scotland, and the spectacle of Macduff's grief compel us to side with the forces of liberation and to rejoice, as we see Macbeth's head on a pole, that the time is free.

8

ANTONY AND CLEOPATRA

Love . . . is capable of infinite degradation and is the source of our greatest errors: but when it is even partially refined it is the energy and passion of the soul in its search for Good, the force that joins us to Good and joins us to the world through Good.[1]   (Iris Murdoch)

Antony and Cleopatra is the second of Shakespeare's love-tragedies, but, unlike *Romeo and Juliet*, it is also an historical play and one dealing with momentous events in the history of the world. Bradley, indeed, supposed that it could not be ranked as one of the 'great' tragedies and some more recent critics have professed to find it episodic, or lacking in tragic effect. Those who allow that it is one of the greatest of Shakespeare's tragedies are divided between those who think that the protagonists are *exempla* of transcendental humanism, and those who believe that the world was ill lost. Mr F. Dickey has no difficulty in showing that Antony and Cleopatra had often been treated as horrid warnings:[2]

Instead of seeing Antony and Cleopatra as patterns of nobility and of a deathless love, the Elizabethan reader must have seen them as patterns of lust, of cruelty, of prodigality, of drunkenness, of vanity, and, in the end, of despair. Nowhere does an author hint that their love enriched their lives.

Mr Dickey admits that Shakespeare was not bound to follow this tradition in his depiction of the lovers; and it is worth noting that Horace in the Ode in which he celebrates the defeat of Antony has a word of praise for Cleopatra's suicide;[3] that she is depicted by Chaucer as one of love's martyrs; and that Daniel's portrait is by no means hostile.[4] Shakespeare, we may suppose, was more likely to be influenced by the poets than by the preachers and moralists.

Faced with the conflicting interpretations which appear to be based squarely on the text, Professor John Danby argued[5] that Shakespeare presents us with the Roman and Egyptian points of view, the one symbolising the world and the other the flesh, without committing himself to either:

The Roman condemnation of the lovers is obviously inadequate. The senti-mental reaction in their favour is equally mistaken. There is no so-called 'love-romanticism' in the play. . . . The love of Antony and Cleopatra . . . is not asserted as a 'final value' . . . To go further still in sentimentality and claim that there is a 'redemption' motif in Antony and Cleopatra's love is an even more violent error.

Professor Ernest Schanzer is similarly moved by the play's dialectic to claim that it is one of Shakespeare's problem plays and that an audience will leave the theatre debating whether the world was well, or ill, lost.[6]

It is true that there is a deliberate juxtaposition of the two points of view. We first hear the counsel for the prosecution with Philo's scathing commentary on Antony's lust:

> Nay, but this dotage of our general's
> O'erflows the measure: those his goodly eyes,
> That o'er the files and musters of the war
> Have glow'd like plated Mars, now bend, now turn
> The office and devotion of their view
> Upon a tawny front: his captain's heart,
> Which in the scuffles of great fights hath burst
> The buckles on his breast, reneges all temper,
> And is become the bellows and the fan
> To cool a gipsy's lust . . .
>   You shall see in him
> The triple pillar of the world transform'd
> Into a strumpet's fool.   (I.i.1–13)

After watching the endearments of Antony and Cleopatra, Demetrius comments:

>   I am full sorry
> That he approves the common liar, who
> Thus speaks of him at Rome.

In the fourth scene Caesar continues the indictment. Antony, he tells us,

>   fishes, drinks, and wastes
> The lamps of night in revel; is not more manlike
> Than Cleopatra; nor the queen of Ptolemy
> More womanly than he; hardly gave audience, or
> Vouchsafed to think he had partners; you shall find there

> A man who is the abstract of all faults
> That all men follow. . . .
>   let's grant, it is not
> Amiss to tumble on the bed of Ptolemy;
> To give a kingdom for a mirth; to sit
> And keep the turn of tippling with a slave;
> To reel the streets at noon, and stand the buffet
> With knaves that smell of sweat . . .
>   But to confound such time
> That drums him from his sport, and speaks as loud
> As his own state and ours, 'tis to be chid
> As we rate boys, who, being mature in knowledge,
> Pawn their experience to their present pleasure
> And so rebel to judgement.   (I.iv.4–33)

Even if we discount some of this attack because Caesar feels he has been slighted and perhaps resents the way in which the disreputable Antony inspires more love and loyalty than he can himself, and even if we do not regard angling as a serious misdemeanour, the accusations are true. Antony, then, indulges in 'lascivious wassails' and he himself speaks of his poisoned hours, admits that he is grown hard in viciousness, his clear judgement dropped in his own filth. His own soldiers are afraid of being too victorious, lest he should become jealous of them, and he bungles his suicide.

Nor is Cleopatra romanticised. We have an exhibition of all the arts of harlotry, critics tell us, and we may assume that they have expert knowledge. 'She owes more to a study of prostitutes than to a knowledge of how even the worst queens behave.' (In view of this remark, it may be mentioned that others have suggested that two details of the characterisation were borrowed from Queen Elizabeth I.)[7] She dallies with the idea of making a treacherous peace with Caesar and commits suicide only when she learns that she is to be exhibited at Rome in Caesar's triumph. This summary would seem to support Dickey's view that Antony and Cleopatra were depicted by Shakespeare in the traditional way as two rulers 'who threw away a kingdom for lust'.

What then are we to make of the rival interpretation—that the play is the expression of transcendental humanism (Wilson Knight); that it is Shakespeare's 'hymn to man' (Dover Wilson); that it contains 'the greatest affirmation' in the world's literature of 'the supreme value' of human love (Harold Wilson); and that Shakespeare 'asserts, without either moral censure or romantic compromise, his belief in the resurrection of the flesh' (Robert Speaight)? If one concentrates on other

passages in the play most of these remarks could find some support. In
the first scene, for example, after we have heard Antony described as
a strumpet's fool, the dialogue which follows destroys this impression:

> *Cleop.* If it be love indeed, tell me how much.
> *Ant.* There's beggary in the love than can be reckon'd.
> *Cleop.* I'll set a bourn how far to be beloved.
> *Ant.* Then must thou needs find out new heaven, new earth.

Antony refuses to hear the messengers from Rome:

> Let Rome in Tiber melt, and the wide arch
> Of the ranged empire fall! Here is my space.
> Kingdoms are clay: our dungy earth alike
> Feeds beast as man: the nobleness of life
> Is to do thus; when such a mutual pair
> And such a twain can do 't, in which I bind,
> On pain of punishment, the world to weet
> We stand up peerless. (I.i.33–40)

When we hear these lines—with one echo from *Revelation* and probably one from *Daniel*—we are not likely to suppose that they are the
delusions of an ageing sensualist, unable to distinguish between love
and lust.

Antony's final tribute to Cleopatra in this first scene as a

> wrangling queen
> Whom every thing becomes, to chide, to laugh,
> To weep; whose every passion fully strives
> To make itself in thee, fair and admired!

is borne out later both by his own behaviour and by the tributes of her
enemies. Enobarbus is her unwilling admirer. He testifies that 'her
passions are made of nothing but the finest part of pure love' and that
she is 'a wonderful piece of work'. It is Enobarbus who is made to
describe the first meeting of the lovers and explain why Antony will
never leave her:

> I saw her once
> Hop forty paces through the public street;
> And having lost her breath, she spoke, and panted,
> That she did make defect perfection,
> And, breathless, power breathe forth. (II.ii.232–6)

When Maecenas declares that Antony, having married the holy
Octavia, must leave Cleopatra, Enobarbus replies:

> Never; he will not:
> Age cannot wither her, nor custom stale
> Her infinite variety: other women cloy
> The appetities they feed, but she makes hungry
> Where most she satisfies: for vilest things
> Become themselves in her, that the holy priests
> Bless her when she is riggish.

Even Caesar talks of 'her strong toil of grace'.[8]

There are many aspects of the relationship of Antony and Cleopatra which cannot be written off as lust. As he had an actor playing the part of Cleopatra, Shakespeare may have deliberately avoided physical manifestations of her passion; but it is clear that she is a wife and companion as well as a mistress. Caesar sneers at the way Antony wanders in disguise through the streets of Alexandria, although wandering through the streets to 'note the qualities of people' has always been a favourite pastime for lovers. Cleopatra plays billiards and fishes; she could be a drinking-companion; and she liked dressing up in Antony's clothes or as the goddess Isis.

Shakespeare deliberately reminds us of the divine attributes of his protagonists. In Plutarch's account of their first meeting it is mentioned that

there went a rumour in the people's mouths, that the goddess Venus was come to play with the god Bacchus, for the general good of all Asia.

Shakespeare does not make use of this sentence but he nevertheless conveys the idea in his description of the barge. The boys who fan Cleopatra are 'smiling Cupids' and she herself is not merely (as Plutarch says) 'apparelled and attired like the goddess Venus', but rather

> O'er picturing that Venus, where we see
> The fancy out-work Nature.

Antony is not only identified with Bacchus—and it is appropriate that the one song in the play should be an invocation of that god—but Philo and Cleopatra both compare him with Mars. Even more significant is the way Shakespeare makes use of his supposed descent from Hercules. When he is enraged with Cleopatra he compares himself to his ancestor:

> The shirt of Nessus is upon me: teach me,
> Alcides, thou mine ancestor, thy rage:
> Let me lodge Lichas on the horns o' th' moon,

And with those hands that grasp'd the heaviest club
Subdue my worthiest self. (IV.xii.43–7)

Earlier in the same act, the supernatural music in the air and beneath the earth is interpreted by one of the sentries to mean that

> the god Hercules, whom Antony loved,
> Now leaves him.

But the god-like quality of Antony is brought home to us by the remorse of Enobarbus, by the reaction of the soldiers to his suicide— 'The star is fall'n'—by Cleopatra's words—

> Had I great Juno's power,
> The strong-wing'd Mercury should fetch thee up
> And set thee by Jove's side— (IV.xv.34–6)

and by her hyperbolical portrait of Antony to Dolabella:

> His face was as the heavens; and therein stuck
> A sun and moon, which kept their course and lighted
> The little O, the earth . . .
> His legs bestrid the ocean: his rear'd arm
> Crested the world: his voice was propertied
> As all the tuned spheres, and that to friends;
> But when he meant to quail and shake the orb,
> He was as rattling thunder. For his bounty
> There was no winter in't; an autumn 'twas
> That grew the more by reaping: his delights
> Were dolphin-like; they show'd his back above
> The element they lived in: in his livery
> Walk'd crowns and crownets: realms and islands were
> As plates dropp'd from his pocket. (V.ii.79–92)

This portrait of Antony as a demi-god, although Dolabella is bewildered by it, stays with the audience as one aspect of truth. We cannot altogether dismiss the portrait as the delusion of grief, any more than we can altogether discount the obituary treatment by his enemies:

Caes.   it is tidings
To wash the eyes of kings.
Agr.   And strange it is
That nature must compel us to lament
Our most persisted deeds.
Maec.   His taints and honours
Waged equal with him.
Agr.   A rarer spirit never
Did steer humanity: but you, gods, will give us
Some faults to make us men. Caesar is touch'd. (V.i.27–33)

F

The conflicting views on the protagonists and, even more, the complex way in which they are presented, makes it tempting for us to accept the Danby or the Schanzer interpretations of the play: that Shakespeare, more than customarily, leaves us with unresolved contradictions. Yet I think it is true to say that most members of an audience come away from a performance neither perplexed nor argumentative, as after a problem play, and certainly not feeling that they have witnessed a sermon against lechery. On the contrary they feel that Cleopatra's death is a triumph which thwarts Caesar's. It was his realisation of this that led Schücking to argue that the Cleopatra of the last act was completely inconsistent with the character depicted throughout the first four acts and led Bernard Shaw to complain[9] that

after giving a faithful picture of the soldier broken down by debauchery, and the typical wanton in whose arms such men perish, Shakespeare finally strains all his huge command of rhetoric and stage pathos to give a theatrical sublimity to the wretched end of the business, and to persuade foolish spectators that the world was well lost by the twain.

As so often in his remarks about Shakespeare, Shaw gets the right end of the stick and then proceeds to clobber the bard with it. He saw instinctively that the last act of the play was impossible to square with his interpretation of the earlier acts; but 'rhetoric and stage pathos' are derogatory terms for what should more properly be termed great dramatic poetry and 'theatrical sublimity' is what most good critics would call sublimity *tout court*.

Plutarch describes how after Antony's defeat at Actium, and after the desertion of some of his followers made him abandon hope, he determined to enjoy the few weeks left to him. At the same time Cleopatra began experimenting with poisons. Plutarch says

there was kept great feasting, banqueting, and dancing in Alexandria many days together. Indeed they did break their first order they had set down, which they called Amimetobion, (as much as to say, No life comparable) and did set up another, which they called synapothanumenon (signifying the order and agreement of those that will die together) the which in exceeding sumptuousness and cost was not inferior to the first. For their friends made themselves to be enrolled in this order of those that would die together, and so made great feasts one to another: for every man, when it came to his turn, feasted their whole company and fraternity.

Shakespeare does not actually mention the order of those who will die together; but the sense of doomed fellowship and forced gaiety are brilliantly suggested in the fourth act of the play. The third act had ended with Antony's decision to 'have one other gaudy night' and with Enobarbus's soliloquy in which he decides to desert to Caesar:

> I see still
> A diminution in our captain's brain
> Restores his heart: when valour preys on reason
> It eats the sword it fights with. (III.xiii.197–200)

In the second scene of Act IV, as a prelude to the gaudy night, Antony shakes the hands of five of his household servants, an equalitarian gesture which Cleopatra seems to find inexplicable though she almost repeats it in her own death-scene. Antony tells his servants:

> Tend me to-night;
> May be it is the period of your duty;
> Haply you shall not see me more; or if,
> A mangled shadow: perchance to-morrow
> You'll serve another master. I look on you
> As one that takes his leave. Mine honest friends,
> I turn you not away; but, like a master
> Married to your good service, stay till death:
> Tend me to-night two hours, I ask no more,
> And the gods yield you for't. (IV.ii.24–33)

This scene begins the rehabilitation of the god-like Antony; and the process is continued by his magnanimity after the desertion of Enobarbus. Indeed, the episode of his desertion does more than anything to raise our opinion of Antony. Enobarbus is shrewd and cynical, but fundamentally loyal. He has confessed earlier that

> The loyalty well held to fools does make
> Our faith mere folly: yet he that can endure
> To follow with allegiance a fall'n lord
> Does conquer him that did his master conquer,
> And earns a place i' th' story. (III.xiii.42–6)

The breaking-point comes when he realises that Antony cannot face realities, but even after he has decided to desert, Antony's treatment of his followers makes him, as he characteristically puts it, 'onion-eyed'. Before he learns that Antony has sent his treasure after him he decides

that he has made a mistake since Caesar will give him no honourable
trust; but when the treasure arrives he dies of a broken heart, in his
last words using words that remind us of Judas:

> O Antony,
> Nobler than my revolt is infamous,
> Forgive me in thine own particular,
> But let the world rank me in register
> A master-leaver and a fugitive:
> O Antony! O Antony!   (IV.ix.18–23)

On receiving the false news of Cleopatra's death, Antony decides
forthwith not to live without her; or, to be more precise, no decision
is necessary since there is no conflict in his mind. The name of the
servant who unarms him—taken from Plutarch—is Eros. He is
unarmed by love, as he had been made less of a warrior by his love for
Cleopatra; but when he tells Eros, in fulfilment of his oath, to slay
him, he slays himself instead, after speaking of Antony's 'noble
countenance, / Wherein the worship of the whole world lies', his 'dear
master', captain and emperor. Antony dies Eros' scholar, though he
cannot get anyone to put him out of his misery. Too much, perhaps,
has been made of the bungling of Antony's suicide. Its primary
purpose is not to contrast a sordid reality with noble pretensions, but
to spare Antony for a last meeting with Cleopatra, a meeting described
by Plutarch, already dramatised by Garnier and Daniel, and obviously
necessary for more than reasons of historical accuracy. Antony's final
speech is not intended to be self-deception, any more than Othello's
is:

> The miserable change now at my end
> Lament nor sorrow at, but please your thoughts
> In feeding them with those my former fortunes
> Wherein I lived, the greatest prince o' th' world,
> The noblest, and do now not basely die,
> Not cowardly put off my helmet to
> My countryman, a Roman by a Roman
> Valiantly vanquish'd.   (IV.xv.51–8)

The rehabilitation of Cleopatra was a more difficult feat of drama-
turgy. She flies from the battle at Actium, followed by the 'doting
mallard', Antony. In the Thidias scene, it is not certain whether she is
intending to desert Antony or not:

> Say to great Caesar this: in deputation
> I kiss his conquering hand: tell him, I am prompt
> To lay my crown at's feet, and there to kneel:
> Till[10] from his all-obeying breath I hear
> The doom of Egypt.   (III.xiii.74–8)

But her repudiation of Antony's accusation sounds convincing, until we learn in Act IV that the fleet has surrendered to Caesar's:

> This foul Egyptian hath betrayed me:
> My fleet hath yielded to the foe; and yonder
> They cast their caps up and carouse together
> Like friends long lost. Triple-turn'd whore! 'tis thou
> Hast sold me to this novice, and my heart
> Makes only wars on thee.   (IV.xii.10–15)

Antony tells Eros that Cleopatra has 'packed cards with Caesar' and the denial of this comes only with the false report of her death. It is not until Diomedes comes with the news that she is alive do we get a more convincing denial from a more reliable messenger:

> for when she saw—
> Which never shall be found—you did suspect
> She had disposed with Caesar, and that your rage
> Would not be purged, she sent you word she was dead.

When Antony dies, Cleopatra's grief is manifestly sincere. Her eloquent lament that the world is no better than a sty, and that

> there is nothing left remarkable
> Beneath the visiting moon,

is followed, when she recovers from her swoon, by her determination to die, expressed by the final couplet of Act IV:

> Come; we have no friend
> But resolution and the briefest end.

The last act of the play is devoted to the death of Cleopatra, 'after the high Roman fashion':

> *quae generosius*
> *perire quaerens nec muliebriter*
> *expavit ensem nec latentis*
> *classe cita reparavit oras.*

Because of her past behaviour, the audience may doubt at times whether she will carry her resolution into effect, and whether her main

motive for suicide is not so much grief for the loss of Antony as fear
of being part of Caesar's triumph. There is irony in Antony's injunction to trust only Proculeius when he is the man chosen by Caesar to
entrap her; and it is Dolabella, the last man she succeeds in enchanting,
who reveals that Caesar intends to lead her in triumph.

The wrangle with Seleucus about the amount of her treasure is often
misinterpreted. It is taken to mean that Cleopatra is still wavering in
her resolution. But there is no reason to doubt that Shakespeare was
following Plutarch—and a marginal note in North's translation—and
that Cleopatra was pretending that she wanted to live so that Caesar
would be hoodwinked. It is not even necessary to suppose that
Seleucus was privy to her scheme. Her first words after Caesar's exit
make her motives clear and till then the audience may have been duped
like Caesar:

> He words me, girls, he words me, that I should not
> Be noble to myself.

Iras interprets for us:

> Finish, good lady; the bright day is done,
> And we are for the dark.

We need not deny that Cleopatra's motives remain mixed. She does
not wish to undergo the shame of being part of Caesar's triumph; she
cannot endure the thought of seeing

> Some squeaking Cleopatra boy [her] greatness
> I' th' posture of a whore.

But one has to remember that this speech is mainly designed to
strengthen not her own, but Iras' resolution to die. She had already
dispatched Charmian to arrange for the asps to be brought; and when
Charmian returns Cleopatra calls both her, and the deed they are about
to do, 'noble'. She declares that she has overcome any female weakness:

> now from head to foot
> I am marble-constant; now the fleeting moon
> No planet is of mine.

The ritual of death, which Cleopatra herself compares with her first
meeting with Antony on the River Cydnus, has sometimes been taken
as illustrating her continued self-deception. Her 'Immortal longings'
are said to be undercut by the Clown's malapropism about the asp:

'his biting is immortal; those that do die of it do seldom or never recover'. The Clown's anecdote of one of the victims of the asp, his comment that a woman should not lie 'but in the way of honesty', and his assertion that five women in every ten are marred by 'these same whoreson devils' are thought to remind the audience not to approve of Cleopatra's morals. In taking leave of life her first thought is that she will never again drink wine. She refers to the stroke of death in sexual terms

> as a lover's pinch,
> Which hurts, and is desired.

Above all, her character is revealed in her jealous fear that Antony will meet Iras in the underworld and spend his first kiss on her. Her suicide, William Rosen assures us, is 'her most accomplished self-dramatisation'.[11] Professor Roy Battenhouse goes further and claims that there is an element of parody in the scene.[12] He suggests that there is a pun on *Nilus*, 'nihilism is being imagined as liberty'; that the asps at Cleopatra's breast are a parody of love and motherhood, while she is neglecting her own children; that the fact that her crown is awry, gives 'her queenship a comic aspect'; that her very kiss kills Iras; that by claiming to be marble-constant she is 'negating true womanhood for the stony immortability of an Egyptian mummy'; and that underlying Charmian's tribute—

> Now boast thee, Death, in thy possession lies
> A lass unparalleled—

is the idea that 'a lover of death, *alas*, can become *possessed* with unparalleled lies'.

There are not many readers of the scene who would accept such an interpretation and in the theatre it would be totally unacceptable, and in continual conflict with the poetry. As many critics have recognised, the ending of the play is not wholly tragic, not because the hero is disposed of in Act IV, nor yet because Cleopatra lacks the stature of a tragic heroine, but because she transforms herself after Antony's death, and because she tricks Caesar. Instead of being led to Rome to take part in Caesar's triumph, she herself triumphs in death—whether or not she actually meets Antony in another world than this and make 'the ghosts gaze'.

All Cleopatra's speeches in this final scene suggest to most members of most audiences that she is becoming worthy of her lover:

> Methinks I hear
> Antony call; I see him rouse himself
> To praise my noble act; I hear him mock
> The luck of Caesar, which the gods give men
> To excuse their after wrath. Husband, I come:
> Now to that name my courage prove my title!   (V.ii.281–6)

This is the first and only time that Cleopatra refers to Antony as her husband and its significance, coming as it does after 'noble act', hardly needs emphasising, especially as her cowardice in battle had contributed to Antony's ruin. The scornful reference to 'the luck of Caesar' and the after-wrath of the gods not merely implies a life after death, but also poses in the most direct way the basic opposition of the play. It is not primarily a question of luck, although Antony, warned by the Soothsayer, admits that 'the very dice obey' Caesar. He is, as Cleopatra declares earlier, 'Fortune's knave'. Caesar is not merely fortunate, he is also single-minded in his pursuit of power, and not too scrupulous in his choice of means. This is the point of Cleopatra's wish that the asp could speak:

> That I might hear thee call great Caesar ass
> Unpolicied!

Charmian's love and loyalty are apparent not merely in her decision to die with her mistress, but in all her words and actions in this scene. She calls Cleopatra 'eastern star' and 'a lass unparallel'd'; she shuts her eyes with the words,

> Downy windows, close;
> And golden Phoebus never be beheld
> Of eyes again so royal!

She makes certain that the final tableau shall be worthy of the royalty by adjusting the Queen's crown; and her last words to the guard are an affirmation of the rightness of the suicide:

> It is well done, and fitting for a princess
> Descended of so many royal kings.

Middleton Murry was right to stress the importance of the ideas of loyalty and royalty in the play, and Cleopatra's stature in this last scene is enhanced by the attitude of her maids.

The 'lass unparallel'd', however, has proved a stumbling-block to critics besides Battenhouse. They link the phrase with Cleopatra's confession that she is not royal or Empress,

> but e'en a woman, and commanded
> By such poor passion as the maid that milks
> And does the meanest chares,

as a proof that she cannot rise above the vices of her sex and that she is 'governed by no specifically noble passion'. To which we may retort that a queen may compare herself with a milkmaid without ceasing to be royal. When Queen Elizabeth I was urged by Parliament to marry, she replied:

If I were a milkmaid with a pail on my arm, whereby my private person might be a little set by, I would not forsake that poor and single state to match with the greatest monarch.

Shakespeare used similar touches in his portrait of Cleopatra not to suggest her weakness or commonness, but rather to bring out the essential humanity of the glittering monarch in her best attires.

Coleridge called *Antony and Cleopatra* the finest of the historical plays and Bradley argued that there was little action in the first three acts, the first half of the play not being tragic in tone. Other critics have complained that the treatment was episodic and that the play as a whole was lacking in unity. Shakespeare, of course, sacrifices the unities of place and time—as he does in all the tragedies—but in this play he wanted to show by transporting us from Egypt to Rome and back again that the fate of the Roman Empire and the future of the world depended on what happened. Even so, he is careful to preserve the unity of action. Antony is invariably the subject of conversation when he is not present on the stage; and Cleopatra is likewise frequently mentioned when she is not present. The longest lapse of time without her being mentioned is only seventy lines and even in this scene (III.ii) Cleopatra is much in the minds of the characters on the stage. Caesar is saying good-bye to his sister and he tells his brother-in-law:

> Most noble Antony,
> Let not the piece of virtue, which is set
> Betwixt us as the cement of our love,
> To keep it builded, be the ram to batter
> The fortress of it; for better might we
> Have loved without this mean, if on both parts
> This be not cherish'd.

Caesar is obviously afraid that Antony will return to Cleopatra.

Another example of the way Shakespeare preserved the unity of

action is to be found in the curious arrangement of scenes in the second
and third acts. Cleopatra begins her interrogation of the messenger
from Rome in Act II Scene v and continues it in Act III Scene vii.
Between these scenes, which are really one, are sandwiched four other
scenes—the meeting of Antony and Caesar with Pompey, the feast
aboard Pompey's galley, the triumph of Ventidius in Parthia,
and the departure of Antony with Octavia. Shakespeare means
us to understand that these events were taking place at about
the time when Cleopatra was questioning the messenger about her
rival.

On one point Bradley is surely wrong. He complains that we do not
see the inner struggles of the characters, as we do in *Hamlet* or
Macbeth.[13] But we see Antony's vacillation between his desire for
power and the enchantment of Egypt. It is true that we do not see the
actual moment of Antony's return to Cleopatra, but the arrival is
dramatically unimportant. What matters is the moment when he
decides to return; and this decision is not made between the fifth and
sixth scenes of Act III, as Bradley seems to think, but long before,
after the scene with the soothsayer:

> I will to Egypt:
> And though I make this marriage for my peace,
> I' th' East my pleasure lies.

Antony's tragedy is due more to vacillation than to lust. He desires
power as well as Cleopatra; but in marrying Octavia to preserve the
triumvirate he offends Caesar beyond forgiveness. After that his ruin
is certain. Whether the nobleness of life is to do as Antony does or to
exercise the arts of power Shakespeare is not concerned to decide; but
there is no doubt that he makes the strumpet's fool more sympathetic
than Fortune's knave. Caesar is too much like Prince John of Lan-
caster for us to like him. The sordid realities of the pursuit of power
are revealed in the Pompey scenes. Menas suggests that they
should cut the cable and slit the throats of the triumvirate, so that
Pompey would be the sole ruler of the world. Pompey declines
the offer, but regrets that Menas had not done it without consulting
him.

George Saintsbury was right when he said that Antony was at once
ruined and ennobled by his passion. As Mr Dickey rightly reminds us,
we ought not to read into the play modern conceptions of the absolute

value of sexual love; but if our views on love differ from those of Elizabethan moralists this may be due partly to the fact that we have inwardly digested Shakespeare. Iris Murdoch's words quoted at the beginning of this chapter might have been written with *Antony and Cleopatra* in mind.

9

CORIOLANUS

*. . . Coriolanus, too late pious and penitent after his wickedness
committed.* (Seneca)

I

Coriolanus is the least popular of the great tragedies and this is probably
due to the character of the hero with whom modern audiences find it
more difficult to sympathise than with those who commit murder or
adultery. Even Coriolanus' enjoyment of the 'royal occupation' of
fighting is regarded with some measure of disapproval and his bad
qualities seem a good deal worse because of one major difference
between the Jacobean age and ours. We profess to believe in democracy: they did not. The story of Coriolanus was nearly always told to
illustrate the evils of the democratic form of government; and the odd
man out, Machiavelli, who defends the tribunes, serves only to underline the general view. Bodin, for example, uses the Coriolanus story
as part of an attack on democracy; Fulbecke likewise regards the
banishment of Coriolanus as an example of the evils of democracy.
Goslicius praises the piety of Coriolanus and complains of the fury
and insolence of the Tribunes; and Leonard Digges, Shakespeare's
neighbour and admirer, refers with approval to the way the Romans
used the war against the Volscians to quell their rebellious plebs.

Shakespeare had many precedents for excusing the treachery of his
hero and for laying all the blame on the plebeians and their leaders. It
is therefore significant that the alterations he made in Plutarch's
account have the effect of presenting us with a more favourable idea
of the citizens. It is usual in the theatre to assume that the patricians
are right in their views and the plebeians are therefore presented as
cowardly, ungrateful, inconsistent and stinking. For good measure
they are given accents which suggest that they are illiterate. But if one
were to rely on the text, it would be difficult to show that they were

illiterate. They are given genuine grievances; and, if his style is at all a guide, their spokesman is more an intellectual than a proletarian rabble-rouser:

We are accounted poor citizens, the patricians good. What authority surfeits on, would relieve us: if they would yield us but the superfluity, while it were wholesome, we might guess they relieved us humanely; but they think we are too dear: the leanness that afflicts us, the object of our misery, is an inventory to particularize their abundance; our sufferance is a gain to them. Let us revenge this with our pikes, lest we become rakes; for the gods know I speak this in hunger for bread, not in thirst for revenge.   (I.i.14–23)

This is not in the least like Jack Cade's illogical clap-trap, with which it is too often compared. It is much closer to the speech of Lear in which he urges pomp to take physic and shake the superflux to the poor and needy or to Gloucester's parallel prayer that 'distribution should undo excess'. When Menenius claims that the patricians care for the citizens like fathers, the citizens are grimly sardonic:

Care for us! True indeed they ne'er cared for us yet: suffer us to famish, and their store-houses crammed with grain; make edicts for usury, to support usurers; repeal daily any wholesome act established against the rich; and provide more piercing statutes daily, to chain up and restrain the poor. If the wars eat us not up, they will; and there's all the love they bear us.
                                                                                                    (I.i.77–84)

It has often been pointed out that similar grievances sparked off the Midlands insurrection not long before *Coriolanus* was written; and Lear, in his madness, came to the conclusion that there was one law for the rich and one for the poor. Whether the shortage of grain was caused by hoarding or a bad harvest is left uncertain, but we do know that the patricians welcomed the war as a means of killing off the surplus population:

> I am glad on't; then we shall ha' means to vent
> Our musty superfluity.

Not only does Shakespeare give the citizens genuine grievances, he shows that they are prepared to forgive Coriolanus' deplorable rudeness to them. They are not ungrateful: they want only their minimal constitutional rights. It is obvious, moreover, that the accusations made by the Tribunes are perfectly justified: Coriolanus wished to overthrow the constitution and abolish the office of Tribune; he would have been a tyrannical consul and used the office to further the interests of his class.

All this may be granted; but the Tribunes, Brutus and Sicinius, have few defenders. Dr Johnson deplored their plebeian malignity and tribunitian insolence, a judgement to be expected of one who was not entirely free of party bias. They have been called comic and detestable villains. Comic they sometimes are; detestable they may seem to an audience that commiserates with the tragic hero; but villains they are not. Their only defender was John Palmer in *Political Characters of Shakespeare*, who called them 'the natural products of a class war'.[1] They defend the interests of the people they represent and, realising that Coriolanus was a bitter enemy to those interests, they determine to outwit him by fair means or foul. They cunningly refrain from opposing the nomination of Coriolanus as consul, because they know his victories have made him a popular hero. He tries to avoid the usual electoral procedure and, when he is compelled to comply, he treats the electors with inexcusable rudeness. The Tribunes advise the citizens to reconsider their promises to vote for Coriolanus and, wanting 'the senators to feel that the rejection of Marcius is a spontaneous and representative act of the people', they tell the citizens to pretend that in promising their votes they were following the Tribunes' advice:

> Say, you chose him
> More after our commandment than as guided
> By your own true affections; and that your minds,
> Pre-occupied with what you rather must do
> Than what you should, made you against the grain
> To voice him consul: lay the fault on us.   (II.iii.226–31)

Soon afterwards Coriolanus declares that Tribunes are unnecessary, and that their office should be abolished. This attack on the Roman constitution could be construed as treason and Sicinius deliberately enrages Coriolanus by calling him a traitor. He strikes the officers of the state and renders himself liable to capital punishment; but because of his former services to the state, the Tribunes commute the death sentence to one of banishment. There is no reason to doubt the sincerity of Sicinius' words:

> I would he had continued to his country
> As he began, and not unknit himself
> The noble knot he made.

What is curious is that most critics who condemn the unscrupulous behaviour of the Tribunes tend to excuse the equally unscrupulous behaviour of the patricians. Volumnia cheerfully advises her son to play the hypocrite and pretend to be mild and liberal until he has the power in his hands. Menenius, who is regarded by many as the spokesman for sanity—and for Shakespeare—urges Coriolanus to stoop to the herd. Volumnia confesses:

> I would dissemble with my nature where
> My fortunes and my friends at stake required
> I should do so in honour.   (III.ii.62–4)

What she really means is that honour should be jettisoned in order to win. Coriolanus finally agrees to 'mountebank' the loves of the citizens; but he is the only one of his party who appears to suffer from any qualms of conscience.

After Coriolanus' banishment, the Tribunes cut a ludicrous figure in their encounter with the irate Roman matrons and they are foolishly vain and complacent before they hear that Coriolanus has joined the Volscians. But their behaviour thereafter contrasts favourably with that of the patricians. Cominius and Menenius utter not one word of blame of the man who is coming to burn down the city: they appear to think that the 'noble man's' revenge for his banishment is natural and legitimate. Brutus and Sicinius, although Shakespeare does not conceal their fears for their own safety, plead with the reluctant Menenius to intercede with Coriolanus.

This does not mean that the Brechtian adaptation of the play makes explicit what Shakespeare merely implied. What Coleridge called 'the wonderful impartiality of Shakespeare's politics' was neatly demonstrated by the riots that accompanied a production of the play in Paris in the late 'thirties. The communists believed that the play was a libel on the proletariat: the fascists thought it was a satire on dictatorship.

II

The attitudes expressed by the characters are not necessarily Shakespeare's own. It has often been observed that his main concern in dramatising his material was to find a way in which it could be made dramatically most effective. With *Coriolanus*, much of the spade work had already been done by Plutarch, and some of actual language

provided by North. Plutarch's analysis of the virtues and defects of
the hero's character is basically the same as Shakespeare's. It is also
relevant to mention that Shakespeare, as Coleridge, Hazlitt and Keats
recognised, had the power of identifying himself with a wide range of
characters. The ability of a dramatist varies directly with this power;
and in *Coriolanus* Shakespeare speaks from behind a dozen different
masks.

It is therefore hazardous to assume that Menenius is Shakespeare's
main spokesman, even though the fable of the body and its members,
which is given a prominent position in the first scene of the play, is
plainly an important clue to the political theme. The fable was a
popular one and Shakespeare would have read it in Sidney's *Defence
of Poesy*, in Camden's *Remaines*, and probably in Livy and Aesop. It
had already served as the kernel of two substantial books—Averell's
Marvellous Combat of Contrarieties and Forset's *Comparative Discourse*.[2]
Averell used it at the time of the Armada as an argument that all classes
should unite against the common danger; and it was more generally
used in support of an hierarchical society. Menenius' application of the
fable is on traditional lines:

> Your most grave belly was deliberate,
> Not rash like his accusers, and, thus answered.
> 'True is it, my incorporate friends,' quoth he
> 'That I receive the general food at first
> Which you do live upon; and fit it is,
> Because I am the storehouse and the shop
> Of the whole body. But, if you do remember,
> I send it through the rivers of your blood,
> Even to the court, the heart, to th' seat o' th' brain;
> And, through the cranks and offices of man,
> The strongest nerves and small inferior veins
> From me receive that natural competency
> Whereby they live . . .
>   Though all at once cannot
> See what I do deliver out to each,
> Yet I can make my audit up, that all
> From me do back receive the flour of all,
> And leave me but the bran.'   (I.i.126ff.)

The First Citizen asks how Menenius applies the story, and he replies:

> The senators of Rome are this good belly,
> And you the mutinous members; for, examine
> Their counsels and their cares, digest things rightly

Touching the weal o' th' common, you shall find
No public benefit which you receive
But it proceeds or comes from them to you,
And no way from yourselves.

Menenius evades criticism by calling the First Citizen the big toe of
the assembly; and the entrance of Marcius prevents further argument.
Yet the fable does not really give a satisfactory answer to the popular
grievances. The citizens had not complained of the idleness of the
senate or even that they were unproductive. They had complained
that they themselves were starving and that the laws favoured the
wealthy. For Menenius to pretend that the hungry citizens received
the flour while the senators were left with the bran is hardly convincing.

Even if we do not enquire too closely into the economic realities of
the situation—and Shakespeare probably did not wish us to do so—it
is a fable that cuts both ways. If the Commons are rebellious members,
Coriolanus, we are told later, is a disease that must be cut away. Even
Menenius, his staunch admirer, admits he is a diseased limb. So
Sicinius argues that

The service of the foot
Being once gangrened, is not then respected
For what before it was.

Critics have noted that there is a considerable amount of disease
imagery in the first four acts of the play, but the significant images
from the present standpoint—those relating to the sickness of the
commonweal—are concentrated in the first scene of the third act. This
imagery is used by both parties. Coriolanus thinks that the disease
afflicting Rome is the contagion of democracy:

Those measles
Which we disdain should tetter us, yet sought
The very way to catch them.

He speaks of those

that prefer
A noble life before a long, and wish
To jump a body with a dangerous physic
That's sure of death without it.

Brutus, as Forset had done in his treatise, realises that desperate
diseases of the state require desperate remedies:

G

> Sir, those cold ways,
> That seem like prudent helps are very poisonous
> Where the disease is violent.

Later he speaks of Coriolanus' treason as an infection. The common-
wealth is sick: but the rival parties differ in their diagnoses and pre-
scribe different remedies. Shakespeare sees the situation steadily and
sees it whole.

III

There is an element of satire in the play. The Tribunes are often
ludicrous; the fickleness of the citizens is wryly comic; Menenius is a
humorous *raisonneur*; and even Coriolanus is not spared. It was therefore possible for Bernard Shaw to call it paradoxically 'the best of
Shakespeare's comedies' and for Oscar J. Campbell to class it as a
satire.[3] Sir Edmund Chambers, too, regarded[4] the play as a tragical
satire on the heroic ideal: Coriolanus' honour is rooted in pride and
egoism. If the play is regarded in this light, it would explain the dis-
appointment that some critics have felt with the actual poetry. Bradley
thought that there was 'a lack of imaginative effect or atmosphere in
the play as a whole'; Granville-Barker thought that it contained 'few
passages of really magnificent poetry' and that it lacked the 'transcen-
dent vitality and metaphysical power' of the greatest tragedies; and
J. C. Maxwell has pointed out that momentous statements are made in
the most literal—one might almost say, prosaic—form.[5] Instead of
Ulysses on the effects of disorder—

> Appetite, an universal wolf,
> So doubly seconded with will and power,
> Must make perforce an universal prey,
> And last eat up himself—

or Albany's fear of cannibalism—

> Humanity must perforce prey on itself
> Like monsters of the deep—

we get the flat expression of the same idea:

> You cry against the noble senate, who
> Under the gods, keep you in awe, which else
> Would feed on one another.

It cannot be an accident that in one of the scenes invented by Shakespeare, Valeria is introduced for the sole purpose of describing the behaviour of Coriolanus' son. Volumnia says that 'He had rather see the swords and hear a drum than look upon his schoolmaster' and Valeria replies:

O' my word, the father's son! I swear 'tis a very pretty boy. O' my troth, I look'd upon him a Wednesday half an hour together; has such a confirm'd countenance! I saw him run after a gilded butterfly; and when he caught it he let it go again, and after it again, and over and over he comes, and up again, catch'd it again; or whether his fall enrag'd him, or how 'twas, he did so set his teeth and tear it. O, I warrant, how he mammock'd it!

(I.iii.57–65)

Volumnia's approving comment, 'One on's father's moods', under-lines the fact that the child is father of the man. Coriolanus exhibits the same ungovernable rages and we are reminded of Valeria's speech later in the play when the Volscian army, led by Coriolanus, approaches the gates of Rome:

> they follow him
> Against us brats with no less confidence
> Than boys pursuing summer butterflies
> Or butchers killing flies.   (IV.vi.93–6)

It is not surprising that Bradley should speak of Coriolanus as a huge boy or that Wyndham Lewis should say that he possesses 'the qualities and defects of the English Public Schoolboy',[6] even though we may think that Lewis was unfair to the Public Schools and certainly unfair to Coriolanus who cannot properly be described as 'crabbed, sullen and pompous'. But that Shakespeare was fully conscious of his hero's boyishness can be seen from the fact that his last paroxysm of rage is caused by Aufidius' taunt:

Name not the god, thou boy of tears.

Shakespeare also makes it plain that Coriolanus never really escapes from his mother's dominance. This is suggested in the very first scene of the play where the First Citizen says that 'though soft-conscienc'd men can be content to say it was for his country, he did it to please his mother and to be partly proud'. When we are introduced to Volumnia in the third scene, we are soon made to realise the influence she has had on her son. Although allowance must be made for the supreme value set on the military virtues in the early years of the Roman republic, Volumnia has allowed her maternal feelings to be warped by a perverted kind of patriotism. She is contrasted with the tender Virgilia, and boasts that if she were married to Marcius she would rather he were at the wars 'than in the embracements of his bed where he would show most love'. If she had had a dozen sons she 'had rather had eleven die nobly for their country than one voluptuously surfeit out of action'. She speaks of her son's 'bloody brow' and calls Virgilia a fool because she shrinks at the idea:

> The breasts of Hecuba,
> When she did suckle Hector, look'd not lovelier
> Than Hector's forehead when it spit forth blood.   (I.iii.40–2)

Shakespeare in this scene directs our sympathies to Virgilia. It could be argued, indeed, that Doll Tearsheet's behaviour on the eve of Falstaff's departure for the wars shows more natural human feeling than Volumnia's obsession with blood and with her pleasure at her son's wounds. Menenius asks: 'Is he not wounded? He was wont to come home wounded.'

Vir. O, no, no, no.
Vol. O, he is woundèd, I thank the gods for 't.
Men. So do I too, if it be not too much . . . Where is he wounded?
Vol. I' th' shoulder and i' th' left arm; there will be large cicatrices to show the people when he shall stand for his place. He received in the repulse of Tarquin seven hurts i' th' body.
Men. One i' th' neck and two i' th' thigh—there's mine that I know.
Vol. He had before this last expedition twenty-five wounds upon him.
Men. Now it's twenty-seven; every gash was an enemy's grave.
                                                                (II.i.113–48)

This macabre gloating over Coriolanus' wounds is bound to make an audience critical of both Volumnia and Menenius; and it contrasts with the silent tears of Virgilia—Coriolanus' 'gracious silence'—when she sees his wounds.

It is noteworthy that on his return from the wars Coriolanus kneels to his mother before greeting his wife, and when she comes to plead for Rome in the last act he seems to be ashamed that he has spoken a few words to his wife and kissed her before kneeling to his mother. The bond between mother and son is a very close one. It is manifest that all her ambitions are centred on him and that she has brought him up to share her opinions, carry out her desires, and bask in her admiration. The education he has undergone is the main cause of the tragedy. Volumnia has taught him not merely that he should seek martial glory but that he should despise the plebs. Later on she criticises his pride, not realising that this also is the result of her training. Add to this the fact that she admires his rages and that he has never been taught to restrain his anger and it is clear that he is doomed to be a political failure, especially when he is matched against the professionals, Brutus and Sicinius.

At the beginning of Act II Scene ii two officers, while laying cushions in the capitol, discuss the qualities and defects of Coriolanus, and they act as a chorus. They agree that he is a worthy man but, says one, 'he's vengeance proud and loves not the common people'. The other replies that it is 'his noble carelessness' that makes him 'neither to care whether they love or hate him'. The first one replies that 'to affect the malice and displeasure of the people is as bad' as 'to flatter them for their love'. The second officer says that Coriolanus has risen by merit, not by being 'supple and courteous'. At the end of Act IV, Aufidius, who plans to destroy Coriolanus, makes a notable attempt to give an objective assessment of his great rival:

> First he was
> A noble servant to them, but he could not
> Carry his honours even. Whether 'twas pride,
> Which out of daily fortune ever taints
> The happy man; whether defect of judgement,
> To fail in the disposing of those chances
> Which he was lord of; or whether nature,
> Not to be other than one thing, not moving
> From th' casque to th' cushion, but commanding peace
> Even with the same austerity and garb
> As he controll'd the war; but one of these—
> As he hath spices of them all—not all,
> For I dare so far free him—made him fear'd,
> So hated, and so banish'd. But he has a merit
> To choke it in the utt'rance. So our virtues
> Lie in th' interpretation of the time.

This is a curiously careful analysis of the possible causes of Coriolanus' banishment. Not merely does Aufidius offer three different explanations—pride, defect of judgement, behaving like a soldier in civic affairs—but then he cannot decide whether Coriolanus was guilty of one of these or all of them. As Professor Hibbard suggests, 'The inconclusive nature of the analysis suggests that Shakespeare wishes his audience to realise that there is an element of mystery at the heart of the tragedy'.[7]

The mystery depends partly on Shakespeare's refusal to give his hero soliloquies of self-analysis. Antony has few, Coriolanus has none. The one soliloquy he is given, outside Antium, occurs after he has decided to fight against Rome. The actual moment of decision takes place off stage. We have last seen him saying farewell to his friends and relations and promising them to be constant:

> While I remain above the ground you shall
> Hear from me still, and never of me aught
> But what is like me formerly.   (IV.i.51–3)

He calls the patricians 'My friends of noble touch' and there is no suggestion that he regards them then, as he calls them to Aufidius, 'dastard nobles'. He declares that he will be loved when he is lacked and the image he uses to describe himself only seems sinister in retrospect:

> though I go alone,
> Like to a lonely dragon, that his fen
> Makes fear'd and talk'd of more than seen—your son
> Will or exceed the common or be caught
> With cautelous baits and practice.   (IV.i.29–33)

Certainly his later actions 'exceed the common' and he is caught 'with cautelous baits and practice' by Aufidius; but, as far as the audience can tell, he has no intention of fighting against Rome. The decision is made somewhere between Scene i and Scene iv.

In his final tragedies Shakespeare appears to have been confident of the ability of his actors to convey to the audience, and the ability of the audience to grasp, the unexpressed motivations of his characters. He could dispense with direct addresses to the audience, who would be able without them to catch behind the dialogue unconscious thoughts and feelings. It is by such means that Shakespeare is able to convince us that Coriolanus is something more than the valiant, proud, intolerant, choleric, impolite and treacherous patrician he seems at first to be.

It is in the climactic scene in Act III that we are made to realise that Coriolanus is greatly superior not merely to the plebs but to his fellow-patricians and to the mother whom he mistakenly worships.

Volumnia urges him to play the hypocrite to obtain the consulship
and not to annoy the citizens before the power is safely in his hands:

> Because that now it lies you on to speak
> To th' people, not by your own instruction,
> Nor by th' matter which your heart prompts you,
> But with such words that are but roted in
> Your tongue, though but bastards and syllables
> Of no allowance to your bosom's truth.
> Now, this no more dishonours you at all
> Than to take in a town with gentle words,
> Which else would put you to your fortune and
> The hazard of much blood . . .
>   I prithee now, my son,
> Go to them with this bonnet in thy hand;
> And thus far having stretch'd it—here be with them—
> Thy knee bussing the stones—for in such business
> Action is eloquence, and the eyes of th' ignorant
> More learned than the ears—waving thy head,
> Which often thus correcting thy stout heart
> Now humble as the ripest mulberry
> That will not hold the handling.   (III.ii.52–80)

Volumnia is assuming that in the class war one ought to use the most
Machiavellian means. Coriolanus first unwillingly consents, realising
that to adopt such a plan he must be possessed by a harlot's spirit.
Then he revolts against sacrificing his inner integrity:

>   I will not do't,
> Lest I surcease to honour mine own truth,
> And by my body's action teach my mind
> A most inherent baseness.   (III.ii.120–3)

His mother scolds him and he again consents to mountebank the loves
of the Roman populace. But when in the following scene he is face to
face with the Tribunes, he does not flatter. He is truest to his ideals, as
Bradley said, when he tries to be false to them.[8] Sicinius calls him a
traitor, he declares that he

>   would not buy
> Their mercy at the price of one fair word.

Before the end of the scene he addresses the mob as

> You common cry of curs, whose breath I hate
> As reek o' th' rotten fens, whose loves I prize

> As the dead carcasses of unburied men
> That do corrupt my air—I banish you.   (III.iii.122–5)

The hero's inability to be false to himself and his defiance of his enemies arouse the sympathy and admiration of the audience.

As we have seen, Coriolanus promises to 'mountebank' the loves of the citizens. The revulsion he feels at playing the hypocrite is expressed by a number of theatrical images. Before the election he says:

> It is a part
> That I shall blush in acting, and might well
> Be taken from the people.

He asks his mother:

> Would you have me
> False to my nature? Rather say I play
> The man I am.

When he is told to conceal his thoughts from the people, he tells Volumnia:

> You have put me to such a part which never
> I shall discharge to th' life.

In the last act Coriolanus twice uses theatrical imagery. When the deputation arrives to beg him to spare Rome, he tells Virgilia:

> Like a dull actor now,
> I have forgot my part and I am out
> Even to a full disgrace.

Mr Charney interprets[9] this to mean that

Coriolanus cannot maintain the pretense of acting, although mercy will mean his own destruction. He cannot feign a 'part' so discordant with nature, and his yielding to his family is again a sign of inherent honesty.

This seems a wrong interpretation of the lines for Coriolanus does not capitulate until much later. He tells his mother:

> Tell me not
> Wherein I seem unnatural; desire not
> T'allay my rages and revenges with
> Your colder reasons.

He is a dull actor who has forgotten his lines. He cannot, he believes, forgive Rome; and he shrinks from telling his wife that her mission is in vain.

In the later passage using theatrical imagery, where (Coriolanus says)

> The gods look down, and this unnatural scene
> They laugh at,

the scene is not unnatural because Coriolanus was acting as a destroyer of his native city, nor because it is unnatural for the proud Coriolanus to yield to his mother's pleadings, but because it is unnatural for a mother to kneel to her son. The gods laugh because they know that his mercy will cost him his life.

Not only is Coriolanus a much nobler figure than his associates—except Virgilia; he is ignorant of his own nature, imagining that pride is a virtue and loving-kindness a weakness. Professor Ellis-Fermor was right to see that 'the easily articulated code of his community, at once heroic and insidiously base' was 'the only system of values' he had seen defined, but that his real 'need is for wholeness of life', with 'the balancing silences, graces and wisdom' associated with Virgilia.[10]

Even in the scene of surrender, Coriolanus does not realise what has caused his change of heart. He assumes that it is his mother's eloquence and the bond with her which has made him the man he is; but when the women arrive on their mission, he confesses he is melted by the doves' eyes of his wife 'which can make gods forsworn'. Yet he determines not to obey the promptings of instinct, the call of human kindness, but with a boast grimly echoing the self-sufficiency of Shakespeare's villains,

> stand
> As if a man were author of himself
> And knew no other kin.

He struggles against the tenderness which is eroding his resolution; and he rises at the end of Volumnia's first oration, because he is moved by the intervention of Virgilia and the boy Marcius.[11] This is made clear by the words he uses at this point:

> Not of a woman's tenderness to be
> Requires nor child nor woman's face to see.

Volumnia, the old battle-axe, is without tenderness. Coriolanus is thinking of the doves' eyes of his gracious silence. Despite the ruinous education he has received, he is converted almost against his will to a recognition of the claims of tenderness, 'the human heart by which we live'. But the conversion is too late to save his life.

G. R. Elliott has argued that the flaw in all Shakespeare's tragic heroes is pride and that this is what brings about their downfall. This would seem to ignore the difference between proper pride which is inseparable from self-respect and the pride which is the deadliest of the seven deadly sins. Coriolanus *is* guilty of pride, which though evil is the basis of his integrity. He is whooped out of Rome because he cannot control either his pride or his passion; but Aufidius is able to destroy him not because of his vice, but because his vice is conquered by love.

TIMON OF ATHENS

Like as false and couterfeit pieces of gold which will not abide the touch
(Plutarch)

I

Timon of Athens presents a number of insoluble problems: its date, its text, even its single authorship have been questioned. It has been regarded as 'a first sketch of *King Lear* set aside unfinished', as an 'after vibration' of *King Lear*, as a close neighbour of *Troilus and Cressida*— Apemantus echoing Thersites—and as the last of the tragedies, the subject of which being suggested by the account of Timon in Plutarch's life of Antony, and by the account of Alcibiades in the life of Coriolanus. The text of the play given in the Folio cannot have been acted. The scene in which Alcibiades pleads for a nameless friend (III.v) is not properly linked with the rest of the play. As Una Ellis-Fermor said, 'It tumbles suddenly into the action with the bewildering inconsequence of an episode in a dream'.[1] In the middle of IV.iii Apemantus hails the approach of the Poet and the Painter, but they do not actually appear until Timon has talked with some Bandits and had a long conversation with Flavius. Then, as many critics have noted, there is a great contrast between the magnificent verse of Timon's best speeches and the feeble, disjointed verse in other scenes of the play. Professor Bradbrook, who believes[2] that *Timon* was staged at the Blackfriars, and that the text we have is rough rather than corrupt, nevertheless admits that some inconsistencies may have been caused by recopying.

It is not necessary to go over the arguments afresh. As *Coriolanus* was probably written after Shakespeare had retired to Stratford, it would be very difficult to place *Timon* as late as that. It seems much more likely, as Bradley maintained, that the date of the play was close to that of *King Lear*. The most plausible explanation of the play's defects is that, whether Shakespeare ever completed it or not, we have to do with a fragmentary first draft and that the poet, as his custom apparently was, revised first those scenes which he found most stimulating to his imagination, and that the Folio editors did what they could with the scenes which had been left unrevised.

II

The most obvious pointer to the meaning of the play is the dialogue between the Poet and the Painter in the opening scene. The allegory of Fortune, which the Poet is presenting to Timon, is intended to guide the response of the audience to what follows, just as Menenius's pretty tale illustrates the political moral of *Coriolanus*. It is true that the Poet deserts Timon when he goes bankrupt and returns to him when he discovers gold; but the Poet lives on patronage and, after all, his desertion of Timon is merely an illustration of his own fable:

> When Fortune in her shift and change of mood
> Spurns down her late beloved, all his dependants,
> Which labour'd after him to the mountain's top
> Even on their knees and hands, let him slip down,
> Not one accompanying his declining foot.   (I.i.87–91)

The allegory prepares the audience for the central action of the play, the ingratitude of Timon's friends, though it does not tell how Timon will react to it.

Plutarch has an essay on 'How a man may discerne a flatterer from a friend', and its length is some indication of the difficulty. 'Where there is authoritie and power', Plutarch says, thither flatterers flock; but 'no sooner is there a chaunge of fortune but they sneake and slinke away, and are no more seen'. As Wyatt put it, echoing the same essay,[3]

> Like lyse awaye from ded bodies thei crall.

To Wilson Knight, Timon's all-embracing love is turned to hatred through man's ingratitude.[4] At the other end of the scale are those critics who regard the play as a tragical satire, in which the hero is as absurdly prodigal in the opening scenes as he is absurdly misanthropic after his self-imposed exile. Neither view is satisfactory. On the one hand, Timon's susceptibility to flattery, his refusal to listen to warnings, and his later indiscriminate rage make it impossible to agree with Knight's extravagant eulogy; on the other hand, his splendid genero-

sity, the affectionate loyalty of his servants, and the poetic grandeur
of his curses do not fit the satiric genre.

We sympathise with Timon, even in his excessive prodigality and
equally excessive hatred, because he is so much nobler than his environ-
ment. Athens is a corrupt society, mean, sordid, and hypocritical, its
values entirely commercial. Timon himself, although it could be
argued that he tries to buy love with gold, is entirely unaware of the
nature of the society in which he lives; but, after his disillusionment,
he gives a penetrating analysis of the power of gold in society. It
resembles the great speech at the beginning of *Volpone*, but appropriately transposed into a tragic key. Volpone worships gold, 'the
world's soul', 'the price of souls':

> Thou art virtue, fame
> Honour, and all things else! Who can get thee,
> He shall be noble, valiant, honest, wise.

Timon acknowledges the truth of Volpone's words but his reaction to
the truth is one of violent revulsion. He refuses to worship:

> I am no idle votarist . . .
> Thus much of this will make black white, foul fair,
> Wrong right, base noble, old young, coward valiant.
> Ha, you gods! why this? What, this, you gods? Why, this
> Will lug your priests and servants from your sides,
> Pluck stout men's pillows from below their heads—
> This yellow slave
> Will knit and break religions, bless th' accurs'd,
> Make the hoar leprosy ador'd, place thieves
> And give them title, knee, and approbation,
> With senators on the bench. This is it
> That makes the wappen'd widow wed again—
> She whom the spital-house and ulcerous sores
> Would cast the gorge at this embalms and spices
> To th' April day again.   (IV.iii.27–41)

Later, he speaks of gold as 'king-killer', 'defiler / Of Hyman's purest
bed', a 'delicate wooer / Whose blush doth thaw the consecrated
snow / That lies on Dian's lap'. Volpone thinks of the advantages and
honours bought by gold; Timon thinks only of the crimes and sins.

These speeches of Timon were quoted and analysed by Karl Marx
in 1844, at the period in his life when he was moving towards commun-
ism. Nor is this surprising, for the attack on the cash-nexus has never
been more powerfully or more terrifyingly expressed. The revelation

that drove Timon into the wilderness drove Marx to write the Communist Manifesto.[5]

We can see from the parallel attacks on the acquisitive society by Jonson, Massinger and others that Shakespeare was expressing a common feeling of disquiet. He chose as his hero, not a king, a statesman or a warrior, but a man whose eminence depended entirely on his wealth, and whose power vanished with his wealth. It is as though he realised at the beginning of the capitalist era that power was shifting from one class to another and that authority was decreasingly invested in the nominal rulers. It is for this reason that the play may be said to continue the debate on order and authority, begun in the Histories and continued in the great tragedies, the praise of order and the criticism of authority being the thesis and antithesis of the Shakespearian dialectic. Money, the new basis of authority, is the destroyer of order. The all-embracing idea of order, inherited from the medieval world, may have been undermined by Luther, Copernicus, and Machiavelli; but Hooker's conception of order differs very little from that of pre-Reformation thinkers, the new astronomy substituted a new order for that which it disproved, and Machiavelli, whatever his effect on political morality, was primarily concerned with the maintenance of order in the state. Shakespeare, though he may have nominally accepted the Copernican theory, continued in his poetry to assume the Ptolemaic system; he could regard Machiavellism as a temporary aberration; but the new money-power was clearly a threat to the traditional conception of order. It substituted for it an order divorced from morality, an authority without responsibility, a power which was animated by self-interest alone.

One characteristic of Timon's curses remains to be mentioned. Although he is concerned generally with the overthrow of order—

> Degrees, observances, customs and laws,
> Decline to your confounding contraries
> And let confusion live—

he returns again and again to sexual examples. Matrons are instructed to 'turn incontinent'; 'green virginity' is told to convert to 'general filths'; maids are directed to their masters' beds; youths are told to give themselves up to lust, with its accompanying diseases. In a later scene, when he gives gold to Phrynia and Timandra, he instructs them with obscene relish to spread venereal disease.

Critics, who accept the appropriateness of Thersites' curses on 'those that war for a placket', have been puzzled by Timon's diatribes, since there is nothing in the early part of the play to suggest that he has any cause for what the critics call 'sex-nausea'. But it may be observed that the only women invited to Timon's banquets are professional masquers and that the Fool's mistress is a whore who writes to Timon. It is surely appropriate that, in a society in which everything is subordinated to gold, sexual relations should also be bound by the cash-nexus. Marx in the unfinished treatise referred to above made the same point: that from the sexual relationship in any society can be seen 'how far the natural behaviour of man has become human, how far another person has become one of his needs as a human being, how far existence depends on mutuality'.

Lear's ravings about sex have naturally been associated with Timon's curses and both have been attributed to the intrusion of Shakespeare's personal feelings: yet it is worth noting that Lear proceeds directly from his invective against the simpering dame to analyse the corruption of society through the power of gold. So in *Timon of Athens* love is a commodity like everything else.

Plutarch argues that the most effective protection against flatterers is self-knowledge:

That every man would labour and strive with himselfe to roote out that selfe-love and overweening of their owne good parts and woorthinesse: For this is it that doth flatter us within, and possesseth our minds beforehand, whereby we are exposed and lie more open unto flatterers that are without, finding us thus prepared already for to worke upon.

If we sought to know ourselves, we should

finde there an infinite number of defects and many vanities, imperfections and faults, mixed untowardly in our words, deeds, thoughts and passions.

As a result we should not so easily be taken in by flattery.

When Caroline Spurgeon rediscovered the multiple imagery linking flatterers, dogs and sweets, she claimed that this constituted the iterative image of *Timon of Athens* and she dismissed in a footnote Wilson Knight's essay in *The Wheel of Fire* because he stressed the central importance of gold-symbolism, a 'contrast between gold and the heart's blood of passionate love of which it is a sacrament'. She was right to point out that there is not, properly speaking, any gold imagery in the play; but as the essential nature of an image is that it should throw light on an idea or object by means of a comparison, Shakespeare was precluded from using gold as the basis of imagery because of the numerous references to it in the course of the play and its visible presence when Timon is digging for roots.

Timon's discovery of gold is not mentioned by Plutarch or Painter and Shakespeare took the incident, directly or indirectly, from Lucian's dialogue. But in Plutarch's essay on flatterers there is a passage, which may have caught Shakespeare's eye, that links the theme of flattery with gold symbolism:

> Like as false and counterfeit pieces of gold which will not abide the touch, represent onely the lustre and bright glittering of gold: So a flatterer resembling the sweete and pleasant behaviour of a friend sheweth himself alwaies jocund, mery and delightsome, without crossing at any time.

Timon cannot tell the difference between true and counterfeit friendship, any more than Lear can distinguish between love and flattery, or Othello can penetrate the hypocrisy of his Ancient.

Many critics feel that Timon lacks the stature of a true tragic hero, since he is a foolish and credulous prodigal in the first three acts of the play and equally unbalanced in his 'beastly' hatred of his fellow-men in the last two. Shakespeare, however, is careful to show that Timon has initially a certain grandeur and nobility which evokes a response from characters who act as a kind of chorus. After three strangers have observed the way in which Lucius has refused to send Timon money, they make the following comments:

> *1 Stranger*   Why, this is the world's soul;[6] and just of the same piece
> Is every flatterer's spirit. Who can call him his friend
> That dips in the same dish? for, in my knowing,
> Timon has been this lord's father,
> And kept his credit with his purse;
> Supported his estate; nay, Timon's money
> Has paid his men their wages. He ne'er drinks
> But Timon's silver treads upon his lip;
> And yet—O, see the monstrousness of man
> When he looks out in an ungrateful shape—
> He does deny him, in respect of his.
> What charitable men afford to beggars
> *3 Stranger*   Religion groans at it.   (III.i.63–76)

The First Stranger says that although he himself has never been indebted to Timon, he admires 'his right noble mind, illustrious virtue / And honourable carriage', so much that he would have gladly made him a present of half his wealth. This scene shows both that Timon is genuinely noble and also that he is wrong to condemn the whole population of Athens.

Equally significant is the way Timon's servants react to the ingratitude of his friends. Flaminius is disgusted at Lucullus's refusal, and throws his bribe in his face:

> Let molten coin be thy damnation,
> Thou disease of a friend, and not himself!
> Has friendship such a faint and milky heart
> It turns in less than two nights? O you gods,
> I feel my master's passion!   (III.i.51–5)

Another of Timon's servants, horrified at the ingratitude of Sempronius, calls him 'a goodly villain'.

After Timon's ruin, four of his faithful servants lament the fall of a noble master and attack the ingratitude of his false friends:

> *2 Servant*   As we do turn our backs
> From our companion, thrown into his grave,
> So his familiars to his buried fortunes
> Slink all away; leave their false vows with him,
> Like empty purses pick'd; and his poor self,
> A dedicated beggar to the air,
> With his disease of all-shunn'd poverty,
> Walks, like contempt, alone . . .
> *3 Servant* Yet do our hearts wear Timon's livery;
> That see I by our faces. We are fellows still,
> Serving alike in sorrow . . .   (IV.ii.8–19)

Flavius, the honest steward, shares what money he has with his fellow-servants, telling them 'Let's yet be fellows'; and in a soliloquy in gnomic couplets he points the moral—the 'fierce wretchedness' of wealth, 'a dream of friendship', and his dearest lord

> brought low by his own heart,
> Undone by goodness!

This touching scene of affection and loyalty is strategically placed between two of Timon's soliloquies in which he curses the whole of mankind for its ingratitude; but although it shows that Timon is as absurd in his hatred as in his universal benevolence, it also makes the audience feel that there is something magnificent about both.

In the last act the deputation of senators makes the audience reassess Timon's position in Athens before his self-imposed exile. That they urge him because of the threat from Alcibiades to be a virtual dictator

—'The captainship . . . Allowed with absolute power'—suggests that he must have had martial qualities as well as wealth. It is these qualities which are implied by Alcibiades' final speech and the roll of drums with which the play concludes.

There is one other method by which Shakespeare ensures our sympathy for his hero: both in prosperity and adversity he is contrasted with Apemantus, whose very name suggests a subhuman figure. A churlish, envious, cynical, selfish railer, Apemantus, like Thersites, is inferior to the men he satirises; and, though his attacks on Timon's friends are shrewd, and his criticisms of Timon himself largely valid, he comes in Act IV to jeer rather than sympathise. He is wrong to imagine that Timon would return to Athens if he were not penniless, and wrong to prefer beasts to men. Timon becomes a misanthrope because he has been disillusioned and his tragedy is that his attitude superficially resembles that of Apemantus. Yet he is right to be indignant at Apemantus' sneering:

> Thou art a slave whom Fortune's tender arm
> With favour never clasp'd, but bred a dog.
> Hadst thou, like us from our first swath, proceeded
> The sweet degrees that this brief world affords
> To such as may the passive drugs of it
> Freely command, thou wouldst have plung'd thyself
> In general riot, melted down thy youth
> In different beds of lust, and never learn'd
> The icy precepts of respect, but followed
> The sug'red game before thee. But myself,
> Who had the world as my confectionary;
> The mouths, the tongues, the eyes, and hearts of men
> At duty, more than I could frame employment;
> That numberless upon me stuck, as leaves
> Do on the oak, have with one winter's brush
> Fell from their boughs, and left me open, bare
> For every storm that blows—I to bear this,
> That never knew but better, is some burden.
> Thy nature did commence in sufferance; time
> Hath made thee hard in't. Why shouldst thou hate men?
> They never flatter'd thee. What hast thou given?
> If thou wilt curse, thy father, that poor rag,
> Must be thy subject; who, in spite, put stuff
> To some she-beggar and compounded thee
> Poor rogue hereditary. Hence, be gone.
> If thou hadst not been born the worst of men,
> Thou hadst been a knave and flatterer.   (IV.iii.249–75)

After this splendid piece of invective, however, Timon descends to the level of Apemantus, and the two men are reduced to mere abuse—'Beast! . . . Slave! . . . Toad! . . . Rogue, rogue, rogue!' The misanthropes become indistinguishable. But Timon recovers dignity as his death approaches, when his 'long sickness / Of health and living . . . begins to mend'. His actual death is almost as mysterious as the passing of Oedipus:

> Say to Athens,
> Timon hath made his everlasting mansion
> Upon the beached verge of the salt flood,
> Who once a day with his embossed froth
> The turbulent surge shall cover. (V.i.212–16)

III

The best passages in the play are so splendid that one can understand why some critics have waxed enthusiastic about the whole play. But although one recognises its splendours, one must accept the more usual verdict that, even when one makes allowances for its unfinished state, it is not quite on a level with the other great tragedies. Wilson Knight goes so far as to say that the play transcends *Hamlet*, *Troilus and Cressida*, *Othello* and *King Lear* and that it expresses 'the central essence of tragic drama'.[7] But even the histrionic abilities of Wilfred Walter, Paul Scofield and of Wilson Knight himself did not make it seem wholly satisfying as an acting play: some scenes were comparatively inert. Yet the last two acts are Shakespeare's most powerful statement of what he seems to have regarded as the worst of sins—ingratitude. The theme was touched lightly in one of the songs in *As You Like It* and in one scene in *Twelfth Night*; ingrateful man was excoriated by Lear in the storm; and it was the ingratitude of Athenian society that drove Timon into voluntary exile.

The chronology of the last three or four tragedies is uncertain. *Timon of Athens* may have followed, or even preceded, *King Lear*; and *Coriolanus* may, as we have seen, belong to Shakespeare's final period. What is certain is that with his writing—or rewriting—of *Pericles*, he became interested in the possibilities of tragi-comedy. This may have been due to the popularity of the plays of Beaumont and Fletcher, Heywood and others; to revivals of early romantic dramas, to a realisation that he had gone to the limits of the tragic form; to a wish (in

Keats's phrase) to devote himself to other sensations; perhaps even to a change of mood, traces of which may be found in *Antony and Cleopatra*.

In the tragedies the hero's error is irreparable. In the last plays he is given a second chance. Pericles and Leontes regain their wives and daughters; Posthumus Leonatus regains his wife; Prospero regains his kingdom. The daggers of the murderers miscarry. The wronged ones—Imogen, Hermione, Prospero—forgive their wrongers. To some critics these plays represent a decline in Shakespeare's 'imaginative vision', 'an old man's compensation for the harshness of man's lot', a turning away from reality, the expression of boredom or sentimentality.[8] Human life being inescapably tragic, it is assumed that tragedy is a higher form of art than comedy. Yet it is not necessarily sentimental to show the workings of Providence in human affairs and the parabolic art of *The Tempest* is as legitimate as that displayed in the tragedies.

NOTES

R.E.S.: Review of English Studies   PMLA: Publications of the Modern Languages Association of America   S.Q.: Shakespeare Quarterly   T.L.S.: Times Literary Supplement   S.A.B.: Shakespeare Association Bulletin   P.Q.: Philological Quarterly   H.L.Q.: Huntingdon Library Quarterly   N.Q.: Notes and Queries   M.L.R.: Modern Language Review

Chapter 1: Introduction

1. *Shakespearean Tragedy* (ed. 1950), pp. 3–4.
2. It has also been argued by H. D. F. Kitto that Aristotle is a poor judge of some Greek tragedies.
3. op. cit., p. 21.
4. op. cit., p. 39.
5. G. R. Elliott, *Flaming Minister* (1953), pp. xix–xxi.
6. *The Story of the Night* (1961), p. 150.
7. *The Harvest of Tragedy* (1956), pp. 161–2.
8. *The Mirror up to Nature* (1965), p. 52.
9. George Puttenham, *The Arte of English Poesie* (1589), p. 27.
10. Thomas Heywood, *An Apology for Actors* (1612).
11. *The Revenge of Bussy D'Ambois*, Epistle dedicatory.
12. See the Epilogue to *The Tempest*.
13. *Letters*, Ed. Rollins, I.224.
14. ibid., II.213.
15. In Miss Prism's novel, 'The good end happily and the bad unhappily: that is what fiction means.'
16. J. Dover Wilson, *The Essential Shakespeare*, V.
17. *Shakespeare and the Nature of Man* (1942).

Chapter 2: Apprenticeship

1. Ben Jonson, *Bartholemew Fair*, Induction.
2. *Pericles* and *The Two Noble Kinsmen* were excluded from the First Folio.
3. *Shakespeare Our Contemporary.*
4. *Shakespeare Survey 10*, pp. 39–49; *The Early Shakespeare* (1967); *Shakespeare's Early Tragedies* (1968); *Essays in Criticism*, X (1960), pp. 275–89.
5. *Shakespeare Survey 10*, p. 33.
6. 'Seneca in Elizabethan Translation.'
7. *Shakespearean Criticism*, Ed. T. M. Raysor (1960), II.27.
8. See note 4.

9. Ovid, *Metamorphoses*, trans. R. Humphries (1957), p. 147.

10. II.iii.172–83.

11. *Shakespeare and Elizabethan Poetry* (1951), p. 107.

12. See A. Somers' article in note 4.

13. See *The Massacre at Paris*.

14. *King Lear*, IV.i.35.

15. See J. B. Steane, *Marlowe* (1964), pp. 363–4.

16. l. 340.

17. See *Richard II*, Ed. K. Muir.

18. cf. Kenneth Muir, 'Shakespeare among the Commonplaces', *R.E.S.* (1959), pp. 283–9.

19. *A Study of Shakespeare* (ed. 1918), p. 39.

20. *PMLA*, LXII (1947).

21. *Biographia Literaria*, XV

22. *Shakespeare* (1927), pp. 69–70.

23. *Shakespeare's Life and Art* (1938), p. 115.

24. *Shakespeare's Imagery* (1935), p. 310.

25. See K. Muir, 'The Imagery of *Romeo and Juliet*', *Literary Half-Yearly* (1968), pp. 71ff.

26. *Romeo and Juliet*, Ed. John E. Hankins (1960), p. 24.

Chapter 3: Julius Caesar

1. *A Midsummer Night's Dream* is partly based on Plutarch's life of Theseus.

2. *Lives*, ix (1899), p. 305.

3. *The Problem Plays of Shakespeare* (1963).

4. op. cit., vii (1899), p. 141.

5. II.i.20.

6. F. R. Leavis, *The Common Pursuit* (1962), pp. 136–59.

7. 'A New Look at Julius Caesar' in *Essays in Honor of Walter Clyde Curry* (1954), p. 177.

8. *Character and Motive in Shakespeare* (1949), III.

9. S. T. Coleridge, *Shakespearean Criticism* I, p. 14.

10. *Political Characters of Shakespeare* (1945), p. 7.

11. 'Brutus, Virtue, and Will', *S.Q.*, X (1959), pp. 367–79.

12. See Wilson's edition and Granville-Barker's *Prefaces*.

13. See *Shakespeare Survey* 2, p. 40.

14. *S.Q.*, IV (1953), pp. 153–61.

15. M. W. MacCallum, *Shakespeare's Roman Plays* (1935), p. 242.

16. op. cit., p. 244.

17. *Julius Caesar*, Ed. M. Macmillan (1902).

Chapter 4: Hamlet

1. *The Defence of Poesie* (1595), Sig. E4.^{V}

2. See, e.g., Spurgeon, op. cit., W. H. Clemen, *The Development of Shakespeare's Imagery* (1951).

3. See Kenneth Muir's article in *Etudes Anglaises* (1964), pp. 352–63.
4. See Ernest Jones, *Hamlet and Œdipus* (1949).
5. *Hamlet—the Prince or the Poem* (1943).
6. S. T. Coleridge, *Table Talk*, June 15, 1827.
7. J. M. Robertson, *The Problem of 'Hamlet'* (1919).
8. *The Wheel of Fire* (1949), ch. II.
9. *On 'Hamlet'* (1948), pp. 103, 105.
10. *Explorations* (1946), pp. 66ff.
11. *An Approach to 'Hamlet'* (1960), p. 47.
12 *Hamlet and Revenge* (1967).
13. op. cit., p. 178.
14. I. Gollancz, *The Sources of 'Hamlet'* (1926), p. 197.
15. Cited Fredson Bowers, *Elizabethan Revenge Tragedy* (1940), p. 36.
16. J. C. Maxwell, 'The Ghost from the Grave', *Durham University Journal* (1956), pp. 55–9.
17. III.i.50.
18. Perhaps we should read 'now'.
19. II.ii.8–24, 53–60, 163–88.
20. *Hamlet and Ophelia* (1964).
21. A stallion is a masculine whore.
22. T. M. Parrott, *Tragedies of George Chapman* (1910), p. 573.
23. *The Revenge of Bussy D'Ambois*, IV.iv.14ff.
24. V.ii.43–5.
25. III.iii.362.
26. *The Wheel of Fire* (1949), p. 37.
27. In a lecture.
28. III.iv.202, IV.ii.12.
29. See note 3 above.
30. III.iv.197–9, IV.i.27.
31. IV.vii.111.
32. op. cit., 15 June 1827.
33. *Selected Essays* (1932), p. 144.
34. See note 3 above.
35. See *Shaw on Shakespeare*, Ed. E. Wilson, p. 89.
36. *T.L.S.*, 20 March 1969.
37. Sonnet 66.
38. *Hamlet and Ophelia* (1964), pp. 135–51.
39. ibid., p. 146.
40. 'The Death of Ophelia', *S.Q.* (1964), pp. 345–8.
41. E. K. Chambers, *Shakespeare*, I, p. 25.
42. *Hamlet and Ophelia*, p. 148.
43. See William Montgomerie, 'More an antique Roman than a Dane'.
44. Kenneth Muir, *Shakespeare: Hamlet* (1963), p. 40.
45. L. C. Knights, *An Approach to 'Hamlet'* (1960).
46. E. Jones, *Hamlet and Œdipus* (1949).
47. Fredson Bowers, 'Hamlet as Minister and Scourge', *PMLA*, LXX (1950), pp. 740–7.

48. *The Court and the Castle* (1967), p. 31.
49. *The Idea of Great Poetry* (1925), p. 181.
50. *The Tragic Sense in Shakespeare* (1960), p. 73.
51. *Shakespeare: Hamlet* (1963), p. 61.

Chapter 5: Othello

1. Henri Troyat, *Tolstoy* (1970), p. 790.
2. *Speculative Instruments* (1955), pp. 198ff.
3. V.ii.130.
4. Oscar Campbell's phrase.
5. See R. Flatter, *The Moor of Venice* (1950).
6. cf. M. C. Bradbrook's article in *A New Companion to Shakespeare Studies* (1971).
7. *Table Talk*, 29 December 1822.
8. op. cit., p. 186.
9. C. Stanislavsky, *Stanislavsky Produces 'Othello'* (1948).
10. Cited E. K. Chambers, *Shakespeare*, II.233.
11. E. E. Stoll, *Othello* (1915).
12. ibid., pp. 21–3.
13. cf. John Holloway, *The Story of the Night* (1962), pp. 155ff.
14. *Selected Essays* (1932), p. 126.
15. *The Common Pursuit* (1962), p. 142.
16. *The Wheel of Fire* (1949).
17. *The Common Pursuit*, p. 145.
18. *Character and Characterisation in Shakespeare* (1962), p. 150.
19. Leavis, op. cit., p. 138.
20. *Othello's Countrymen* (1965).
21. *The Revenge of Bussy D'Ambois*, IV.iii.80–1. Cited by Wyndham Lewis, *The Lion and the Fox* (1927).
22. *Paradise Lost*, III.682–3.
23. F. R. Leavis, *The Common Pursuit*, p. 138.
24. ibid., p. 141.
25. *Shakespeare Survey 5* (1952), pp. 62–80.
26. William Hazlitt, *Characters of Shakespeare's Plays* (1906), p. 41.
27. *A Study of Shakespeare* (1918), p. 178.
28. op. cit., p. 231.
29. *Prefaces*, II.104.
30. *Essays of Elia* (1901), p. 185.
31. Quoted in New Variorum edition.
32. *Characters and Commentaries* (1935), pp. 295–6.
33. *Shakespeare and the Allegory of Evil* (1958), p. 448. cf. J. Lawlor, *The Tragic Sense in Shakespeare* (1960), p. 98.
34. D. J. Snider, *System of Shakespeare's Dramas* (1877).
35. 'The Wronged Iago', *S.A.B.* (January 1937).
36. Snider, op. cit.
37. Cited in New Variorum edition.

38. *Sixteen Plays of Shakespeare* (1946), p. 217.
39. Chapter XLII.
40. *Shakespeare's Tragic Heroes* (1961), pp. 148ff.
41 *Essays* (1897), p. 25.
42. See W. H. Clemen, *The Development of Shakespeare's Imagery* (1951), ch. 13.
43. G. Bonnard, *English Studies* (1949), pp. 175–86.
44. *Studies in Shakespeare* (1927).
45. Thomas Rymer, *A Short View of Tragedy* (1693).
46. Bradley, op. cit., p. 180; Granville-Barker, *Prefaces*, II.
47. See *Shakespeare Survey 21*, p. 47.
48. *Imaginary Conversations* (1891), IV.52.
49. E. M. Wilson in *The Listener* (1952), p. 926.

Chapter 6: King Lear

1. *Journals*, Ed. Justin O'Brien (1956), II.345–6.
2. *Shakespeare* (1936), pp. 337–51.
3. *Tolstoy on Shakespeare* (1906).
4. Y. D. Levin, 'Tolstoy, Shakespeare, and Russian Writers of the 1860s' (*Oxford Slavonic Papers*, 1968, pp. 85–104).
5. R. H. Perkinson, *P.Q.*, xxii (1943), pp. 315–29.
6. *Shakespeare: King Lear* (1963), p. 60.
7. *Pelican Guide to English Literature*, II, p. 240.
8. But see L. Kirschbaum, *Character and Characterisation in Shakespeare* (1962), pp. 33–50.
9. *This Great Stage* (1948).
10. op. cit., p. 266.
11. Florio's Montaigne (1897), III.216,268.
12. op. cit., p. 339.
13. *Shakespeare* (1907), p. 27.
14. *Character and Motive in Shakespeare*, p. 23.
15. See G. M. Young, *Shakespeare and the Termers* (1948).
16. *Life and Flowers* (1907), p. 200.
17. *Selected Essays* (1957), p. 116.
18. *Hamlet*, III.iii.57–60.
19. op. cit., pp. 186–9.
20. New Arden edition, p. lx.
21. III.i.16.
22. V.ii.
23. Cited in New Variorum edition.
24. Ovid, *Metamorphoses*, trans. Golding, XV.74ff.
25. *A Declaration* (1603), p. 94.
26. *A Treatise of Melancholy* (1586), sig. N1^r.
27. *Arcadia*, II.10.
28. *MLR*, xlv, pp. 142ff.
29. *King Lear and the Gods* (1966), p. 107.
30. ibid., pp. 75ff.

31. ibid., p. 334.
32. op. cit., p. 60.
33. op. cit., p. 60.
34. cf. R. W. Chambers, *King Lear* (1940), p. 48.
35. *The Sketch Book* (1823), II.158.

Chapter 7: Macbeth

1. See Emrys Jones, 'Othello, Lepanto and the Cyprus Wars', *Shakespeare Survey 21*, pp. 47ff.; J. W. Draper, *S.P.* (1937), pp. 178–85; J. W. Bennett, 'Measure for Measure' as a Royal Entertainment (1966).
2. See H. N. Paul, *The Royal Play of 'Macbeth'* (1950).
3. *The Idea of Great Poetry* (1925), pp. 176–7.
4. W. M. Merchant, 'His Fiend-like Queen', *Shakespeare Survey 19*, pp. 75ff.
5. H. N. Paul, op. cit., p. 359, argues that IV.iii.97–100 was interpolated.
6. *Political Works*, Ed. McIlwain, p. 19.

Chapter 8: Antony and Cleopatra

1. *The Sovereignty of the Good* (1970), p. 103.
2. *Not Wisely But Too Well* (1957), p. 159.
3. *Odes*, I.37.
4. *The Legend of Good Women: Cleopatra.*
5. *Elizabethan and Jacobean Poets* (1965), pp. 128ff.
6. *The Problem Plays of Shakespeare* (1963).
7. See Helen Morris' article, *H.L.Q.* (1968–9), pp. 271–8, and Kenneth Muir's, *Renaissance Drama* (1969), pp. 197–206.
8. V.ii.345.
9. *Three Plays for Puritans*, Preface.
10. cf. *N.Q.* (1961), p. 142.
11. William Rosen, *Shakespeare and the Craft of Tragedy* (1960), p. 158.
12. *Shakespearean Tragedy* (1969), pp. 161–83.
13. *Oxford Lectures* (1909), p. 286.

Chapter 9: Coriolanus

1. *Political Characters of Shakespeare* (1945), p. 259.
2. See Kenneth Muir, 'The Background of *Coriolanus*', *S.Q.* (1959), pp. 137–45.
3. G. B. Shaw, *Man and Superman*, Preface, and Oscar J. Campbell, *Shakespeare's Satire* (1943), p. 198.
4. E. K. Chambers, *Shakespeare: A Survey* (1925), p. 260.
5. 'Animal Imagery in *Coriolanus*', *M.L.R.* (1947), pp. 417–21.
6. A. C. Bradley, *A Miscellany* (1929), p. 88, and Wyndham Lewis, *The Lion and the Fox* (1927), p. 202.
7. *Coriolanus*, Ed. G. R. Hibbard (1967), p. 242.
8. op. cit., p. 87.
9. Maurice Charney, *Shakespeare's Roman Plays* (1961), p. 176.

10. U. Ellis-Fermor, *Shakespeare the Dramatist* (1961), pp. 60–77.
11. Harold C. Goddard, *The Meaning of Shakespeare* (1951), makes this point.

Chapter 10: Timon of Athens

1. *Shakespeare the Dramatist*, p. 169.
2. M. C. Bradbrook, *Shakespeare the Craftsman* (1969), pp. 144–67.
3. *Collected Poems*, Eds K. Muir and P. Thomson (1969), p. 241.
4. *The Wheel of Fire* (1949), pp. 207ff.
5. See Kenneth Muir, 'Timon of Athens and the Cash Nexus', *Modern Quarterly Misc.* (1947), pp. 57–76.
6. cf. Volpone's words quoted on p. 189.
7. *Principles of Shakespearian Production* (1949), p. 177.
8. See H. B. Charlton, *Shakespearian Comedy* (1938) and L. Strachey, *Books and Characters* (1929), p. 41.

INDEX